THE HAIGHT-ASHBURY

The Haight-Ashbury

 A HISTORY

Charles Perry

A RANDOM HOUSE
ROLLING STONE PRESS BOOK
NEW YORK

*Grateful acknowledgment is made to Suzanne Locke
for photo research.*

Library of Congress Cataloging in Publication Data
Perry, Charles, 1941–
The Haight-Ashbury.
Includes index.
1. Haight-Ashbury (San Francisco, Calif.)—History.
2. San Francisco (Calif.)—Social conditions.   I. Title.
HN80.S4P47 1984   979.4'61   83–43187
ISBN 0–394–41098–X

Manufactured in the United States of America
Typography and binding design by J. K. Lambert
98765432
First Edition

There are only two constants
in the San Francisco hippie scene:
music, grass and LSD.

Tom Donahue, *Billboard,* May 6, 1967

CONTENTS

Preface ix

1. Strange Clouds Gather   3
2. The First Flash   25
3. The Flash Goes On   51
4. Big Plans   87
5. The Be-In Era   120
6. The Deluge   173
7. What Was That?   245

Epilogue   283
Index   301

"Have you ever been in a riot?" asks a former marijuana dealer named Roger. "You could be standing there minding your own business and all of a sudden this thing, this feeling or magnetic force from the crowd, just engulfs you and you actually start participating in the riot. There's an opposite end of the spectrum. If everybody goes around with the love and brotherhood thing that they had in the Haight, when you walk into it you can be engulfed by it.

"That's why so many people walked into that thing and within two hours had their heads so turned around they took off their wingtips and put 'em down on the sidewalk and walked off into some commune. That kind of thing happened hundreds of times a day. You got into that feeling and it was just like the whole world was revolving around this thing that was growing and you could see it grow."

The Haight-Ashbury explosion of 1965–67 was perhaps the most written-about and least understood event of the sixties. The reporters who descended on the neighborhood in the summer of 1967 found it frightening or amusing, but in any case insane. They could not conceive how it happened because they didn't realize that it had a history—this thing that was growing and you could see it grow.

Its history was what made it the apparent madhouse that it was.

For some time the Haight had been shaped by events that came from all sorts of surprising quarters, but were obviously part of a single event. These events seemed at the same time unexpected and inevitable—the essence of drama. Life in the Haight had the exaltation of a play.

But people in the Haight weren't talking to reporters about history. Things had developed so far beyond anybody's expectations that the only honorable course was to take every idea to an extreme —anything less was a cowardly evasion of destiny. So it was their ideas that people in the Haight were telling reporters, ideas so wildly hopeful that they can scarcely be recalled without a pang of regret for lost hopes, mixed with a little embarrassment: "The paradox of a culture reincarnated by itself: that the 'white-eye' who once annihilated the buffalo must now, in action-reacted, be 'saved' from slaughtering himself by the Indian incarnate." "The unnatural state of the universe will not disappear until the last vestige of hierarchy is destroyed." "Mafia is a state of mind—drop it."

When I began researching this history in 1975, I was afraid that a lot of the people involved in the Haight would be burnt out on the subject and reluctant to talk to a reporter about it, even a reporter like me who had been a Berkeley hippie with a number of friends in the Haight. A few years earlier they probably would have been, but now people were just starting to reassess the period, and nearly everybody was eager to talk. Of the half-dozen people who refused to talk to me, four were still associated with the hard core of original Diggers and refused on grounds that I would misrepresent them because I didn't share their ideology. There has been talk of an authorized Digger history. I hope they write it, and I hope this book of mine provides them, and anyone else who writes about the Haight-Ashbury, with a reliable chronology.

I am indebted to the following informants:

Keith Abbott, Chester Anderson (com/co), Ray Anderson (Holy See Light Show), Tony Kaufman Anderson (groupie), Willard Bain (author of *Informed Sources*), Paree Bakhtir (Love Burgers), Teddy Bear, Larry Blackburn, Bobby Bowles (Peg 'n Awl Leathers), Stewart Brand (Prankster, Trips Festival), Ashleigh Brilliant (street poet),

Lynn Brown (Mime Troupe, Digger), Joan Dierkes Carlisle, Luria
Castel (Family Dog), Richard Cherney (House of Richard), John
Cipollina (Quicksilver Messenger Service), Allen Cohen (*Oracle*),
Vince Cresciman (Digger, I/Thou Coffee House), Faybeth Dia-
mond, Bob Durso, Nancy Evans, Ernie Fosselius (Final Solution),
David and Girl Freiberg (Quicksilver), Jerry Garcia (Grateful Dead),
Patrick Gleeson (Happening House), Lou Gottlieb (Morning Star
Ranch), Bill Graham (Fillmore Auditorium), Linda Gravenites, Car-
glin Green (The Righteous Rag), Luther Greene (Straight Theater),
Bill Ham (Pine Street, light-show artist), Ellen Harmon (Red Dog
Saloon, Family Dog), Father Leon Harris (All Saints Church), Chet
Helms (Family Dog), Mendel Herscowitz (straight Haight Street
merchant), Howard Hesseman (The Committee, KMPX disc
jockey), Gary Hirsh (Country Joe), Tom Hobson, Richard Hodge
(lawyer), Richard Hundgen, George Hunter (Charlatans), Roland
Jacopetti (Open Theater, Morning Star), Gary Jackson (Matrix),
Jorma Kaukonen (Jefferson Airplane), Al Kelly (Red Dog, posters),
Ken Kesey (Prankster), Harvey Kornspan (Digger), Mary Anne
Kramer, Paul Krassner, Peter Krug (Wild Colors), Chandler Laugh-
lin (Red Dog, KMPX), Seymour Locks (light-show inventor), Si
Lowinsky (Print Mint), Tom Mazzolini (music archivist), Michael
McClure, Don McCoy (Rancho Olompali), Walter Medeiros
(poster archivist), Barry Melton (Country Joe), Mervyn Millar, Larry
Miller (KMPX), Victor and Gail Moscoso (posters), Moe Mosko-
witz, Stanley Mouse (posters), Ron Nagel (Mystery Trend), Patt
Nathe (Blue Unicorn), Richie Olsen (Charlatans), Steve Porterfield
(Family Dog), Norwood Pratt (Love Conspiracy), Dean and Lee
Quarnstrom (Pranksters), Cindy Reade (Digger), Greg Reisner, Bill
and Hillel Resner (Straight Theater), Roger the Dealer, Elias
Romero (light show), Jon Sagen, Max Scherr (*Barb*), Rock Scully
(Grateful Dead), Jerry Sealund (Far Fetched Foods), Ramon Sender
(Tape Center, Trips Festival, Morning Star), Greg Shaw, Edmund
Shea, Gretchen Sherman, Bob Simmons, Dr. David Smith (Free
Clinic), Jeff Stallard, Rob Sutherland (All Saints Digger), Nathan
Terré, Ron Thelin (Psychedelic Shop), Bill Thompson (Jefferson
Airplane), Hunter S. Thompson, Jack Towle (Family Dog), Teresa

Tudury (All Night Apothecary), Hall Van Vlack (Hearth Coffee Shop), Ben Van Meter (light show), Bill Wheeler (Wheeler's Ranch), Wes Wilson (posters), Leonard Wolfe (Happening House), Don Works (Red Dog).

Needless to say, their opinions are not necessarily those expressed in this book, and I alone am responsible for any errors. I am more particularly indebted to the following people, who gave me access to their files: Chester Anderson, Howard Hesseman, Tom Mazzolini, Gary Jackson and Jann Wenner. Anderson's donation of a nearly complete file of com/co output from January to July 1967 was invaluable.

The books that proved useful to me were Ralph J. Gleason's *The Jefferson Airplane and the San Francisco Sound*, which contains the first attempt to tell the early history of the Haight; Tom Wolfe's *The Electric Kool-Aid Acid Test*, about the Merry Pranksters; *We Are the People Our Parents Warned Us Against*, Nicholas Von Hoffman's attempt to understand the scene as of early summer 1967; two books of interviews, *Voices from the Love Generation*, by Leonard Wolfe, and *Garcia*, by Jann Wenner and Charles Reich; and *Cooptation: The Story of a Radio Station*, an academic thesis by Susan Krieger on KMPX/KSAN. *Scenes*, a sociology of the hippie and surfer movements by John Irwin, greatly helped me clarify my thinking about the dramaturgical elements of life in the Haight. The best contemporary journalism on the Haight was Jeff Jassen's weekly report in the *Berkeley Barb*, but there was also useful coverage in the *San Francisco Chronicle* and the *Oracle.*

Much light is cast on the mood and thinking of the time by Emmett Grogan's *Ringolevio: A Life Played for Keeps* and Marco Vassi's *The Stoned Apocalypse*, although the historical value of both books is limited by their authors' grandiose self-images. Only a handful of straightforward novels have come from the psychedelic movement, the best being Willard Bain's head-twisting *Informed Sources*, Billy Craddock's *Be Not Content*, which parodies the unspoken conclusion of Leary's "tune in, turn on, drop out" mantra—"freak out, fuck up, crawl back"; and the little-known *Tripper*, by Jocelyn (Exposition Press, 1972), which exquisitely portrays the psychedelic life in all its anguish and aimless gorgeousness.

THE HAIGHT-ASHBURY

Why was he doing this? Wasn't it bad enough to get busted? Why did Owsley have to ask for trouble?

On February 21, 1965, California state narcotics agents had raided his home in Berkeley—a squat building nicknamed the Green Factory—and charged Augustus Owsley Stanley III with operating a Methedrine laboratory. Now that the case had come to a hearing, every rule in the book demanded he should get a haircut and a conservative suit and start looking like a misunderstood choirboy.

But Owsley wasn't playing along. At one hearing, the short, dark ex-radar technician showed up in denim trousers and jacket; at the next he wore a sharp Italian suit. He broadcast dangerous, edgy resentment rather than decent fear. He managed to beat the charges anyhow. His lawyer argued that although Owsley's home might have *looked* like a Methedrine lab—could scarcely be said to look like anything else, in fact—nevertheless no completely synthesized Methedrine had been found. So Owsley was free.

At this point, according to the scenario held in common by narcs and drug people, a chemist who was lucky enough to escape the law should disappear gratefully into the woodwork. However, the state of California still held the lab equipment it had confiscated during the bust, and Owsley wanted it back. It was his equipment, and he meant to use it. He sued the state for it and got it back.

Only then did Owsley disappear, slipping off for a few weeks to Los Angeles with his girlfriend, who until a few months before had been a graduate chemistry student at the University of California. When they returned to Berkeley in April they had what he'd really been wanting to make: LSD. Somewhat dubiously his Berkeley friends said they'd try the funny-looking vitamin capsules that were slightly deformed from having been dosed with LSD out of an eyedropper.

To their astonishment, it really was LSD. In fact it was very strong LSD. It was the strongest LSD they'd ever had, devastatingly strong in an almost heavy-handed way that recalled Owsley's own insistent manner.

"Oh, hey," he told them in his mysterious, faintly irritable way, "those first ones were too heavy. You only should have taken half." But even when he claimed he'd gotten the dosage worked out, this was still exceptional LSD. Under the name Bear Research Group, Owsley had already ordered the raw materials to make a million and a half doses.

The United States was a busy place in early 1965. The civil rights movement was in full heat. President Johnson was ordering the bombing of North Vietnam. "Student movement" radicalism was still news on college campuses. The pop art/camp movement had spawned a national fad for corny old Batman movies, and there was a whole new wave of rock and roll coming from England, of all unexpected places, led by the wistful-irreverent Beatles and accompanied by a raft of silly, energetic-looking Mod fashions. An ad campaign reminded everyone that this was a fun-loving, uninhibited Pepsi Generation.

But there was a strange feeling of desolation in the middle of all this activity. Maybe it was the persisting shock effect of President Kennedy's assassination or residual terror from the nuclear confrontation over Cuban missile emplacements. Whatever the reasons, it sometimes seemed that despite all the noise the party was over, and the world was settled, compartmentalized and devoid of high deeds and adventures.

One thing that could cut away at the cut-and-dried feeling, if you were crazy enough to chance it, was taking certain drugs that altered mental processes—marijuana, amphetamines and psychedelics such as LSD. Here was territory that seemed pretty new. In fact, if you wanted a model for mind-drug use, there wasn't much to find. The Beat Generation had experimented with a lot of drugs, but the Beats were now dispersed—at the moment their old San Francisco neighborhood of North Beach was a tourist trap full of topless bars. Then there were the hipsters, who followed black ghetto fashions in drugs as well as slang, clothing, jazz and so on. But like the Beats, the hipsters were in their thirties and forties now, and the ones a young person was likely to meet preferred alcohol and heroin to mind drugs.

There was a new generation of bohemian-minded kids who were very interested in these mind drugs. They were also interested in such traditional bohemian subjects as art, psychology, pacifism, exotic religions and anything else that stretched the limits of understanding. They had no name for themselves comparable to the Beat Generation, though the Beats derisively called some of them hippies (junior grade hipsters), and by default that group had started using the name itself. The Beats looked down on hippies as imitation bohemians who were only interested in getting stoned and having a good time rather than doing something serious, like writing poetry or playing jazz. Another grievance was that while the Beats were always down and out, the hippies seemed to have money. Most of them were selling a little marijuana.

Closest kin to the hippies were the folkies, the bohemian fringe of the long-established folk music scene. They were the same age as the hippies and had the same sense of being disinherited by their elders-in-nonconformity, in their case the "protest song" radicals who saw folk music as a political tool rather than a way of life. Of course hippies and folkies had different tastes in music. The hippies went for the rock and roll of the British Invasion groups and of Bob Dylan after he scandalized the folk purists by adopting the electric guitar. A lot of hippies, in fact, were folkies who had followed Dylan in his switch to rock.

What was unique to the hippies was their attitude—an expansive, theatrical attitude of being cool enough to have fun. They called themselves dudes and ladies rather than cats and chicks. Unlike Beats in their existential black and folkies in their homespun and denim, they wore flashy Mod clothes. Miniskirts, patterned stockings and "Beatle boots" would do, and Beatles-long hair was definitely becoming the mode for hippie men. Even better than the English fashions, though, were the Victorian and Edwardian clothes you could get for next to nothing at thrift shops. They were finely made garments, and you could wear them with a mustache and a swagger.

Better still was to do all this and live in a Victorian house. San Francisco was full of Victorians, since much of the city was rebuilt after the 1906 earthquake, and like Victorian clothes they were now unfashionable and cheap. The best neighborhood in the city for the Edwardian-Victorian motif was an area where many San Francisco State College students lived, a rather forgotten part of the city called the Haight-Ashbury district, which was convenient by trolley to the State College campus and full of once-expensive houses. You could rent two floors of an old mansion for $175 a month, and get leather wallpaper and expansive window seats and art nouveau stained glass and scrollwork. Some of the State crowd were carrying the motif to the limit, dressing like Edwardian toffs every day, furnishing their apartments entirely in period style, even unscrewing the light bulbs and hooking up the old gaslights.

Hippies were scattered around in other places in the country, too, mostly near college campuses. The scene blossomed best where there was a high concentration of hippies. Take Pine Street: three blocks of the San Francisco street of that name where there were fully half a dozen apartment houses full of hippies and grass dealers. Pine Street was what people called outrageous—people there simply ignored the possibility that neighbors or the police would find anything suspicious about their dress or behavior. Pine Streeters had it all figured out. North of Pine was California Street, part of the wealthy Pacific Heights area; south of Pine was the black ghetto, the Fillmore

District. Pine Streeters believed the police were turning a blind eye to their blatant weirdness and open traffic in drugs because they were keeping the foothills of Pacific Heights from becoming entirely black.

In April and May, the new LSD with the brand name Owsley began making its way through the psychedelic communities around the San Francisco area. However many people that might be.

That was one of the mysteries of psychedelics. Taking LSD was like being in a secret society. Hardly anything was being said about it publicly. As a matter of fact, LSD was not an illegal drug, but people acted as if it were; it *seemed* illegal. About the only place where psychedelics were openly discussed was in a tiny magazine called the *Psychedelic Review*, edited by ex-Harvard professor Timothy Leary and some associates. Leary's own writings reinforced the secrecy of the whole thing, though, because he dwelt on the importance of avoiding a panic situation, so people who followed him took their LSD in isolation, in their homes or out in the woods. There was no way of knowing how many people might be messing with psychedelics. If you thought about it, you might conclude the only people taking LSD were Leary and the Harvard crowd, some Beats, and a few others, possibly not many more than your own circle of insane friends.

Around the same time that Owsley's name was becoming a household word in some households, there were rumors of a project that seemed designed to alleviate the adventure shortage. Some crazies were opening a totally Old West saloon with folk music in, of all places, the semi-ghost town of Virginia City, Nevada.

Virginia City wasn't actually such an odd place for a hippie saloon. The old boomtown capital of the Comstock Lode silver rush already had a colony of exotic people, including some psychedelic users. The latter group was centered around a second-generation bohemian named Don Works, a member of the peyote-eating Native American Church who had moved out to the Comstock country to be with his coreligionists among the Washoe and Paiute Indians.

Works lived on a little plot named the Zen Mine after a pair of nonproducing mine shafts running into the dusty hillside behind his cinder-block cabin. The idea for the Red Dog Saloon had been formed there a few months before, when Works, a tall desperado type named Chan Laughlin (who had once owned a Berkeley folk music coffeehouse), and a rich folkie named Mark Unobsky were stranded in Works' two-room cabin by a blizzard. With nothing to do but get stoned and play the board game Risk, they started fantasizing about a folk nightclub to enliven the mountain evenings. It actually sounded plausible, because there was no decent nightlife around for competition, and particularly because folk musicians were always passing through Nevada on their way between the Boston-New York scene and San Francisco-Berkeley. Some fairly big names might be willing to stop off and play a relaxed night or two.

That was the original plan, anyway. Unobsky bought the old Comstock House building on C Street, near the original claim of the wild silver rush that financed the Civil War and drove Germany off the silver standard. Bohemian carpenters were called in from Marin County, and Laughlin was dispatched to San Francisco for antique red velvet drapes and brass fittings.

On one of these buying trips Laughlin stopped off at Pine Street, where he'd hidden out for a while a few months before when he figured the police were after him for smuggling marijuana. While he was talking up the excitement of this stylish folk cabaret in the hills to a Pine Street friend, he met a fellow with a long blond Dutch boy haircut and a missing front tooth who was dressed to the nines in Edwardian duds. It so happened that this Edwardian dude with the elusive, slightly formal manner had put together a musical group that might fit right in.

His was not a folk group, though, but a rock and roll band called the Charlatans. Well, why not? The Beatles, Dylan, this band in Los Angeles named the Byrds that was being called a folk-rock group—suddenly it was clear that a hip rock and roll band was just what the Red Dog needed. And the Charlatans already had a following. Bob Hunter, the Dutch boy blond with the missing tooth, was a culture hero in certain circles at State College for his elegant Edwardiana.

The pianist, Michael Ferguson, had the same sort of stature and had once run an unheard-of kind of store at the edge of the Haight-Ashbury. Magic Theater for Madmen Only had sold nothing but antique clothes, knickknacks, a little art and a lot of marijuana stash jars.

The only problem with the band was that Hunter, an artist and boy-wonder architect, had conceived the Charlatans as a sort of pop art statement, an American response to the British rock groups. At the moment it was really only the concept of a rock band; they had hundreds of publicity stills, featuring Edwardian clothes and twenties rowing-crew uniforms, but had never rehearsed. For months now they'd been growing their hair down to their shoulders—much longer than the Beatles' hair—and carrying on like a rock band at parties, and now it was time to get down to finding out what they could play. A lot of work needed to be done. Hunter, for instance, couldn't play anything but tambourine and autoharp, and there were those who said he couldn't play that.

The Red Dog became a sort of Pine Street project. A collage artist and one-time motorcycle racer named Al Kelly went up to Virginia City to work on the remodeling. Ellen Harmon, the rangy woman who shared his tiny room in Pine Street where the walls were painted with pop art sound effects ("Poww!" "Bawannnnggggg!"), went as a waitress. There was an abstract expressionist painter on Pine Street who managed two of the apartment houses, a shaggy-bearded Southerner named Bill Ham. His light shows, which were like moving abstract paintings projected in brilliant colors on a screen, were Pine Street's favorite evening entertainment. He designed a light box for the Red Dog that would pulsate with color in time with the music.

Altogether, a couple of dozen people from San Francisco moved up to Virginia City for the Red Dog project. After a number of delays and false starts, the Red Dog Saloon finally opened on June 29, 1965, advertised by a poster drawn by the Charlatans' pianist in a sort of old-timey medicine-show style that described the band as "The Limit of the Marvelous." The band moved up to Virginia City on opening day with one loudspeaker and a ten-watt amplifier.

The sheriff came to see opening night. The new place was the only nightclub in town, and people had been pushing him to look into it anyway. All these city people dressing in vests and string ties and celluloid collars—and that sign out front, too, with the slavering red dog on it.

But he had to admit they'd done a hell of a job as he mounted the plank sidewalk, rebuilt and roofed over just as it had been in the 1860s. As he pushed in through the swinging doors, he could see they'd spared no expense on the interior, either. All period furnishings, red and turquoise velvet drapes with a lot of gold braid, the whole place painted red with black trim. The bartender was in a striped shirt with sleeve garters, and the waitresses were all in saloon-maid bodices and net stockings. Some of the customers knocking back the beer and bourbon were in old-time getups as well.

A couple of things, you couldn't figure whether they were out of place or not. Maybe in the 1860s there could have been a 380-pound Washoe Indian bouncer in a top hat and a Rainbow Girls sash. The musicians in those days surely didn't play rock and roll, but maybe they did get as looped as these guys on the stage seemed to be, rolling their eyes and staggering and trying to play each other's instruments.

But all told, it was enough to touch a man's heart. The least the sheriff could do was to honor the hallowed Code of the West, which held that when a man entered a bar he checked all his firearms at the door. "Check my gun?"

Without blinking an eye, Don Works plucked the pistol out of the sheriff's hand, threw a practiced glance down the barrel, spun the chambers, cocked the hammer and fired off two quick shots into the floor. "Works fine, sheriff," he said.

Rock and roll meets the Old West—the possibilities were staggering. The Charlatans' gig stretched on far longer than the planned two weeks. People told their friends about it, and some of the posters made it back to San Francisco, where they tended to be handed around from person to person rather than posted. More and more people made the three-hour drive just to see whether it could be true: an Old West Bar with a hip rock band in the Edwardian style.

As a matter of fact, the Charlatans had started changing their style. Stuck in Virginia City week in and week out, they and everyone else working at the Red Dog fell into the Old West style. In a way it was the only thing to do: get a pair of chaps and a ten-gallon hat and spend the afternoons picking off jackrabbits. Owsley's LSD had been around since opening night, and on Mondays, when the Red Dog was dark, the staff would have LSD parties. The sense of the frontier grew stronger and stronger.

Some of the people envisioned the Red Dog as a movie. Chan Laughlin would lecture about it: "This is an Old Western town, and we're more Old Western than anybody else. Remember, when your feet hit the floor in the morning, you're in a Grade B movie. This *is* that saloon down the street where the manager has his office under the stairs and all the gunhands sit around out front and periodically he comes out and motions a couple of them to ride away and rustle some cows. It's *that place*, complete with fancy girls going around bending over tables and the music and people roaring and ordering more drinks and carrying on."

Yes indeed. Everybody started wearing the clothes and carrying fancy firearms. Each bartender as he came on shift brought his own personally selected bar pistol. After a while the Charlatans had a set of matched-caliber Winchester rifles they would carry onstage and lean up against the amplifier before picking up their guitars. Now, what was all this fuss about the Beatles and their so-called flashy style?

Back in San Francisco, a far-out new kind of nightclub opened on July 4, but nobody was going to it.

Actually, there were people who went: people in the music business. The club, called Mother's, was opened by a Rabelaisian rock DJ who went by the name of "Big Daddy" Tom Donahue. He ran the local rock music scene—managed bands, put on big shows at the Cow Palace for teenagers and even had his own record label, Autumn Records, which specialized in teen rock bands like the Tikis and the Vejtables. Before he opened Mother's, the 400-pound Big Daddy had held court over a crowd of promo men, agents and other DJs at a sidewalk restaurant up the block, and that crowd naturally followed him to Mother's.

The new place was nothing like a sidewalk café. Donahue had spent a fortune on it. He'd hired Beat woodworkers from Big Sur, and the walls were covered with undulating sculptured wood and sheets of plastic paneling that pulsed with colored light in time with the music. There were collages in the bathrooms and a big curtain instead of a front door. Pretty far out for a rock DJ who was pushing pimple cream all day. But who did he expect to come besides his music biz friends? The entertainment was his own teen rock bands, but the club's liquor license kept teenagers out.

Then, on August 4, Donahue booked the New York folk-rock band the Lovin' Spoonful, and all of a sudden the place was packed with non-biz people, dressed in Mod flash or Edwardiana—rock fans who were old enough to drink but preferred to dance. There were more of them than they themselves had realized. The music biz people had never even known such people existed.

When the Spoonful left after its four-week gig (which had coincided with their first hit record, "Do You Believe in Magic?"), this bright-feathered tribe of fans vanished, leaving Mother's so empty it started featuring its own semi-nude dancer ("Topless Daughter Maria") like the other North Beach clubs.

Everybody of college age had heard of Ken Kesey, at least as the novelist who wrote *One Flew Over the Cuckoo's Nest.* There were rumors that he'd written the book partly on LSD and that he'd taken all sorts of psychedelics since 1959, when he'd been a $75-a-day guinea pig at Veterans' Memorial Hospital in Menlo Park. He was known as a sort of expert on psychedelics. He'd set a fashion for calling LSD acid (short for lysergic acid diethylamide), to the horror of religious LSD eaters.

In 1964 he had bought a 1939 International Harvester bus with the advance money from his second novel and he and his friends had painted it in splotches of a dozen different colors. They drove to the New York World's Fair in it, and all across the country—even in the South, boiling over with conflict concerning integration—they'd taken acid and acted as crazy as they felt, right out in public.

He was a fearless man, it seemed. *Cuckoo's Nest* was about overcoming fear, and there was a tale that he had given a guest lecture in a creative writing class that consisted of walking up to the front of the classroom and diving out the window. He'd been talking about the potential heroism of the everyday and claiming that the costumed superheroes of Marvel Comics had as much to say about life as a lot of contemporary literature.

Timothy Leary and the *Psychedelic Review* wrote about overcoming fear, too, but in effect they talked about avoiding it. The Leary style was to plan your psychedelic trip in terms of set and setting. In other words, you'd decide what you expected to experience and plan your surroundings and schedule accordingly. Trouble arose, though, when one of life's unexpected events disrupted the setting. Then you might be in for the magnified panic experience known as freaking out, the very thing the set-and-setting model was supposed to prevent.

To the freewheeling people who took psychedelic drugs the way Kesey did, this sounded like exactly the wrong approach. If you set things up to avoid a freak-out, you were in a sense starting the trip with fear in your mind, so a freak-out might well be in the cards. The right way to go about it was to confront fear itself by courting the unexpected. The real lesson of psychedelics was that you couldn't control the trip anyway, so you might as well swing with whatever came up. In Kesey's circle they even used the slogan, "Freak freely."

One of Kesey's friends, another athletic novelist, was Ken Babbs, an ex-Marine helicopter pilot. Babbs introduced the notion of systematically setting up puzzling, unexpected and downright edgy situations to see what would happen. They called these existential practical jokes pranks, and Kesey's crowd started calling themselves the Merry Pranksters.

The Pranksters counted a real underground celebrity among their number. He was Neal Cassady, the legendary prototype of Japhy Rider in Jack Kerouac's Beat novel *On the Road.* Cassady's personal project in life seemed to be achieving total, instantaneous stream-of-consciousness speech, using the amphetamine pills he popped like candies to get his mind and his mouth in synch. Much of the time his nonstop monologue sounded like gibberish, but the moments you grasped might be so acute you wondered whether the rest was really gibberish at all. If you walked past him at a party, where he'd usually be exercising his amphetamine-powered restlessness by juggling a sledgehammer in the air, you were likely to hear unsettlingly sharp observations about yourself worked into his monologue. Cassady was a daredevil driver and had piloted the Prankster Bus across the country in the World's Fair adventure.

The Pranksters mostly had their acid parties at Kesey's six-acre home in La Honda, in the hills that run down the spine of the San Francisco Peninsula. Secluded as it was, Kesey's place had neverthe-less attracted attention. Sheriff's deputies standing on the roadside would study the bizarre activities of the Pranksters, who were likely to have painted their faces in weird designs or taken to wearing goggles. But though they knew in their hearts that something wrong was going on down there, the cops couldn't see any laws being broken. Without a warrant, they couldn't cross the little footbridge to Kesey's property. Neal Cassady would stand naked in the bushes and harangue the cops with impunity in his surreal style.

Then on April 24, 1965, sheriffs got a warrant to search Kesey's place for marijuana, and eighteen law officers descended on La Honda. They found the place perhaps even more bizarre than they'd expected. There were loudspeakers placed out in the woods, all connected to a complex of tape recorders and microphones and electronic sound-synthesizing equipment in the house. There were very peculiar things stuck randomly around the property, inside the house and out: human skulls, incomprehensible signs, grotesque "Funk Art" collages of hair and bent pieces of wire and parts of baby dolls glued together. Many objects had been painted in the slightly poisonous pink and green shades of fluorescent Day-Glo paint.

There was even obscenity. The sculptor Ron Boise, whose welded metal sculptures illustrating the sexual positions of the *Kama Sutra* had caused a scandal, was hanging out at Kesey's. One of his sculp-tures, showing a man and a woman in oral sex, had been modified with a garden hose that shot a watery orgasm up through a leg. Another, one of the "thunder machines" that made sounds when struck, was in the shape of a woman strung with piano wire. To adjust the note, you pushed a knot located where her clitoris would be.

And there was indeed marijuana. The cops claimed to have caught Kesey trying to flush it down a collage-covered toilet. He was arrested and his case commenced dragging through the courts.

This might have looked like a good time for Kesey to lie low, but now he decided he wanted to meet the Hell's Angels. The famous motorcycle club had been thrilling California newspaper readers in June and July with their arrest on a gang-rape charge and the tales that they were going to invade and terrorize a small California town on Independence Day. In August he met Hunter Thompson, a young journalist living in the Haight-Ashbury who was writing a book about the Angels and had gone so far as to buy a motorcycle and to run with them a little. Thompson was on his way to a garage where a couple of Angels worked when Kesey met him, so Kesey invited himself along, struck up a conversation with four or five Angels and invited the whole San Francisco chapter to a party in La Honda.

Heedless of the panic it stirred among his neighbors, on August 7 Kesey put up a fifteen-by-three-foot banner in front of his house that read, "The Merry Pranksters Welcome the Hell's Angels." Sure enough, dozens of Angels showed up on their chopped Harleys, a little dubious about partying with these non-biker "citizens."

The Pranksters didn't know what to expect themselves, but they were stoned on acid and what they might have expected didn't much matter. There was beer available for the Angels and Bob Dylan records playing through the loudspeakers: the makings of a party. The Angels drank the beer and gawked at the Ron Boise statue of the hanged man and all the weird signs and mobiles hanging in the woods.

Most important, the Pranksters were able to get the Angels to try LSD. The Angels had messed around plenty with drugs before. Amphetamines, barbiturates, grass, beer and cough syrup all at once was just an ordinary good time for them. But they had never tried psychedelics, and they were impressed. On acid they could see a screwy logic in all the strange things around Kesey's place, just as the Pranksters could comprehend a rough and unexpected logic in the Angels' ways. Unexpectedly, the acid made the Angels peaceable.

The Angels were impressed with the Pranksters' cool, because most non-Angels had only two ways of reacting to these baddest of all bikers, fear or hostility.

The Angels decided to stick around and party for a while. The party lasted two days and two nights, and continued on and off for a month and a half. It was almost routine: You'd come over the footbridge to Kesey's woodsy retreat, get your LSD-dosed pill, watch the Angels gang-bang some willing girl, chip in for spaghetti, wander around the woods among the sculptures and unexpected microphones, and maybe go into the house, where the Pranksters would be watching the unedited 36 hours of film they'd shot of themselves during the great Bus Trip.

The San Francisco Angels told the Oakland Angels, and the large Oakland chapter spread the word to all the others. The Beat poet Allen Ginsberg came and became a regular fan of the "Angelic barbarians." The parties got bigger and bigger.

On August 11, touched off by a trivial drunk driving arrest, a riot broke out in Watts, the black ghetto of Los Angeles. Widespread arson and looting lasted for over a week and inspired similar race riots in other cities. On August 13, the left-wing student and para-student community of Berkeley got a newspaper of its own, the *Berkeley Barb*, which covered the civil rights and antiwar movements and the waning efforts of the semester-before-last's Free Speech Movement, which had protested the university's right to exclude left-wing recruiters from the campus.

On that same August 13 another nightclub opened in San Francisco with a name curiously similar to Mother's: the Matrix. The baby of Marty Balin—born Martin Buchwald, an actor-turned-singer who was living in the Haight—the Matrix itself was a former pizza house that had been bought—lock, stock and liquor license—by Balin with a group of partners. Balin's own folk-rock group was to be the house band.

This band, Jefferson Airplane, was a peculiar outfit. Balin's choice for rhythm guitar was Paul Kantner, who was rooming at the time with a bunch of people that included a mainstream Prankster; the female lead singer had been to Kesey's parties herself. The lead guitarist was a leading local folk picker, but the drummer was actually a guitarist whom Balin had picked because he "looked like a drummer." As for the name, it came from Berkeley, where in reaction against the heavy political and musical orthodoxy of the Left, the more irreverent folkies had invented a series of legendary blues musicians such as Blind Ebbets Field, Little Son Goldfarb and Blind Thomas Jefferson Airplane.

So there they were, folkies with amplified guitars and the Moddest clothes they could afford, playing rock and roll in what would have passed for a small folk music club with no dance floor. Like the Charlatans off in Nevada, the Airplane were trying everything they could think of in this brave folk-rock experiment: country blues, Chicago blues as played by the Rolling Stones, folk ballads, country and western tunes, and original songs. Balin's roommate was a copyboy at the *San Francisco Chronicle*, where the jazz columnist, Ralph J. Gleason, had recently irritated his jazz readership by speaking kindly of folk rock and actually encouraging people to see the British rock bands. Maybe Gleason would review them, whether or not he could understand the slogan they started using on August 20: "Jefferson Airplane Loves You."

Out in Virginia City, the Red Dog's hazy summer of music, drugs, frontier attitudes and the continual cycling of people between the Comstock country and the Bay Area was drawing to a jittery end. A rival bar owner spread rumors about underage girls and illicit drugs. Some local kids had been turned on to marijuana and their parents figured they knew how. The Red Dog people's fancy for guns led to even more trouble. One week, when the club owner was short of cash, he offered to let the employees take their wages in firearms from the local gun shop, which was willing to give him a wholesale rate. The word spread like wildfire around town when one of those *strange young people* was seen walking up C Street with a double armload of Old West hardware.

The club's managers received a tombstone with their names on it. One of the Miss Kitties had been carrying a porcelain doorknob in her garter for self-protection, but now she replaced it with an elegant silver derringer. And on top of all the trouble with the townspeople, the managers were now at odds. Chan Laughlin was threatening to pull the Charlatans and Miss Kitties out of the Red Dog and take over the Sky Room of the Mapes Hotel in Reno.

Just at this time the Charlatans made their San Francisco debut. One member of the Committee, a North Beach satirical theater group, had made a comic film of himself and wanted a rock band on the same bill when he showed it on August 30. The Charlatans had gotten a lot tighter since their opening night. By this time they had a female singer, Lynn Hughes, who was one of the Miss Kitties (sometimes even billed as "Miss Kitty" or "Crystal Ball") as well as the Red Dog's bookkeeper. The *Chronicle*'s second-string music writer covered their set but did not commit himself except to note their "good sense of rhythm" and the fact that their hair made the Beatles look like chairmen of the board.

The Charlatans' San Francisco debut was the end of the Red Dog summer. On the way back to Nevada the next day, the guitarist and manager got busted for grass in the town of Rodeo by a policeman who was curious about their hairdos. Laughlin had just convinced him they dressed as they did for show biz reasons—the Beatles and all—when he reached up to pull down the hood of the car and the cop saw a bottle of grass stuck in his belt.

This was the last straw for the Red Dog's owner; he fired the Charlatans. Around the same time Ken Kesey's busload of Merry Pranksters showed up to check out the wild kicks said to be going on at the Red Dog. After a day and a night of psychedelic wildness, with electronic equipment set up on the antique floorboards and Neal Cassady flexing his sledgehammer, the owner padlocked the club until sanity returned.

A few weeks later, on September 13, the Committee Theater began hosting a series of Monday-night showings of a multimedia experience called "America Needs Indians." The multiple media were slides, three motion pictures, two sound tracks and four Indian dancers, all at the same time. The effect was an inundation of Indian faces, images of nature, Indian music, everything that America had been before the Europeans came.

One of the two partners who produced "America Needs Indians" was Stewart Brand, who as a photographer shooting at the Warm Springs Indian Reservation in Oregon had become convinced "either the white man or the Indian had to be right." Ken Kesey's first novel, with its Indian narrator, put him in the Indian camp and led him to meet Kesey and become a proto-Prankster.

"America Needs Indians" was not the only multimedia show in the country. In Woodstock, New York, about thirty-five miles from Timothy Leary's psychedelic headquarters in Millbrook, Long Island, two artists working with painted slides on a rear projection screen were known as Leary's show. The most-traveled multimedia show was USCo, of which Stewart Brand was a sometime member. The founder of USCo had been one of the earliest people to follow the "media philosopher" Marshall McLuhan, and his show was emphatically intended to produce "sensory overload," which according to McLuhan was the natural mode of the "electronic age": an overpowering simultaneity that breaks down the confines of rational thought.

Of course, another thing that produced what you could call sensory overload was LSD. Stewart Brand described "America Needs Indians" as "a peyote meeting without peyote." That sounded like fun, and hey—what if you happened to bend the rules a little and come actually stoned on peyote or LSD? Hey!

That obscure neighborhood known as the Haight-Ashbury got some unaccustomed press attention in September. On the sixth the *San Francisco Examiner* ran a story titled "A New Haven for Beatniks." (In the text, however, the locals were referred to as hippies.) It dwelt on the Blue Unicorn, a coffeehouse that had been at 1927 Hayes Street for two and a half years.

As commercialization had driven Beats and hippies alike out of North Beach, a number of them had discovered the State College student private paradise adjoining Golden Gate Park, a neighborhood with beautiful, cheap old Victorians, a tolerably peaceful population with no one ethnic group predominating, and even its own private strip of the park, the eight-block-long Panhandle. There were already two exotic boutiques: the House of Richard, right across the street from the Panhandle at Oak and Shrader, which sold Mexican sandals and ponchos; and a Mod clothing boutique named Mnasidika (usually pronounced "Minsidika") on Haight Street itself.

The Blue Unicorn, in the quieter part of the Haight-Ashbury north of the Panhandle, had begun to attract bohemians who weren't even living in the neighborhood. It advertised the lowest prices of any coffeehouse in town, plus "food, books, music and art" and *no* jukebox." There were chessboards, sewing kits and a piano for the use of patrons, a free secondhand clothes box and a comfortable, saggy old sofa. The food counter displayed used books and records for sale: any little hustle to keep the nickle-and-dime operation going. Bob Stubbs, a tall, laconic naval academy dropout from rural Hawaii, had started the Unicorn with an investment of $100.

It had accepted its responsibilities as a hippie community center. The Legalize Marijuana (LEMAR) movement held meetings there, and a LEMAR activist named Chester Helms organized Wednesday-night poetry readings. The Sexual Freedom League also met there and held a press conference at the Unicorn after one of their nude wade-ins. As word spread of the attractions of the Haight-Ashbury neighborhood, Stubbs started issuing little handbills spelling out the "Unicorn Philosophy." One of them read: "It is nothing new. We have a private revolution going on. A revolution of individuality and diversity that can only be private. Upon becoming a group movement, such a revolution ends up with imitators rather than participants. . . . It is essentially a striving for *realization* of one's *relationship* to life and other people. . . ."

The *Examiner* story celebrated the Blue Unicorn as "a place to relax if you have no money . . . to wash dishes for a meal if you are hungry." Stubbs was dubbed "postmaster general" for his habit of holding mail for regular customers who happened not to have addresses.

Two weeks after the news story, on September 21, city health inspectors cited the Unicorn for a number of violations and ordered it closed as of October 3. Stubbs was ordered to clean all food utensils, purchase a sanitizer to use in the final rinse of dishwashing, put in a "smooth and washable" floor and paint the whole place a "light-colored enamel."

The order that stung most, though, even more than the demand for an un-coffeehousey light enamel, was to remove all items not needed for food preparation from the premises: the encyclopedia, the used books and records, etc. This development stimulated another newspaper story that quoted a customer as saying, "The place is so trippy—that means good—as it is." The Associated Press picked the story up; a columnist in the *Richmond* (Virginia) *Times Dispatch* defended Stubbs' right to run a nonconformist coffee house.

Given all this publicity, the health inspectors called Stubbs to assure him they were not trying to close the Unicorn forever. Reasonable compliance would be enough. If he served nothing but coffee and cold food, for instance, the laws were less stringent. So, after being closed for a couple of weeks in October during which a club called Haight Levels had opened on Haight Street, over on the other side of the Panhandle, and a lot of the Blue Unicorn regulars had started hanging out there, the Unicorn reopened, chess sets and all, both it and the Haight-Ashbury having become mildly famous.

The theater was a busy world late in 1965. Satirical comics like Lenny Bruce and the improvisational theater troupes—in San Francisco, the venerable Committee—had been mocking convention since the late fifties, and were now in their prime. A new avant-garde sort of theater produced not plays but "events" or "happenings" that required audience participation. This new theater aimed for either Zen spontaneity or the re-creation of primitive ritual from which all the arts were thought to have been born. Beat poets such as Lawrence Ferlinghetti had gotten involved with happenings, and several events had been staged at the Tape Music Center at the eastern fringe of the Haight-Ashbury, a building full of studios used for modern dance and painting as well as avant-garde electronic music.

Then there was the San Francisco Mime Troupe, a unique company that sought to combine avant-gardism with radical politics,

Artaud's Theater of Cruelty with Brecht's social didacticism. The name referred to a broad gestural acting style, not wordless pantomime. Founder R. G. Davis was particularly drawn to the burlesque and satiric elements in the Renaissance Italian form of drama called commedia dell'arte.

Renaissance Italy, commedia dell'arte—that sounded enough like Real Art that the Mime Troupe could have applied for funding from the big cultural foundations that had sprung up since President Kennedy had made the arts fashionable. But Davis refused foundation money and its threat of political compromise. His strategy was to spend as little money as possible on sets and props and to try to live off theater gate receipts and whatever donations his troupe could collect at outdoor shows in the parks. In August the Parks and Recreation Commission had lifted their performance permit for alleged obscenity. The Mime Troupe suspected the real reason was political and continued to play without a permit, risking arrest with every performance.

On College Avenue in south Berkeley there was a bizarre building: a Victorian that had been raised up while two storefronts were built underneath it and then settled down on top of them. On October 1 the Open Theater took over both storefronts; some of the actors already lived upstairs.

The leaders of the group were a Berkeley Drama Department dropout named Ben Jacopetti and his wife, Rain, who before getting the storefronts on College Avenue had used the attic of a huge old house at Dwight and Sacramento for rehearsals. One evening they had been experimenting with commercial filmstrips, cutting them up and running them backward and so on. During a Scott Paper educational film about menstruation, Rain had stood up into the projector beam and the result was an animated diagram of menstrual processes projected on her body. She stripped off her clothes to heighten the effect, and thus began a series of experiments with projections on nude bodies.

At first they did these shows for invitational audiences of sixty or seventy in that attic. The projections were films and slides, sometimes light shows of liquid pigment of the sort that the painter Bill Ham was doing for his neighbors on Pine Street. The first to bring a light show was Ray Anderson, whose brother was living with Signe Toly of the Jefferson Airplane. In time the Open Theater actors bought their own overhead projector and started working up more elaborate shows with props, scrim and multiple soundtracks.

They started calling these shows "Revelations," and toyed with the idea of putting them on in public, but after an audition at Mother's they were told by Tom Donahue that the show was too nude even for topless Broadway. They couldn't even perform "Revelations" at their own theater, because they had injudiciously called the police to ask whether they could be arrested for putting on such a show. Instead they returned to their cabaret pieces: a play called *The God Box* written around a high-frequency generator that emitted purple sparks and would make a fluorescent bulb glow if it was brought near; dramatic readings of a nineteenth-century sermon cataloging the hideous effects of masturbation and a 1920s sermon by Aimee Semple MacPherson which exhorted the audience to *"come in numbers, come* in Deuteronomy."

The Open Theater was a sort of multimedia phenomenon itself. To get into the theater section you first passed through the storefront that was an art gallery (featuring works by Pine Streeters such as Hunter and Kelly, and other artists such as Gary Hirsh, sometime drummer in the house jazz band). In the theater section one of the most popular acts proved to be the Congress of Wonders, two young actors who did lively vaudevillian performances of the stories and poems in John Lennon's book *In His Own Write.*

So the Open Theater was flirting with pop art and irreverent fun as well as revelations. The theater prospectus had even begun with a comic strip page, but it showed another side of the project. "The nature of the world around us has changed," said a narrative voice. "(We are slow to believe it,)" replied a fleetingly viewed cartoon figure. "The nature of our roles in the world is being revealed. (We hesitate to accept it.)" The bulk of the prospectus was in more conventional prose and argued for more experimentation with ritual, although it might have to be self-conscious, fragmented or even sham ritual in order to overcome the problem of how art is related to its audience. Rain Jacopetti quoted at length from the Chinese book of oracles, the *I Ching*, which had recently been reprinted in a one-volume edition after many years out of print.

"A time has come," she concluded, "for man again to see Christ —to exalt in fellowship with men—we call it God, all-pervading spirit, state of enlightenment, what you will. . . . The hangup is that we each call it after our own vision. . . . The words are old, worn and misused words which have gathered unacceptable connotations to those who choose others. . . .

"Believe it, and it will exist."

T*ime's* cover story the weekend of October 15 was "The Turning Point in Vietnam." The *Berkeley Barb* counter-headlined:
"VDC Shatters War 'Consensus,' Greatest Antiwar Protest Ever,
U.C. Center of Worldwide Action." A proposal from the Berkeley
chapter of the Vietnam Day Committee had grown into a coor-
dinated event in twenty countries. Of the two American demonstrations, one was going to be in Berkeley.

As it was planned, there would be speakers and antiwar folksingers
all day Friday, then an afternoon march on the army induction
center in Oakland, followed by an all-night vigil and more speakers
on Saturday. But the mayor of Oakland refused to grant the march
a permit. The VDC said it would have a march anyway. Chief
Toothman of the Oakland police said if they did, he would stop it
by any means. There was trouble in the air.

Some 14,000 people came for the event from scores of western
cities, whole busloads from Los Angeles and Portland. Some of them
had sat since morning in a vacant lot on the University of California
campus hearing the war denounced by student and labor radicals and
a slate of antiwar writers, such as Allen Ginsberg, Kay Boyle and

Lawrence Ferlinghetti. Ken Kesey was scheduled in a superstar time slot, just a speaker or two before the march was to start.

The VDC organizers who put together the antiwar cheerleader lineup could not have been up-to-date on Kesey's recent interests, such as pranks, Hell's Angels, Marvel Comics superstars and courting the unexpected. He came with a load of Pranksters in the familiar old bus, painted blood-red for the occasion and covered with nation-alist symbols: swastikas, hammers and sickles, rising suns, stars of David, the Great Seal of the United States, the American eagle. To the VDC's horror, Kesey's speech to the crowd just minutes before the march consisted of a soft-spoken meditation on the similarity between the antiwar movement and the military, punctuated by passages on the harmonica. The VDC couldn't wait for him to get offstage so they could get another speaker up there to sustain a militant mood for the march.

Kesey was just a momentary puzzlement in the antiwar crescendo, however. Everything had been building toward the expected con-frontation between nonviolent marchers and Oakland cops. In addi-tion to the antiwar rhetoric there were protest folk songs and even —though only on record—political rock and roll. A projected folk music newspaper had just published its first "issue," a 45 rpm record entitled "Songs of Opposition," in time for its contents to be wafted out of open apartment windows along the route of the march. It was on sale for 50¢.

One side of the record was orthodox protest songs by Peter Krug, the "Bob Dylan of Berkeley," all solemn and conscientious. The other side was a jug band led by Joe McDonald—who happened to be the musical director of the demonstration—which had taken as its name for the occasion one of those Berkeley left in-joke names, Country Joe and the Fish. It was meant to refer to Mao Tse-tung's dictum that a revolutionist must "move among the people like a fish in water." The Fish's "Feel-Like-I'm-Fixin'-to-Die Rag" delivered its antiwar sentiments in good-timey jug-band style with washboard and kazoo. "Superbird" was even more Pepsi Generation, calling on Marvel Comics superheroes to oppose the war and featuring a cheap Japanese electric guitar. The Fish didn't try using the still controversial electric guitar at the demonstration, but they joined the parade down to Oakland playing their protest jug-band music from the back of a truck.

As might have been expected, the march was stopped flat at the Oakland city line by a phalanx of police 400 strong. Chief Toothman had taken no chances; there were 3,600 more police and National Guardsmen in reserve in case the crowd broke through. The march leaders conferred briefly and decided to lead the march back to a park at Berkeley's civic center for more pep talk. The evening ended dramatically when an unknown party teargassed the park, but not before the organizers had decided to march into Oakland again on Saturday.

It happened that Ken Kesey's circle were not the only intellectuals hanging out with the Hell's Angels. In fact there had always been an intellectual or artistic stratum in the Angels. One former Angel was a city hall reporter for the *San Francisco Chronicle;* other Angels wrote poetry and played folk guitar. An artist who ran with the Angels had recently published a sheaf of silk-screen prints, *Drawings of a Peyote Boy,* to raise money for the legal defense of the Native American Church.

But Kesey had hastened the Angels' contacts with the college community, and during that summer of their notoriety the hulking bikers had become a common sight on Telegraph Avenue in Berkeley. The campus radicals could scarcely believe their luck: the most feared outlaws in California, actually hanging out with them. An old radical dream come true: politicos making contact with delinquent gangs. The radicals who had always chafed under the doctrine of nonviolence started theorizing about "our violent brothers" and their role in the coming revolution. As recently as three weeks before the peace march, the Angels had brawled with police at a café in a working-class San Francisco neighborhood. These were just the shock troops the movement needed: ugly, scary musclemen who were way outside the System.

On the morning of October 16 the radicals found to their dismay that "Sonny" Barger, president of the large Oakland chapter of the Angels, had decided to oppose the second peace march. The rest of the chapter, including most Angel intellectuals, fell into rank behind him, and the Angels formed a solid wall that again stopped the marchers at the Oakland line. Kesey's bus full of people couldn't even get close enough to the Angels to talk to them.

The whole state was thrown into confusion by this turn of events. The Angels were the biggest villains in California, but here they were defending the city of Oakland from the "bearded Vietniks" of Berkeley. For once neither politicians nor newspapers could decide who the bad guys were.

In the evening of that disorienting day there was a big public rock and roll dance in San Francisco—but nothing like the Cow Palace teen shows or the Matrix concerts, and nothing like a sock hop. It was called "A Tribute to Dr. Strange," starring the Charlatans and Jefferson Airplane and was put on by something called the Family Dog. It was Pine Street in action.

One of the Pine Street houses was nicknamed the Dog House. Al Kelly and Ellen Harmon of the Red Dog Saloon lived there, as well as a dealer named Jack Towle who reportedly had established $10 as the ceiling price of an ounce of grass in San Francisco. Another resident was Luria Castell, a political activist and later a psychedelic kid on the Haight–San Francisco State scene, in Big Sur and around the rock and roll nightclubs on Los Angeles' Sunset Strip.

All four had been to Virginia City during the Red Dog summer. Their idea was to create more of that loose, expressive atmosphere with costume and rock music and a sense of frontiers. And besides, the Mexican border had gotten so hot that Kelly didn't want to smuggle marijuana for a living any more. Through her political connections Luria knew of the meeting hall of the International Longshoremen's and Warehousemen's Union near Fishermen's Wharf. They borrowed money from their parents and rented it, doing business as the Family Dog—maybe because of the Red Dog, or the Dog House, or Ellen's dog that had just gotten run over, or maybe even a plan they'd once had to scam up some money by running a pet cemetery in New Mexico. Their idea was to put on a dance every other week.

The Charlatans had played the Matrix by this time, with the Airplane as second bill. The Family Dog people found an Oakland band called the Marbles, who had much the same style as the British rock groups, and a new band called the Great Society that Tom Donahue had just signed up. For MC they got a Top Forty disc jockey named Russ "the Moose" Syracuse, whose *All Night Flight* show featured sardonic gags like the sound of a bomb being dropped on dumb records and even on commercials.

The DJ's radio station ran ads for the dance, as part of the deal by which they got Russ the Moose as MC. The Family Dog also met with the *Chronicle*'s Ralph Gleason because he seemed to be the only public figure who believed rock and roll might be the center of something new and important, and Gleason favored them with a brief mention in his column. Apart from a few silk-screened posters that went up at the Matrix and in North Beach, the only other public notice of the dance was what people called a poster but was actually more like a handbill. It had sketchy decorations reminiscent of the flaming "magic spell" patterns in Dr. Strange comics, hastily scratched by Kelly in the offices of the company that printed them. These posters were sent to Berkeley, Palo Alto, the Haight, anywhere the Dog figured there might be interest.

They got a fellow Pine Streeter to engineer the sound, a nearly impossible task in the echoey octagonal hall. Bill Ham set up his light show at one side of the hall. They had no idea who would come apart from their own friends. The night of the dance Kelly stood out in the street in front of the hall, in the eddies of nighttime traffic flowing to and from the Fishermen's Wharf restaurant district, hoping to sell tickets to passersby.

It was this way. In Marvel Comics, Dr. Strange, "master of the Mystic Arts," stood alone between this universe and hideous forces of supernatural evil which he combated by casting spells—colored patterns of congealed energy emanating from his palms. His ancient enemy, the Dread Dormammu, was a swaggering megalomaniac whose head was hidden in a pillar of smoke. Now here was a rock and roll dance, featuring groups with weird names and MCed by the potheads' favorite DJ, dedicated to Dr. Strange. For a couple of hundred people it was something they'd been waiting for without realizing it.

They came as if there might never be anything like it again. They were in Mod clothes, Victorian suits and granny gowns, Old West outfits, pirate costumes, free-form costumes. There were even a couple of Hell's Angels. They threw themselves into the dance; they formed snake-dance lines that wove through the hall, danced in circles and figure eights with well-met strangers. Allen Ginsberg, in the white hospital orderly uniform he had affected since his visit to India, walked around for the first part of the evening unnoticed and gaping, as astonished as anyone else at the energy in the air and the number of strange people.

It was impossible to make out the lyrics in the crazy acoustics of Longshoremen's Hall, but who cared? The bands were also in costume: the Airplane looked Mod, the Charlatans with their outrageously long hair were dressed as cowboys, and the Great Society had a lead singer who appeared in aggressively Mod miniskirt and stockings the precise color of a grape milk shake. Behind the Great Society stood a poster showing an American eagle, clutching a bunch of bombs in one claw, labeled "Peace," and a bunch of dollar bills in the other, labeled "Freedom"; over the eagle's head was a banner that read, "Bad Taste."

Most astonishing of all, to anybody who had been to a dance in an armory or a high school gym, was the lack of violence. Experienced rock musicians always owned solid-body guitars because they could be used to ward off missiles thrown by a beered-up teenager who had just failed to score with a chick or had some other grudge against the world. There was nothing of the kind here. The bar concession didn't even do any business. In fact, when the dance ended at 2:00 A.M. the audience cleaned up after itself, picked up the litter and deposited it in trash cans.

The next weekend, on October 24, the Family Dog put on another dance at Longshoremen's Hall. It featured the Charlatans again, and the Lovin' Spoonful, who were back in San Francisco for a gig at a North Beach nightclub. This dance they called "A Tribute to Sparkle Plenty."

The people from the Dr. Strange dance came back and brought their friends. On the Beat grapevine there was word that there would be another of these pop art happenings, or whatever you'd call them. Ralph Gleason had written glowingly about the first dance.

One of the MCs this time was a comic from the Committee troupe who tried to tell some dope jokes, but he was cut off by a rumble from the crowd. They were apparently not there to be told they were hip, but to dance and get sweaty with their friends. Even Jefferson Airplane, who were not on the bill for this show, came to the dance after having spent the day getting their new drummer stoned on LSD for the first time. The Palo Alto band that had just changed its name to the Warlocks had also gone tripping around in Marin County that Sunday and got back to San Francisco in time for the dance. Their bassist, a tall, angular blond with glasses, accosted Ellen Harmon in her black Victorian dress and told her with fiendish intensity, "Lady, what this little séance needs is *us*!"

Ever since its obscenity bust in August, the Mime Troupe had been in trouble. It was excluded from the San Francisco Arts Festival. Local police all over the Bay Area had decided the supposedly indecent play shouldn't be performed in their parks. A theater in Sausalito refused to let the Mime Troupe go ahead with an already advertised show on grounds that the rent hadn't been paid; the troupe's business manager, Bill Graham, objected that the theater had returned the check with the claim that it "didn't know what it was for." Finally, on November 1, director R. G. Davis was found guilty of performing in the parks without a permit.

Now the Mime Troupe was even more broke than usual and had to put on a benefit show for itself. This was Bill Graham's sort of thing. Graham was a former business executive who had quit a $25,000-a-year job in order to be involved with the theater, and if anybody could organize a money-making event, he was the one. The Mime Troupe took its last few dollars, rented a white Cadillac and drove through downtown San Francisco passing out leaflets advertising what they called an Appeal, to be held on November 6 at the loft on Howard Street which they shared with the local offices of Students for a Democratic Society.

The censorship issue rallied the art world and Graham was showered with the names of people who wanted to be involved. Some were big names, like the Committee, the folksinger Sandy Bull, Allen

Ginsberg and friends of Ginsberg's from New York, a jug band composed of poets known as the Fugs. Jefferson Airplane would play, of course—the Airplane had used the Mime Troupe loft for rehearsals. A lot of others offered their services, including the Family Dog people, who were willing to put their experience as facilitators of the new kind of rock dance at the Mime Troupe's disposal. Graham, who had never heard of their Tribute dances, cheerfully listed the Family Dog in the Appeal's entertainment lineup under the impression that they were a trained dog act. The Dog ended up putting on another dance of their own the same night as the Appeal.

The loft walls were painted bright colors and bunches of grapes and bananas were hung from the ceiling. Cinematographers brought 16-millimeter film loops and sheets were hung on the walls for screens. An elaborate, comical schedule of tariffs was posted at the door: $48 to get in if you made over $80,000 a year, 16¢ if you lived in a walkup apartment above the sixth floor, and so on. If you didn't have any money at all you were still asked to "leave having left something"—a belt, a ring, anything—or at least to help clean up when the event was over.

The Appeal was a greater success than anybody had expected. People who'd never heard of the Family Dog dances or Kesey's acid parties came out and experienced the same wide-eyed, unforseeable freedom to act as strange as they felt. The crowd waiting to get in stretched around the block, an extraordinary sight in the dingy, light-industrial neighborhood of the Mime Troupe loft.

At midnight the police came and ordered the party shut down. Talking fast, Bill Graham assured them he couldn't close it down now, because the crowd had been waiting all evening for the big celebrities, officer, who had promised to jet in from Vegas to help out the good old Mime Troupe—Sinatra, Liberace, Rudy Vallee, I swear it. . . . They struck a deal: Graham went on stage and asked those who'd been there a long time to leave so that the Fire Department's occupancy limit of 500 would be met. Policemen were stationed at the door to the loft to make sure that the number entering would be the same as the number leaving for the rest of the night (but they didn't know about the freight elevator that was smuggling in more people). At 6:30 A.M. there were still 600 people in the loft, and they cleaned up the place to the accompaniment of Allen Ginsberg's mantras.

For the Mime Troupe the Appeal was a terrific success. It made money and recruited new members into Mime Troupe workshops. But apart from that, the Appeal was the biggest bohemian gathering to date, and despite the long list of acts, it was basically a rock dance. The next day a leading Beat poet, among others, called up and pleaded with the Mime Troupe to put on another appeal, a benefit for anything at all.

The same night as the Appeal, across town at Longshoremen's Hall the Family Dog was putting on its third dance, flushed with success. "An unquestioned power," a poster proclaimed, "the Family Dog presents a Tribute to Ming the Merciless! In the form of a Whambang, wide open stoned DANCE flicking on at dusk."

Whether because of hubris or the ill-omened name of Ming the Merciless, the third Dog dance turned edgy and unpleasant. Curious, sometimes hostile teenagers had heard about these dances by now and there were fistfights in the parking lot and in the hall itself. One of the plate-glass doors was smashed. The Mothers (later the Mothers of Invention), a group invited because Luria Castell remembered them as far-out Sunset Strip characters, presided over the chaotic scene with their sardonic brand of music as if the violence were part of the act. Leader Frank Zappa improvised lyrics about the fights on the floor.

The Family Dog's record stood at two good dances, one mixed, and no money. Now these rock and roll promoters belatedly found out that all along they were supposed to have had a legal permit before putting on dances. They had tried to team up with Bill Graham, the efficiency expert, with themselves as artistic directors; he wasn't interested. Ellen and Jack dropped out and were replaced by two people who were living in the house in the Haight where Luria had just moved.

The top songs in the country were "Eve of Destruction," "Yesterday" and "Get Off My Cloud." A new march on the Oakland Induction center had gone ahead quite peacefully despite the increased popularity of the war in opinion polls and an ominous press conference in which Sonny Barger offered President Johnson the Hell's Angels services as a "crack troop of trained gorillas" in Vietnam. American forces had bombed the "friendly," non-Vietcong village of De Duc by mistake. A Quaker pacifist had committed suicide in front of the Pentagon. Married men were no longer draft-exempt unless they had children.

The Committee Theater had presented two lectures by Richard Alpert, the associate of Timothy Leary who was fired from Harvard in 1963 with him on charges of administering LSD to students. Somehow Alpert had retained his academic standing and was teaching at Stanford University while serving as a director of the *Psychedelic Review*. His lectures had the cautious title, "If LSD and Other Psychedelic Drugs Were Available, How Would One Use Them?" Down on the San Francisco Peninsula, however, Ken Kesey's crowd were actually *advertising* their LSD parties.

For respectable psychedelicans, this was the most shocking thing yet. Kesey never had the right attitude. He was always taking drugs in "uncontrolled circumstances" and calling LSD by the undignified name "acid." Now he was having more LSD parties in very uncontrolled circumstances, and advertising them publicly as Acid Tests. Their slogan was, "Can *You* Pass the Acid Test?"

Test? Was LSD a test? An obvious pun, but how could you pass? Didn't that mean you might fail? The Pranksters wouldn't explain.

The first Acid Test ad went up November 27 at a Prankster-run bookstore in Santa Cruz, on the ocean side of the peninsula. Not a major media campaign, but it may have brought in a few who weren't on the usual word-of-mouth circuit. It was just a La Honda party transferred to Ken Babbs's place near Santa Cruz. Colored light projections and the Bus Movie. Neal Cassady commenting ceaselessly on everything and going through real-life Punch and Judy routines with his volatile girlfriend. Kesey and Babbs taking the microphone to make everybody's trip as weird as possible: "The room is a spaceship and the captain has lost his mind." Speakers and microphones wired through tape recorders for echo effects or delayed playback—all to jog thought in unexpected directions. The Pranksters playing flutes and guitars in a random way that sounded uncannily like the latest school of avant-garde composition, "aleatory" or chance music. And of course acid, plenty of acid, since Owsley had introduced himself to Kesey back in September.

They had done it. They had publicly announced an acid party and no thunderbolts had fallen. Anybody at all could have come, not just friends of friends of friends. Advertising, however, did raise a question: what would you call this sort of party if you were to explain it to a stranger? Art happening, theater with audience participation? Maybe. There was a dollar admission fee, just like a theater event, except that everybody present paid it, even Kesey.

Bob Dylan's Top Ten hit was "Like a Rolling Stone," and he was actually in town. This was a major event for every folkie who had made the leap of acknowledging rock and roll. Dylan always had something of a celebrity quality, was almost as remote as the Beatles themselves in a way, but now he not only was in town but was hanging out. If you knew where to look, you might see him—briefly at a music shop, in and out at an elite folkie party, looking impossibly thin and deathly in black stovepipe trousers.

The day before the first of Dylan's shows, December 3, Ralph Gleason interviewed him on the Public Broadcasting TV station. One of his questions was whether Dylan would take part in a political demonstration. Sure, said the one-time white hope of the folk-song left, only he'd want to carry a sign with a symbol on it rather than words—say, a jack of diamonds or the ace of spades—or a sign reading "Camera," "Microphone" or "Moose."

Toward the end of the interview Gleason asked Dylan about a black and white poster he was holding. "Yeah," he said, "it's a poster somebody gave me. It looks pretty good . . . and I would like to go if I could, but unfortunately I won't be here." He held up the poster and carefully read off the date, place and names of the acts: Jefferson Airplane, Great Society, Mystery Trend, John Handy Quintet and the Gentlemen's Band.

It was a coup for Bill Graham. First, at Ralph Gleason's suggestion, he had rented a handsome old auditorium in the Fillmore district for December 10 to put on a bigger Mime Troupe benefit. He'd gotten the Airplane again, and the Great Society, which by now had played at Mother's with its star, Grace Slick, not only singing but tootling on recorder, occasionally playing bass and even sitting in on drums. The Mystery Trend, a group from the San Francisco Art Institute scene, was certified Art, having played for a party given by the famous ceramist Peter Voulkos and another at the San Francisco Museum of Modern Art. Graham had added a jazz band and a local Fillmore dance band for broader cultural spectrum.

And now he had gotten Dylan's public blessing, simply by fighting his way up to him at the TV station and sticking the poster in his hand. And as the poster ("Appeal II, for Continued Freedom in the Arts") read, "the hall is huge and, like, it's there."

Meanwhile, back in the Haight-Ashbury, they were trying to get a rock band together at 1090 Page. The marijuana legalization activist Chet Helms was running jam sessions in the basement—actually a handsome Victorian music room—of the building, which was an apartment managed by two bluegrass-playing brothers named Albin. There was always an audience for free music, of course, and with the new interest in rock and roll the audience threatened to get too large for the basement. Helms instituted a 50¢ door charge to discourage the crowds, but it unexpectedly had the opposite effect of validating these jam sessions as rock concerts, the only live rock in the Haight. In a few weeks the sessions went from a situation of up to thirty musicians and an audience of eight or ten to one where there were eight to ten musicians and an audience of three hundred.

Helms had been a guy "talking up energies" around town for some time. Even before the first Family Dog dance he'd put on a little dance at the unoccupied Masonic Hall on Haight Street, with an untried band of State College students called the Final Solution. From the time of the first Longshoremen's Hall dance he'd been trying to be part of the Family Dog. Now he was close to having a band that could play in public, with Peter Albin, a gnomish little guy with a startlingly deep voice, as lead singer and a guitarist from Pine Street, the one they called Weird Jim Gurley. They'd just scrapped the name Blue Yard Hill for one that fell together during a stoned conversation about 1984, monopoly capitalism, holding corporations and "holding" in the slang sense of possessing drugs.

"Big Brother and the Holding Company"? Oh wow, could you get busted for having a name like that?

As Bob Dylan was doing the first of his scandalous half-folk, half-rock shows on December 4, a few miles south at the Oakland Civic Auditorium the Rolling Stones were doing their raunchy British version of Chicago blues. When the Stones show ended, leafleteers appeared out front distributing hand-lettered sheets reading, "Can You Pass the Acid Test?" and giving an address. Forty miles south of there, the second Acid Test was unfolding at a private home in San Jose. This was shrewd advertising, and this time the Acid Test drew about four hundred people.

Now there was less chance than ever of confusing this event with one of those arty, self-conscious happenings. In addition to the staggering guitars of Kesey's Psychedelic Symphonette, there was a real rock band—the group of Palo Alto kids who had shown up at a few of Kesey's earlier parties, once as Mother McCree's Uptown Jug Stompers, later as the Emergency Crew, and who were now calling themselves the Warlocks. They were mostly converted folkies, like the former bluegrass banjoist Jerome Garcia, who was playing lead guitar, though the bassist was a sound engineer and electronic composer named Phil Lesh who had occasionally worked with the Mime Troupe.

The Warlocks were playing blues with a fat, solid beat, tape machines were hallucinatizing people's voices, lights were projected all over the walls, fuses were blowing and the Pranksters were playing their mind games on more people than ever before. It was huge, warm, crowded, intense, confused—four hundred people!

The next week the Beatles released an album nobody had quite expected. Of course they had fooled around with a sitar in the movie *Help!* back in August, which was a little far out for a quartet of "lovable mop-tops" whose fans pelted them with jelly beans as love-gifts. On this new album, *Rubber Soul,* they were showing taste and creativity—words one never associated with rock and roll. The arrangements were genuinely elegant, sometimes startling; one song used a sigh as part of the melody. The lyrics were no longer the simple love songs the Beatles were famous for. What was "Norwegian Wood/This Bird Has Flown," with its sitar melody, *about?* Setting fire to somebody's furniture?

How about "The Word"? Say the word "love" and you'll be free, and incidentally, "love" is the only word. "Think for Yourself," "I'm Looking Through You," "You Won't See Me," "Run for Your Life" —the Beatles had dropped much of the coziness that had been their trademark and developed a note of pathos, almost existential desperation. Could it be—was it crazy to think—that they might be getting *stoned?* Would that explain the bizarre foreshortening of the cover photo, the distorted lettering of the title, the phrase "I get high" in one song? More than ever the Beatles were the soundtrack of the Haight-Ashbury, Berkeley and the rest of the circuit. You could party-hop all night and hear nothing but *Rubber Soul.*

On December 9 fireballs were observed in the sky over six eastern states. One was seen in California the next night, the very night of Appeal II at the Fillmore Auditorium.

This time Bill Graham had hired a light show like the Family Dog and was not bothering with any entertainment but music. Unlike the Dog, he knew he needed a dance permit, and he even knew enough about certain Musicians' Union restrictions to skirt them by billing the show as a "dance-concert." There was a sign three feet high at either end of the dance floor reading "Love." The bar sold soft drinks and apples and had a sign over it reading "No Booze."

Admission was $1.50, and as expected, the audience was bigger than ever. There was a block-long double line outside at 9:30 P.M. and at 1:00 A.M. there was still a double line outside, still a block long.

The following night, while Bob Dylan was at the Masonic Auditorium in San Francisco, down on the peninsula the Acid Tests were making their next move: renting a *public* place, a Palo Alto nightclub called the Big Beat. Once again it was the Warlocks' rock, the Pranksters' carry-on and Stewart Brand's Indian show. The Pranksters' semi-official light show, Roy's Audioptics, had a stroboscopic light, and somebody shredded a handful of toilet paper from the men's room into the light beam. In the freeze-frame flicker of the strobe light it looked like something between a petrified snow fall and the wreckage of World War III. People gathered up the paper as it fell and began shredding it further and tossing it around—a toilet paper happening.

In keeping with the increasingly public nature of the Acid Tests, the Pranksters now designed an official poster—a collage of Oriental deities, Victorian cartoon characters and an engraving of a Greek statue that was saying, "Only one way out! I'll take the course myself!" "Happeners," it suggested, were likely to include Ginsberg, the Fugs, the Merry Pranksters, Neal Cassady and the Warlocks, who were changing their name to the Grateful Dead. There was a border on the poster that was labeled "aaaaaaa" and "bbbbbbb." The instructions read, "This grand thing can be made very long and thin by up the middle, pasting (a) below to lower (b) ab it can be left as it is. i.e., schizoid   be cutting g line one.or"

The fourth Test was advertised for Stinson Beach, a remote summer-home community in Marin County. At the last minute the deal for this hall fell through, and the Test was switched to Muir Beach Lodge, in another summer home encampment a few miles south. The change made for confusion, but enough people survived the long, spooky night ride over Mount Tamalpais to find the log-cabinish lodge, set on stilts at the edge of the little marshy crescent of Muir Beach, to make this the biggest Test to date.

No one had ever defined what it meant to pass the Acid Test, outside of the suggestion that if you weren't put off by the connotations of the name you were a safe bet. The December 17th Test weighted the quasi-definition to the side of "survival." If you were still there when the sun came up on Sunday morning, you must have passed.

The confusion at the beginning was part of the trouble, and maybe the cold, echoey lodge helped make people uneasy. That week the

Pranksters had started wearing special "Prankster Shirts" in bright colors, which might have been overbearing. It certainly did no good when Owsley had a classic freak-out: Owsley pushing a chair around on the floor which made a noise akin to fingernails on a blackboard; Owsley, eyes crazed, gasping hoarsely about the necessity of survival; Owsley accusing a Kesey-Beast of draining his acid and his money; Owsley staggering out of the lodge, dragging his expensive tape recorder by the microphone; Owsley running his car up an embankment and gunning the motor until he regained his senses.

Some of the weird trips were comic. One Prankster was found next morning in front of a surprised Marin County resident's empty refrigerator; the Prankster had eaten everything in it. But this Test brought back all the old rumors about Kesey's scene, the hospitalizations and potential suicides. On the other hand, everybody *had* survived.

At the Tribute to Dr. Strange, a guitarist named John Cipollina had climbed up on the stage to see how many people had come. There were so many, he claimed, it hurt his eyes.

He was part of another nascent rock band. Cipollina was a classical guitarist who'd played rock in the rough old days before the Beatles. His roommate David Freiberg had been a hitchhiking folk troubadour for peace, and had roomed with Paul Kantner and David Crosby in Los Angeles before either Jefferson Airplane or the Byrds had formed. Cipollina and Freiberg were briefly part of a band put together by a local folk balladeer, who was busted for grass and sent to jail before their first rehearsal. At the Dr. Strange dance Cipollina ran into two unattached musicians who played the instruments his band was looking for. They were bound to play together, especially when they found that four out of the five musicians were born under the sign of Virgo and a couple even had the same birthday. Because of the influence of Mercury on their astrological charts, they eventually named themselves the Quicksilver Messenger Service, playing on Mercury as messenger of the gods and mercury the metal quicksilver, associated with Venus.

As it happened, the Committee needed more rock and roll. At the beginning of each satirical comedy hour the Committee played a record of Kate Smith singing "The Star-Spangled Banner," which always stirred a few patriots to rise to their feet. For the second hour of the show they decided they wanted a rock version. A Committee actor named Howard Hesseman knew Freiberg, and he commissioned the newborn band to tape a rock version of the national anthem for an ounce of grass.

The band was enthusiastic. "Great! Sure!" they said. "Just get us the lyrics!" Their version was exactly what the Committee wanted, complete with swooping electric guitar lines and even a cowbell, played by a teenage runaway on the Mexico-Big Sur circuit who went by the name of Girl. The Committee was so pleased they paid Quicksilver *two* ounces of grass and invited Quicksilver Messenger Service to play at their Christmas party in Muir Beach for $150. The Christmas party was a great success. The Committee's friends all liked the music, and the band couldn't believe they had earned $150 just for playing six hours of music.

On New Year's Eve, Stewart Brand and some associates staged a parade down Montgomery Street, the heart of San Francisco's financial district. Office workers were celebrating with the traditional ritual of shredding the past year's calendars and throwing the paper out the windows. "What you are doing is beautiful," the paraders told the bankers and secretaries they passed in the street. "Realize that you're in a parade and you'll be as beautiful as what you do."

The real reason for the parade was to get a little press attention for an event three weeks in the future, a sort of circus that would gather together the Acid Test, the Open Theater, Tape Music Center activities, rock bands, light shows and everything else the organizers could think of. Brand and his friends were going to use Longshoremen's Hall and have Bill Graham coordinate it. The name was straightforward: the Trips Festival.

Those Pranksters who, like Kesey, were from Oregon went back to their home state for Christmas and held a small Portland Acid Test on Christmas Eve. There was another small Test on New Year's at Sound City, a San Francisco recording studio, where the events were recorded to be released as an album. For January 8 they planned a bigger Test than ever before. They had the Fillmore Auditorium, with more electronic equipment than ever, since Owsley Stanley had turned his perfectionist attentions to the sound equipment being used by the Dead. He'd bought cratefuls of amplifiers and speakers and monitors and even an oscilloscope. This time the Pranksters had closed-circuit TV portapaks to add to the instantaneity. Ron Boise brought a lot of Thunder Sculptures for this event, including one shaped like a vulture, another shaped like a seashell that you could crawl into and get lost in, and the Tuned Woman.

The owner of the Fillmore's lease was incredulous when a Prankster representative came to him on January 6 asking to rent the place. "Look," he explained patiently, "you can't rent a hall on Thursday for a Saturday date. You'll never be able to advertise it enough to fill it." The Prankster put down the requisite $65 anyway. A former arbitrageur on the international commodities market, he knew business. On Saturday night there were 2,400 people in the Fillmore Auditorium.

The Fillmore was basically a huge dance floor with a balcony running along two walls. The balcony was subdivided into dressing rooms and offices, so the Pranksters were able to wire the place up with microphones and speakers in unexpected places, so you might be downstairs watching somebody make a fool of himself on the closed-circuit TV and suddenly hear something you'd said upstairs a few minutes ago broadcast all over the hall. The floor was littered with electronic boxes and skeins of electrical cable. They had packed in so much electronic equipment the whole hall had a low, dull buzzing sound.

When the doors opened, they set up in the now-standard Acid Test fashion, with Kesey's musicians at one end of the hall and the Grateful Dead at the other. The walls were covered with balloons and streamers and there was a baby's bathtub full of LSD-spiked punch in the middle of the floor. Twenty-four hundred people, some of them as far out as it was possible to get, like the guy in a white mechanic's jumpsuit with a black cross on the front and the message "Please Don't Believe in Magic" on the back.

On one of the balconies Stewart Band found Neil Cassady in an unusual pose, standing still and watching. Not jerking around, not running his mouth, not tossing his biceps-exercise hammer. He was gazing down at the sea-floor riot of blinking electronic equipment, stoned people reeling around blowing whistles, counting their toes, looking for their lost minds in the Thunder Machines. Two electrified guitar bands were playing at cross-purposes; slides and swirls of color were being projected on the walls, as well as sometimes what seemed to be snatches of a Kesey novel in progress, unless this whole event was a Kesey novel in progress. Cassady looked serene and meditative. "It looks," he said placidly, "like the publicity for your Trips Festival is going pretty well."

For most of the acid parties everybody had been able to stay all night, right down to the exhausted, contemplative dawn when the banal rays of the sun appeared. But because of San Francisco city regulations, this event, like the Matrix Test, had to be shut down at 2:00 A.M. But there were 2,400 people at this one. Two policemen came to see to it that the hall was closed. "Who's in charge here?" they wanted to know. The limit of the absurd. Everything had been completely out of control for five hours.

The policemen went around pulling out plugs; Carolyn Adams, whose Prankster name was Mountain Girl, went around after them plugging everything in again. Ken Babbs rubbed his hands together in his expansive ex-Marine manner and bellowed, "Well, gentlemen, how can I help you?" Two members of the Dead disharmonized on a sarcastic rendition of "The Star-Spangled Banner," while Kesey, in a red, white and blue jumpsuit, shouted patriotic slogans. One of the policemen picked up a microphone to announce that the hall was being closed and found that his voice came out weirdly distorted by dial-twirling madmen.

The crowd on the floor milled around in a circle. Whenever the police turned off the lights, it cheered; whenever the Pranksters turned them on again, it cheered. A group of people on the floor found a ladder and started climbing up toward the policemen in the balcony, chanting, "Hug the heat! Hug the heat!" Kesey's lawyers arrived just in time to smooth things over.

That same night the remnant of the Family Dog put on their fourth dance, plainly an unquestioned power no longer. This dance was simply titled "Rock and Roll," not a tribute to anything. They couldn't get Longshoremen's Hall for this night, and the Acid Test was at the Fillmore.

To deal with the Acid Test they had worked out a package: You could buy a double ticket for a special price that would let you into both events, with Kesey's bus running shuttle between the two halls. But the place they got for their dance was California Hall, a heavy, cheerless building at the edge of the Tenderloin that had belonged to the German-American Bund before World War II. Moreover, the Acid Test was in rare form over at the Fillmore. Most of the people who took the bus to the Fillmore stayed there, and hardly anybody went the other way. In fact, Rock Scully and Danny Rifkin, the two new Family Dog partners, ended up staying at the Acid Test themselves.

Publicity for the Trips Festival, which had now hired an advertising agency, was going full blast. With full McLuhanite confidence in the world-historical force they represented, Brand and company took posters and leaflets advertising their event to the posh Mark Hopkins Hotel on Nob Hill. "Trips Festival"? They were directed to the travel desk.

Lou Gottlieb, a folksinger whose highly successful group, the Limelighters, had disbanded two and a half years before, had just started writing a music column for the *San Francisco Chronicle*. Stewart Brand, Ramon Sender of the Tape Center and Ben Jacopetti of Open Theater went to talk to him about a write-up. His column appeared on Tuesday.

"If I were to tell you that an event of major significance in the history of religion is going to take place in this City of Saint Francis this weekend," the column began, "you would say, 'You stayed out of work too long.' And if I were to tell you that an event of major

significance in the history of the arts is going to take place simultaneously, you would pat my hand and say, 'Drink this glass of warm milk
slowly and try to get some rest.'" In a word, what was happening
was that "in His infinite wisdom the Almighty is vouchsafing visions
on certain people in our midst along side which the rapturous trans-
ports of old Saint Theresa are but early *Milton Berle Shows* on a
ten-inch screen." Gottlieb recommended the Trips Festival to the
churches, the intellectuals, the man in the street and even the man
in the ghetto. To the Chamber of Commerce he pointed out that
a tourist attraction during the slump season was nothing to despise.

On Monday, January 17, Ken Kesey was found guilty of the marijuana charge dating from the early spring bust at La Honda. On
Thursday morning he was in court again on a new beef. At 2:00 A.M.
that morning he had been arrested on the rooftop of Stewart Brand's
place in North Beach. Arrested with him was Mountain Girl, a
minor. When police found them on the rooftop, Kesey had scuffled
with them briefly and thrown away a package of brownish plant
material, suspected marijuana, which the police recovered from the
next rooftop.

Now Kesey stood a chance of getting not just six months but the
full three-year sentence on the La Honda bust, plus the automatic
sentence prescribed for a second offense, five years with no parole.
The judge had warned him on Monday not to associate with his
Prankster friends, another strike against him.

The judge also had warned him specifically not to go to the Trips
Festival. Too bad. Kesey and his friends took their garish bus directly
from the courtroom to downtown Union Square to publicize the
Trips Festival. They paraded around in Prankster costumes, which
had come to look like Marvel Comics superhero suits, Kesey in white
jeans with the word HOT printed on one buttock, COLD on the other
and TIBET in the middle. They spoke to the press, set up and played
a Thunder Machine, and unloosed two balloons carrying a sign
imprinted with the word NOW that ascended beautifully until
snagged on an airline's sign on an office building.

Stewart Brand was worried that this publicity—front-page news from rooftop bust to balloon ascent—might jeopardize the Trips Festival's use of Longshoremen's Hall. They had been promoting the event as a "non-drug re-creation of a psychedelic experience," a McLuhanite Global Village/electronic art happening. On the handbills they had suavely defined a trip as "an electronic experience." Now maybe the cat was out of the bag. Brand went down to the union hall to see whether things were still okay.

Outside a longshoreman came up to him and said, "I see Kesey got busted. Is he all right?" Brand allowed that he'd probably be okay. "Well," said the longshoreman philosophically, "at least it's good publicity for your show, isn't it?" It turned out that a lot of Hell's Angels were longshoremen, and there would be no trouble putting on the show.

As at the Family Dog dances, there were two posters: a large silk-screened one showing a gigantic spark, and a cheap black-and-white handbill featuring an oscilloscope pattern surrounded by an op art swirl. To print the latter Bill Graham had gotten hold of Wesley Wilson, an ex-philosophy major from State College who had done printing for the Mime Troupe in the past, largely because his little printing company was the cheapest in town.

The handbill-poster noted that "the general tone of things has moved from the self-conscious Happening to a more JUBILANT occasion where the audience PARTICIPATES because it's more fun to do so than not. Maybe this is the ROCK REVOLUTION. Audience dancing is an assumed part of all the shows, and the audience is invited to wear ECSTATIC DRESS and bring their own GADGETS. (A.C. outlets will be provided.)"

The first night was supposed to be shared by America Needs Indians, now evolved to a stage designated Sensorium Nine, and Open Theater. Or as the handbill explained, "slides, movies, sound tracks, flowers, food, rock 'n' roll eagle lone whistle, indians and anthropologists," plus "Revelations—nude projections, the God Box. The endless explosion. The Congress of Wonders, the Jazz Mice, liquid projections, etc. & the unexpectable." The promoters were also spreading rumors about the possible appearance of Allen Ginsberg, Marshall McLuhan and topless dancers. Of course that was *possible*. Christ knew, anything was possible.

In practice the event engulfed the two shows. Both America Needs Indians and the Open Theater's cabaret theater were mournfully out of place in the rackety, echoing space of Longshoremen's Hall. America Needs Indians was just a little tepee and some slides, so far as most people could tell. But there were things to do. Mikes and speakers and electrical gadgets strewn around. A light show with strobe. A booth selling books on psychedelic subjects, and another selling books about insects. There were Trips Festival T-shirts for sale. And a shopping bag full of Owsley's latest LSD was making the rounds of the hall.

But mostly it was unparalleled chaos in a crowded hall pulsing with undirected energy. A young woman jumped up on stage, stripped to the waist and danced until Brand got her off. This clinched it for the Open Theater, which was supposed to go on at ten—they weren't going to attempt their nude "Revelations" in this wild energy. They read their sermons and got about halfway through the God Box skits when it became obvious that the crowd wanted rock and roll. They quickly brought on the Marbles, who had recently metamorphosed into a band calling itself the Loading Zone.

On Saturday night the Tape Center was going on with films by the Canyon Cinema Group in something called "Options and Contracts at the Present Time." The Ann Halprin Dancers, films by Bruce Baillie and Anthony Martin and a Vortex Light Box were going to be the visuals. Sound would come from a synthesizer invented by Donald Buchla, which would perform on its own and also modulate the rock and roll sounds of Big Brother and the Holding Company in freakish and avant-garde ways. The Acid Test would follow at 10:00 P.M. "Can you die to your corpses? Can you metamorphose? Can you pass the twentieth century?

"What is total dance?"

What, indeed. Big Brother and the Holding Company, fresh from their first gig a week before, barely had time to set up onstage before the Grateful Dead swept them off and the Acid Test was fait accompli. Dancing, strobes, ultraviolet lights that made Day-Glo paint fluoresce all the more brightly, strange things being written on the overhead projector and flashed on the wall (*Anybody who knows he is God go up onstage*) and announced over the loudspeakers.

And through it all, there was Bill Graham running around in a V-neck cardigan sweater trying to keep track of things with his clipboard. One of Brand's duties was to see to it that Kesey and Graham were kept out of each other's way. Kesey's costume at the moment was something between superhero and space suit, complete with a bubble helmet. When Graham finally did run into Kesey, at the back door of the hall where Kesey was letting in a bunch of Hell's Angels, he exploded: "What the fuck do you think you're doing? Goddamn son of a bitch, I'm busting my fucking balls out here to make a dime and you—" Kesey simply closed his bubble helmet.

The Grateful Dead were, as always, playing when the spirit moved them. That is, when the spirit moved them to make music rather than go eat some of the LSD-spiked ice cream or diddle with the Thunder Machines or something. On this particular night Neal Cassady was frequently commandeering the microphones anyway. But a moment came when Jerry Garcia was thinking of playing and picked up his guitar, only to find that the bridge had been smashed. It was just dangling there, with strings flying loose and broken pieces falling off. He was staring at it and absorbing the news when a stranger wearing a cardigan sweater and carrying a clipboard showed up.

"What's the matter," he asked.

"Well, my guitar . . . the bridge . . ."

Without another word, Bill Graham was down on the guitar with his customary furious energy, trying to fix the unfixable the same way he'd been trying to keep track of the incomprehensible all night.

The lines to get into the hall were endless. When the hall closed at 2:00 A.M. there was still a line; probably two or three whole audiences passed through the place in a single night. But the two o'clock close-down left a lot of spectacularly wasted people out on the street with nothing to do but locate somebody's apartment, or find their way down to the beach and listen to the waves until dawn.

Some thought had been given to what people could do in the morning hours when they were still stoned from the night before.

The festival listed some Side Trips. There was a "Worship Service" at the Tape Music Center at 11:00 A.M. with Chloe Scott, dance mistress, and Lou Harrison, composer. Those who showed up found that the room was already scheduled for a light show in the Sunday morning series Bill Ham had been doing there for the past couple of weeks. After confused negotiations the two events combined, sort of. For 3:00 P.M. a mime-dance-sound show was scheduled at a downtown theater:

The Music	Elizabeth Harris, Pauline Oliveros
The Dance	and large Mime Troupe Cast
The Bows	

The SSSSSSSSSSSSSSSSSSSSSSSSSSS
Psychedelic Shop 1535 Haight St.

Sunday evening's events were "still being assembled" when the handbills were printed. The planners tap-danced around this with McLuhanism: "Since the common element of all shows is ELECTRIC-ITY, this evening will be programmed from stimuli provided by a pinball machine. A nickel in the slot starts the evening." The program listed filmmakers, light artists, dancers, more avant-garde music, "Chinese New Year's Lion Dancers and Drum and Bugle Corps, the Stroboscopic Trampoline, the Grateful Dead, Big Brother and the Holding Company, the Loading Zone, America Needs Indians, Open Theater, Tape Center, the Merry Pranksters and

"It's prayer, mostly."

It turned out as another sort of rock dance plus Acid Test. A film consisting of a repeated loop of Jackie Kennedy reaching for a door handle after her husband's assassination was on the screens. Kesey was writing on the overhead projector again, but Stewart Brand's partner in America Needs Indians was squabbling with him and projecting slides of architecture over Kesey's novelistic fragments. The stroboscopic trampolinist actually showed up, a champion ama-teur trampolinist who wore a ski mask to preserve his amateur status. He dove from the balcony onto his trampoline under a strobe light as the Dead played. The crowd was so psychedelicized nobody seemed to pay him any particular mind.

The Mystery Trend hadn't been paying attention to the Trips Festival buildup. Full of plans for another art-rock triumph, they had booked the Gate Theater in Sausalito. The hours ticked by. Only three people came. The bassist finally broke down and in bitter rage destroyed his instrument in front of this tiny audience.

The Trips Festival had decidedly been the place to go this weekend. Not counting those who got in through the back door, over 6,000 people were admitted that weekend. The festival netted $4,000, which to the promoters seemed fabulous wealth. They agreed that the Acid Test was more successful than the films, the theater, the ring-modulator sound machine or the slide show, so Kesey got half the money. Bill Graham, a poor immigrant kid from the Bronx, couldn't believe his eyes—people taking a lower profit voluntarily, with no muscle being applied.

Plenty of things were odd. The program had thanked the company that provided the strobe lights, the printer, an artist for the psychedelic mandala on the program cover . . . the architects who years before had designed Longshoremen's Hall.

The Trips Festival also noted "with approval and great interest the participation in the festival of *Look, Newsweek, Time* and *Life.*" This was the beginning of an era. The Acid Test, snowballing fast, was heading for new horizons. "Rolling east next month," the program announced, "it will soon be international, if not cosmic."

By February 1966 the United States was using arms in Vietnam at an annual rate of 1.8 million air-dropped bombs, 6.8 million air-launched grenades and a billion rounds of .30 caliber bullets. President Johnson repeatedly said he was "willing to negotiate" in Vietnam, but that he would not negotiate with the National Liberation Front all those arms were aimed at. Public opinion polls in March showed 56 percent of the people supporting Johnson's policies on the war with 26 percent opposing, and the polls didn't ask how many of those opposing wanted even more "escalation" of the war than Johnson was providing. Former vice-president Richard Nixon, unofficially campaigning for the 1968 Republican nomination, predicted with hardheaded realism that the war would last five more years at least.

In March an American bomber lost one of its four hydrogen bombs in a midair collision over Spain; radioactive material from two others was sprayed over "a limited area." In May the conservationist Sierra Club took ads to publicize the fact that the federal government was planning to turn the Grand Canyon into a reservoir: "This time," said the ads, "they're going to flood the Grand Canyon. *The*

Grand Canyon." The IRS threatened to revoke the Sierra Club's tax-exempt status. In June a black civil rights worker named James Meredith began a walk from Memphis, Tennessee, to Jackson, Mississippi, to encourage southern blacks to vote by showing them a black man could walk through the South unprotected. He got about twenty miles before being shot in the back.

In the first months of 1966 the Vietnam Day Committee had essentially been dormant. To judge from the newspapers, the public was more concerned about the danger of drugs than about the danger of war. After a highly publicized murder by a thirty-year-old medical school dropout in Brooklyn who told police he had been "flying on acid for three days," Sandoz Pharmaceuticals announced that it would no longer sell LSD.

Although LSD, which had been invented in the Sandoz labs and for a while marketed under the trade name of Delysid, was not yet legally classed as a narcotic, that was bound to change soon. The California senate was considering a bill to declare both LSD and another psychedelic, DMT, dangerous drugs. The U.S. attorney general demanded controls on LSD even in the absence of any studies showing it to be dangerous. *Life* ran a cover story, "LSD: The Exploding Threat of the Mind Drug that Got Out of Control," which approved limited use of LSD in controlled psychotherapy sessions and possibly for a few other purposes, such as a naval officer's use of it to solve a problem on intelligence equipment.

The official news was a dark background of wickedness and stupidity. The only positive news was not in the papers but on the radio, the unexpected flowering of rock and roll. That "simplistic pop music" despised by folk purists was showing taste and intelligence, with a seductive hint that the top rock stars were against the Vietnam War and conceivably even trying drugs. The idea was almost too heady to entertain, especially in the case of the Beatles, who were still the idols of millions upon millions of teenaged Beatlemaniacs.

But the top-selling song all through January was the Beatles' "We Can Work It Out," with what might have been a subtle peace message. They followed it with "Day Tripper," "Nowhere Man" and "Paperback Writer," which were surprisingly like the sarcastic put-on songs of Bob Dylan or the Rolling Stones. (Dylan had titled one of those songs "Like a Rolling Stone.") The Stones themselves had used a cello on "As Tears Go By," following the Beatles' use of cello on "Yesterday," and then sitar on their "Paint It Black" after the Beatles had used sitar on "Norwegian Wood." Dylan had recorded a witty song about getting stoned, "Rainy Day Women #12 and #35." Donovan, an Anglo-Dylanish folk balladeer a year earlier, had become a light rocker with some kind of awareness of things happening in California. "The Trip," for instance, was his song about a Sunset Strip nightclub of that name where, as Donovan observed in the song, Methedrine was used to excess.

It was almost as if an international youth movement were holding a symposium where ideas were taken up, passed around and commented on with great rapidity, all beyond the comprehension of the world's grown-ups. One grown-up who did seem to understand was Ralph Gleason. He had already envisioned a world youth underground centered on music; throughout the early sixties he had often written about Colin MacInnes's novel *Absolute Beginners,* which portrayed English youth seeking refuge from the compartmentalization of the adult world in jazz nightclubs. In the summer of 1965 Gleason started covering rock and roll.

What made the Beatles so attractive to the Haight-Ashbury was their strangely compelling music, which could suggest expansiveness and grief at the same time, but they were also winning hearts with their ever more daring style. *Yesterday and Today,* their June album of recent singles, had a cover showing the lovable mop-tops wearing bloodstained butcher uniforms, wielding knives and carrying hunks of meat and chopped-up baby dolls—an obvious statement about the war. Capitol Records refused to release it with that "tasteless" cover, and all copies of the album were hastily pasted over with an inoffensive shot of the Beatles sitting on packing crates. However, as they found out in the Haight, you could steam the tasteful cover off.

Then on the eve of their American tour the Beatles got in real trouble. The *London Evening Standard* published an article in which John Lennon was quoted as saying, "Christianity will go. It will vanish and shrink. I needn't argue about that, I'm right and I will be proved right. We're more popular than Jesus now." Fundamental-ist reaction was swift. A southern evangelist publicly destroyed a stack of Beatles records and the group's music was banned from some southern radio stations (which, admittedly, had never played their music anyway). The American Bible Society pointed out that in 1965 only 13 million Beatles records had been sold as against 150 million Bibles. The Beatles spent several days backtracking and finally Len-non apologized: "I'm sorry I said it, really. I never meant it as a lousy, anti-religious thing." He had actually been "sort of deploring" the decline of Christianity.

Their American tour, which had so suddenly seemed fraught with danger, was to promote their new album *Revolver* (a gun? something that revolves on a turntable? that makes a revolution?), their most daring project yet. "Yellow Submarine" was a fantasy of living under the sea. "I Want to Tell You" and "Got to Get You into My Life" were miniature psychodramas about the struggle to confess love, the same sort of thing that ran through Dylan's ambitious two-record album *Blonde On Blonde.* "Good Day Sunshine" had a positively acid-drenched sound, a bold but slightly stumbling march tempo that threw the accent on unnatural syllables and made the singers sound as if they were forgetting the meaning of the words as they sang them.

And "Tomorrow Never Knows" was unbelievable. It scarcely sounded like the Beatles' old "yeah, yeah" rock at all. In between what sounded like sallies by a vindictive flock of intergalactic crows, the lyrics—about turning off your mind and floating down an undy-ing stream (unless the meaning was that turning off your mind was not the same as dying)—were actually quotations from Timothy Leary's *The Psychedelic Experience.* The Beatles explained to report-ers that they found Leary's philosophy interesting.

Philosophy, indeed. And this was coming from the most popular entertainers in world history, whose records topped sales charts in Hong Kong and Singapore as well as in England and Ameerica.

Back in San Francisco, far removed from the international spotlight, the rock and roll scene was going through a development of its own.

This was not a time of watershed events, as had occurred in the preceding six months, but an expansion and refinement of what had already emerged.

Throughout the spring and summer of 1966 there were at least two rock dance concerts each weekend night, all marked by the same accepting spirit that presumed that anyone who came was hip to psychedelics and probably stoned. The mere fact of being immersed in a sea of hundreds of like-minded heads produced an intoxication of its own. San Francisco LSD users developed a special confidence about what they were doing and a freedom from that reflex of trying to conceal one's association with mind drugs that was typical of other psychedelic enthusiasts. They were publicly outrageous. Nothing terrible had happened when the public gatherings began, and the proceedings had taken on an aura of destiny.

You could see the phenomenon expand and refine itself week after week. The dance posters went through exciting artistic development. The light shows moved from brilliance to brilliance. The bands improved all the time, too, and had an even more exalted place than the poster or light-show artists. Not only did the bands cause the gatherings, in a way, by providing the attraction of music, but they also were singing songs about the psychedelic life. They were speaking of the Great Unspeakable of being stoned, like prophets emerging from the community to address its deepest concerns. Whether they were singing community anthems like "Let's Get Together" or simple love songs, existential blues like "All Is Loneliness" or familiar rock standards, there was a special poignancy to their performance because they themselves had faced the situation described in the lyrics in all the vulnerability of being stoned on psychedelics.

The audience made its own contribution to the event. Many individuals came in costume, painting their faces and carrying on more like a running Beaux Arts Ball than a spectator show. People brought things to share, such as food or Day-Glo paints with which to decorate each other's bodies or paint designs on the floor (the dance halls soon set up ultraviolet lights at various places to make Day-Glo patterns fluoresce more brilliantly). Or little toys: soap-bubble blowers, bells, convex mirrors. An Arab kid who wore a button saying, in Hebraic letters, "We're No. 2" brought something new every week: sparklers, yo-yos or pens that glowed in the dark. The Family Dog's ballroom featured a puppet theater in the balcony run by a puppeteer named Demetrios, who lived in a miniature house underneath the puppet stage shaped like a gigantic mouth. Sometimes he would hang a life-size marionette down from the balcony to dance with the girls on the floor.

Not everyone involved with psychedelics went to the dances every week, but many hundreds did, and their lives revolved around them. The dances were everything: creative but selfless, serious but high-spirited, exalted but down to earth. Given the mystical turn of mind that has almost always accompanied any attempt to take psychedelics seriously, the dances were like religious rituals. There was a sense of confronting ultimate reality, moving toward a breakthrough—even perhaps on the political level, as when the musicians sang songs touching on the prospect of nuclear war (Quicksilver's "Pride of Man" or the Grateful Dead's "Morning Dew").

But this was all taking place in San Francisco. Once in a while people wondered what could be happening along the same lines elsewhere; certainly there were good out-of-town bands such as the Spoonful and the Byrds. So when Andy Warhol's highly publicized Plastic Exploding Inevitable show came to the Fillmore Auditorium at the end of May, a number of hippies went in hopes of finding out what New York, the capitol of the avant-garde, was doing. After all, here was Warhol, an official Artist and the very father of pop art, with rock and roll and what the news magazines said was a far-out light show.

What they found was the Velvet Underground, which seemed to be nothing but a self-consciously decadent rock group playing a mannered paraphrase of amateurish high school rock. They sang about perversion and heroin addiction; there was a "whip dancer" on the bill. The light show was nothing but ordinary stage lighting spotlights (though when the spots were flashed on the revolving mirror ball hanging from the Fillmore's ceiling, it was like being in a room full of galaxies), supplemented by static Warhol movies like *Sleep* and *Empire State Building.* There were raised platforms on the dance floor so you could stand up above the crowd to see and be seen.

So this was what was happening in New York. Heroin, perversion, vanity, stasis. No breakthroughs here, and maybe San Francisco wasn't so provincial after all. The psychedelic crowd went home relieved of the burden of keeping track of what might be going on elsewhere.

THE DANCES   Beginning two weeks after the Trips Festival, the Fillmore Auditorium held dances every weekend. Bill Graham, who had put on one last Mime Troupe Appeal in January, scheduled his first non-benefit dance on the weekend of February 4–6, complete with a light show featuring films taken during the Trips Festival. The benefit motif still prevailed: the door charge was listed not as "Admission: $2.00" but "Donations: $2.00". The price had already gone up from $1.50 at the last Appeal because the musicians were no longer willing to work free.

That same February 4 saw the last Family Dog concert at California Hall. This time the Dog actually made a profit, but as an organization it was in collapse. Scully and Rifkin had gotten caught up in the Grateful Dead scene and were now the Dead's managers, insofar as the Dead could be managed. A despairing Luria Castell went off to Mexico with two of her original partners, leaving only the poster artist Kelly and the Charlatans' leader George Hunter to carry on the name—if they could.

On the night after the Family Dog dance there was an Acid Test in Los Angeles, and the Dead naturally attended. By this time Owsley's laboratory was in L.A., and Owsley wanted to be the Dead's patron, on a vaster scale than the contributions other prominent dope businessmen were offering their favorite rock bands. He wanted to give them a whole house (minus the space for his lab) to woodshed in, plus ever more electronic equipment and his own insistent spiritual input. The Dead stayed in L.A. There was another Acid Test the following Friday, February 12, boldly scheduled at the Youth Opportunities Center at 13331 South Alameda on the fringes of Watts, site of the previous summer's race riots. "To integrate Watts," said the handbill, on Lincoln's Birthday.

The question was whether Los Angeles was ready for the Acid

Test. There was no community of Acid Test alumni to spread news of the event by word of mouth, so it was publicized entirely by conventional advertising. To enlightened Los Angeles liberals hoping as ever to elevate the quality of life in the "cultural wasteland," it must have sounded as if they were in for just another happening, probably with an edifying civil rights motif. The Pranksters, though, proceeded as if everybody knew what to expect and gleefully filled a large plastic trash can with what they announced was "electric" Kool-Aid.

But the 200 people in attendence had not come with the habit of reckless participation an Acid Test required. As Ken Babbs repeated with controlled mania into the microphone the words "Freak, freak, freak!" they began to realize the Kool-Aid had been dosed. Then there were lines of woozy, frightened people at every pay phone calling friends or doctors. One woman shrieked, "It's LSD! It's LSD! My shrink told me never to take it again, I can't handle it!" Out in the middle of the floor a young woman sat for hours screaming, "Who cares? Who cares?" with the loudspeakers amplifying her voice all through the hall. Policemen—city police, sheriffs, narcs and even the California Highway Patrol—stood around inside the hall all night long. The final score of the night: one Prankster held in jail for a few hours (rumor said the charge against him was "dream drunk") and seven people committed to hospitals. There were people who'd had a wonderful time, but for once the Pranksters had been unable to save a ticklish situation. The Pranksters split up, some heading for Mexico.

Kesey had not been there, nor had he attended the Acid Test the week before, nor his bail hearing on February 2. In fact he had disappeared after the last night of the Trips Festival. On February 6 police investigated a bus parked beside the road near Eureka, California, up by the Oregon border. The bus was painted cerise, magenta and chartreuse, and bore a sign that read "Intrepid Traveler." On the front seat was a suicide note signed by Kesey:

Last words. A vote for Barry [Goldwater] is a vote for fun.
Ah, the Fort Bragg sign and that means the ocean and that means time

to drop the acid (not that I really need it, mind you; I've courage enough without chemical assistance. It's just that I'm scared. . . .)

Driving along checking the abyss at my left like I'm shopping for real estate prospects. Ocean, ocean, ocean, I'll beat you in the end. I'll go through with my heels at your hungry ribs.

I've lost the ocean again. Beautiful. I drive hundreds of miles looking for my particular cliff, get tripped behind acid. I can't find the ocean, end up slamming into a redwood just like I could have slammed into at home. Beautiful!

So I Ken Kesey being of (ahem) sound mind and body do hereby leave the whole scene to [wife] Faye, corporation, cash, the works. And Babbs to run it. (And it occurs to me here that nobody is going to buy this prank and now it occurs to me that I like that even better.)

The police weren't taking it very seriously, although Kesey's friends assured them that he was impulsive and possibly suicidal. The police were inclined, on the contrary, to think that Kesey might have abandoned the bus and continued over the border into his home state. Newspapers learned that Kesey's father didn't credit the suicide note. The story finally fell apart when police heard that the Prankster who owned a bookstore in Santa Cruz had received a phone call from Kesey, by then in Puerto Vallarta.

So everybody had gone to Mexico: Kesey, then much of the Family Dog, then the Pranksters. In the hazy wake of the Family Dog bus, Chet Helms moved in to take charge of the Family Dog operation. He had been eager to join since the first dance, and now it needed a firm hand. For his part, he had a responsibility to get gigs for the band he now managed, Big Brother and the Holding Company.

Helms's first Family Dog production was at the Fillmore on Saturday, February 19. The night before, the Fillmore was the venue for a dance put on by one of the new ephemeral promotion groups: "Alldance Dervish # 1," with King Kong Light Machines; or maybe it was "Alldance # 1," presented by King Kong Dervish. The poster was a little hard to read. Helms's first dance was titled "Tribal Stomp," and the poster had a brand-new Family Dog logo with a wizened old Indian's face on it.

Suddenly it seemed everybody wanted to put on rock dances. Half a dozen parties were bidding to rent the Fillmore, including a Beat poet named Lew Welch who eventually put on dances at California Hall. Another group with the Doggish name Stray Cat rented the same hall for dances. There were benefit dances for the Student Nonviolent Coordinating Committee, the Vietnam Day Study Group, the Farm Workers' Union strike and for an underground filmmaker. A repertory theater in the well-to-do Laurel Heights district divided its building—an old firehouse—into a theater section and a club with a dance floor, and started putting on dances as No. 26 Engine Productions. The profusion of rock dances killed the Bay Area folk music scene dead, just as folk music in its time had ruined the jazz scene. The North Beach folk clubs started booking rock bands.

Bill Graham had not had the Fillmore to himself, and as of March 18 he was putting on only his fourth dance since leaving the Mime Troupe. This one was a three-day Batman Festival featuring a drawing for a mynah bird on the last day, a talking mynah like the stock figure in the *Batman* TV series. Unfortunately for the winner, three days in a cage over the rock and roll bands had rendered the bird deaf.

With the Batman dance Graham had sewn up a three-year lease on the Fillmore, acing out all the other bidders. He nevertheless alternated weekends with Helms's Family Dog for the rest of March and the first half of April. For his third dance Helms booked the Paul Butterfield Blues Band from Chicago, with great success. As Graham and Helms counted the money after the show they chatted about getting the band back for another weekend. Graham got up early the next morning and phoned Butterfield's manager in New York to set up a date three weekends away—one of Graham's own weekends. When Helms found out, he accused Graham of betraying what he saw as a partnership. Partnership or whatever, the relationship was too strained to last, and after one more Family Dog weekend in early April, Helms was out of a hall. He resurfaced two weeks later and eight blocks to the east in another walk-up dance hall with a balcony, the Avalon Ballroom.

During Helms's first Friday night at the Avalon, a stage announcement urged anybody under eighteen to leave. Over at the Fillmore police were enforcing a 1909 law forbidding minors to attend public dances unless accompanied by an adult.

It looked like police vindictiveness. When Graham applied for a dance permit of his own a few weeks before, the cop on the beat in the Fillmore neighborhood had presented a petition signed by twenty-eight shop owners opposing Graham's application. Graham then dressed up in a suit and resolutely went around to all the shop owners to argue his case, dwelling on the grocery and cigarette business he would bring the neighborhood. By the time of his second permit hearing, he had reduced the opposition to just the policeman himself and the rabbi of the synagogue next door to the Fillmore.

On April 22 the *Chronicle* had published an editorial defending Graham and a cartoon showing dancers and a policeman, captioned, "They're dancing with tears in my eyes." That night when a paddy wagon came to take away four rowdy young men who had been arrested outside the Fillmore for swearing, policemen went through the Fillmore checking everybody's ID. Graham himself was arrested and held until 3:00 A.M. for allowing kids under eighteen into his hall.

Over at Longshoremen's Hall that same eventful night there was the latest of the recent ersatz Trips Festivals. There had been a Trips A Go Go in Berkeley and something in a North Beach theater called Blast! This one was simply called Trips, and was notable chiefly for the return of the Grateful Dead from Los Angeles. Like the Family Dog dance at the Avalon, it was not checked for underage patrons.

Graham and Helms had the two best halls anybody had found so far. Each had a legal capacity of just under a thousand and was designed as a dance hall. By contrast, Longshoremen's had bad acoustics, California a dismal atmosphere, and the other places, like the now frequently closed Mother's, were small. No place out of town could draw much of a crowd, though dances were tried in Berkeley at the Veterans' Memorial Hall and the Finnish Brotherhood Hall. Helms and Graham had the rock scene to themselves.

Each man had his own style and his own partisans. Helms was the artist creating an event; like the original Family Dog, he often gave his dances names, such as "Euphoria," "A Stone Facade" or "Earthquake." Graham spoke only of trying to "create a situation where each individual can create his own atmosphere." Helms had long, wispy blond hair and a beard to match. He wore richly embroidered clothes and sometimes even a deaconish frock coat; as he walked around in his ethereal manner savoring the tone of his dances, he would sometimes greet newcomers by saying, "Welcome to our church." Over at the Fillmore, Graham would be running around with his clipboard making sure everything happened on time.

Whole communes had complimentary passes to the Avalon, while Graham waged perpetual war against expanding comp lists and had a sign next to his coatroom reading, "Once Inside No Outsy-Insy." Helms had an Australian with a fashionably Liverpoolish accent to make announcements from the stage. Graham, an ex-character actor, barked announcements at the Fillmore himself in pungent and unfashionable Brooklynese. The difference was even carried down to the style of lighting. Where at the Avalon the musicians were half invisible in the murk at the bottom of the light-show screen, just like the dancers, at the Fillmore there was always a spotlight on the lead musician, making the band the center of the event.

Part of the difference was Graham's stage and biz school background, but part was the fact that Graham was not an acid head, despite continual efforts by the musicians to slip him a dosed apple or soft drink, and he did not want to cater exclusively to the psychedelic community. He had balloons and a tub of free apples in the hall in the hope that having something to hold would make newcomers or outsiders feel less self-conscious. He also booked non-rock acts, such as the Russian poet Andrei Voznesensky (reading in Russian, with Lawrence Ferlinghetti translating) on the same bill with the Airplane, or Lenny Bruce in his last public appearance June 24.

It was astonishing. Hundreds of people—five or six hundred people a night in each of these two halls—were having the wildest visions, the most extreme emotional experiences, in a public place every weekend, but the general public scarcely knew of it. The newspaper coverage was limited to Ralph Gleason's music reviews and the story of Bill Graham's hassles with the police over the under-eighteen law. (Graham had gotten his dance permit on June 6, having won over the rabbi on the condition that dances would not be scheduled for nights when there were religious services. Asked by a reporter how he had gotten everybody to change his mind, Graham snapped back, "By pressure.")

The only other place where the dances were publicly acknowledged was the *Berkeley Barb,* and until mid-March the *Barb* listed only the benefit dances. But it proved impossible to ignore the scene. Editor Max Scherr was hawking his paper on Haight Street and at the Avalon, and soon the *Barb* started carrying his unsigned reports on developments in both places.

It was at the beginning of summer that the *Barb,* and the Berkeley scene in general, started paying close attention. The turning point was the May 21 rally to celebrate the first anniversary of the Vietnam Day Committee. The *Barb* had announced it all over page one and published a detailed program of all the speakers on page two. Then the day came, and the rally drew fewer than a thousand people. The radical orators were at their most tedious and self-regarding, and even the *Barb* described the event as "an endurance contest." Shortly afterward, the *Barb*'s folk music columnist changed his tune about rock and roll. In the middle of April he had downplayed the idea that rock was the music of the future. In June he was admiring at least one band, Country Joe and the Fish, who he said "radiate the Berkeley hip-innocence." He had also become their manager.

Around this same time fashionable society also started taking notice. A few doctors and lawyers had attended the Trips Festival and already there were children of wealthy families living in the Haight, but in May some of the society page faces themselves began to appear in the dance halls and visit the cluster of hip shops on Haight Street.

How fast it had happened, this creation of a whole way of life centered around psychedelic dances. The usual reaction of someone seeing it for the first time was amazement. The most amazed of all, when they returned from Mexico in September, were three people who had left six months before, the original Family Dog.

THE DANCE POSTERS   First there was Michael Ferguson's sketchy handbill for the Red Dog Saloon, then Kelly's cartoon-style handbills. Both the Family Dog dances and the Trips Festival had used fancy silk-screen posters as well as more surreal black-and-white handbills. Chet Helms quickly scrapped the silk screens and upgraded the printed posters with color, and an avalanche of poster art began.

When Helms took over the Family Dog, the poster artist he used was the young printer who had done the Trips Festival handbill and all the Appeal posters, Wes Wilson. Helms had actually used his work once before on the poster for Big Brother's premiere at a benefit concert for the Open Theater.

Wilson was very close to being completely untrained, his only art instruction being three months of figure drawing classes. But he had the advantage of owning Contact Printing Company, which consisted of an ancient 17-by-22-inch handpress. It was so old that the color registration would slip every couple of dozen sheets, and consequently Wilson specialized in one-color posters. His big account was Chico-San, the macrobiotic food supplier.

As Helms named his early dances, he also conceived how he wanted the posters to look and often supplied the art. For "Tribal Stomp" he used an engraving of Plains Indians; for "The Laugh Cure," a forty-year-old photo of a man with a breezy smile captioned, " 'The smile that won't come off.' It is worth practicing to get this sort of smile. Try it in your mirror." Helms had also supplied the art for the Family Dog logo, a photo of an Indian with long hair, an absurd stovepipe hat and a huge cigarette dangling out of his battered, stoical face. In April the Indian got a motto: "May the Baby Jesus Shut Your Mouth and Open Your Mind." Wilson would take this art and letter the information about the dance—musicians, date, place—around it freehand, distorting the letter shapes in the manner of the *Rubber Soul* album cover, and squeezing the lines together to form a turbulent overall design. The result was eye-catching, if hard to read.

Bill Graham had paid no attention to the artistic design of his posters. The Mime Troupe posters were strictly informational. For his first independent dance Graham had an artist sketch the wings and fuselage of a biplane onto an old engraving of a Byronic hero strapped down naked on a horse's back. Two months later, on April

1, with Jefferson Airplane again on the bill, he used the same art again. For the Batman dance he started using Wes Wilson, but Graham had fewer suggestions for the content of the posters than Helms. He didn't supply any art until June, when he asked Wilson to include photos of the musicians. What he wanted was readability, and sometimes the title of an out-of-town band's hit song. So Wilson began doing quite different posters for Graham and Helms, and for the five months he worked for both men you might have thought two separate poster artists were at work. For Helms he did posters in a collage style full of pop art images and nearly unreadable lettering. For Graham he explored bold abstract designs—circles, flames, mushrooming or twisting shapes—formed or filled by plain block letters.

Wilson kept working for Graham and Helms even after they were in competition. Then on June 17 Helms started using a Pine Streeter named Stanley Miller, usually known as Stan Mouse. Before becoming a spiritual hippie, Mouse had supported himself for years by sketching monsters on T-shirts at car shows. He brought a gentle, humorous, slightly romantic pop art feeling to his posters. The first one he drew, for Captain Beefheart and His Magic Band with Oxford Circle as second bill, showed a bull's head posing in a heart-shaped hole in a circle, his tongue lolling clownishly out of his cheek. He was stamped "Choice" behind the ear. For the next few months Mouse and the original Family Dog artist Kelly collaborated (as Mouse Studios) on posters into which they threw any kind of imagery that made sense when you were stoned: op, pop, art nouveau, collage, cartoon, even high school "hot-rod surrealism" art.

Mouse and Kelly's first poster together featured Mr. Zig-Zag, the trademark of Zig-Zag cigarette papers and probably the best-known face in the pot-smoking world. Around the same time Mouse saw Gut Turk, a gangling Hell's Angel who looked like a raffish church-calendar Christ, walking past the old firehouse on Henry Street where Mouse lived. Gut had sketched Mr. Zig-Zag on his T-shirt with felt-tip pens. Idea! Mouse went looking for a press where he could print Mr. Zig-Zag T-shirts. After all, Mnasidika was selling Dylan T-shirts; Mr. Zig-Zag was easily as important.

As the summer went on, Wes Wilson's style became more assured as he learned the rudiments of graphic design by trial and error. In August, Wilson chanced on the work of Alfred Roller, a turn-of-the-century Viennese artist who had worked in posters. Roller had developed an extraordinary way of lettering. In an ordinary alphabet, each letter is a pattern of lines on a roughly rectangular background. In Roller lettering, the lines that make up a letter swelled to fill that imaginary rectangle, while the spaces between the strokes of the letter shrank down until they resembled lines, so that a word became a sequence of rectangular cells differentiated by oddly angled lines coming in from the sides.

It was the hardest thing to read yet: a totally abstract series of squares with strange fernlike growths in them. It was now possible to subordinate the text entirely to the overall design, both because the Roller letters could be twisted to fit any space without becoming clumsy and because it was possible to ignore the content of the text while looking at the poster; it took a special effort to decipher the Roller letters. Now it made sense to look on the posters as works of art, uncluttered by ephemeral dance information.

Of course this violated the first principle of advertising, which subordinates design to content. But even before the discovery of Roller lettering, the posters had become items people collected for their own sake. One day Bill Graham was tacking up posters along Telegraph Avenue in Berkeley, and when he finished four blocks he discovered that the posters had been taken down as fast as he could put them up. That was the last time he printed only five hundred posters for a dance. His first two weekends in May he advertised "Free posters to all advance ticket purchasers," but then bowed to the inevitable and offered free posters to all who attended.

THE LIGHT SHOWS The Thunder Machines, self-interfaced TV equipment, tape recorders and other electronic toys of the Acid Tests did not survive into the dance halls. Graham and Helms basically continued the form of the original Family Dog dances. As at those dances, the element that inspired people to call them multimedia experiences and to speak of media overload was the light show.

There were several kinds of psychedelic light shows around the country similar to the companies Stewart Brand was involved with and to the group in Woodstock, New York, that was associated with Timothy Leary. They were all based on slide projection. What made the San Francisco shows different was that they projected light through liquid pigments in motion, producing radiant abstract paintings that covered a whole wall and changed from instant to instant.

When the psychedelic dances burst on the scene, it was suddenly evident that literally dozens of people in the San Francisco area could perform this kind of show, although it was virtually unknown elsewhere. The reason was that a San Francisco State College professor had invented it thirteen years before.

In 1952 State College had just moved out of its funky old campus near the Haight-Ashbury and wanted something impressive for a national conference of art educators it was hosting. The idea was to revive the European experiments of the twenties and thirties in projected scenery and have dancers running in and out of scrim projected with designs. Professor Seymour Locks used hollow slides filled with pigment in a regular projector to get plantlike growth patterns. But he also experimented with Viewgraph overhead projectors, the kind used by teachers in many large classrooms. The light shot vertically rather than horizontally, up through a glass plate before being reflected by a mirror onto the screen. In his experiments Locks found that paints could be stirred, swirled and otherwise manipulated in a glass dish with slightly raised edges to keep the liquid from spilling. Plastic clock face covers were perfect.

The show for the art educators was a great success, with a jazz group improvising to the lights while Locks added abstract vocal sounds. Two of the musicians—one was among Locks's advanced art students—quickly tied up with a promoter to take the show on the road and went to Los Angeles, where it quickly broke up. One of the last shows was seen by an art student named Elias Romero, who went to San Francisco three years later to learn the technique from one of the artists he'd seen.

Locks kept teaching his course on Light and Art, but Romero was the real Johnny Appleseed of light shows. In 1958 he was doing shows in the Beat colony of Los Angeles, with a college classmate named Christopher Tree on percussion. In 1962 he was living on Pine Street in San Francisco and performing at parties, galleries and coffeehouses. When R. G. Davis formed the Mime Troupe, he and Romero rented an old church in the Mission district where Romero did regular Sunday night shows. He also came to the Open Theater's attic gathering where the "Revelations" nude projection idea was born.

The building manager where Romero lived was Bill Ham, who had been working in the gestural and action painting genres of abstract expressionism; to him these light shows looked like the natural next step. Romero collaborated with Ham on a theater piece and ended up loaning him a projector. Ham started doing his own shows in his basement studio. Later he moved his shows to another basement he maintained for just that purpose, with musicians from the after-hours jazz club around the corner for music and most of the Pine Street gang for an audience. Romero had also collaborated with Anthony Martin, the Tape Music Center's lighting director, and encouraged him in the use of liquid pigment shows.

Already at least a dozen people in the area owned overhead projectors for light shows, and more got involved as the dance scene expanded. One was Ben Van Meter, a State College graduate in filmmaking who not only knew the Pine Street crowd but had even rehearsed with the Charlatans as a potential drummer. He had already shown interest in projections with his film *Poon Tang Trilogy*, where films of the crash of the airship *Hindenburg* were projected on a woman's body, docking at her navel and exploding on her pubes.

Bill Ham naturally did the light shows for the original Family Dog dances. Martin's assistant Roger Hilyard did lights for the Trips Festival, and Martin himself took care of Graham's dances and a few of Helms's until Bill Ham replaced him. Van Meter took Martin's place at the Fillmore for a couple of weeks in the spring while Martin was on tour with the Tape Center. Ironically, Romero never performed at the dance halls. He was about to retire from light shows, fatigued after ten years of pushing the form.

To the careless observer all these shows looked alike: brilliant swirling colors supplemented with slides and film and often with ultraviolet lights to make Day-Glo paint fluoresce and a flashing strobe light that might hit a hypnotic alpha-wave rhythm. But each light artist had a distinct approach. Romero was known for brilliance and saturation of colors in his all-liquid show. Ham, like Romero, came from an abstract expressionist background and liked working with jazz musicians so the lights and the music could be a combined improvisation. For the dances he had to supplement the liquid projections, which needed one man's total attention, with slides and film to create a dance-hall-sized light environment covering two or three walls.

Martin had worked in events and environment-shaping art and thought of himself as a fine-arts performer, not improvising but executing a worked-out composition. Indeed, he wanted to avoid being identified with the dance halls and never fought to get his name mentioned on the posters. Only two Family Dog posters carried his name, and with Bill Graham the problem didn't exist: Graham never mentioned light-show artists on his posters. Martin also avoided such psychedelic motifs as the mandalas and concentric patterns which in light shows symbolized psychedelic glory. His opposite might have been the Holy See light show where Ray Anderson of the Matrix worked. Holy See not only reveled in concentric imagery but also worked in literal images from songs, creating shapes through which a liquid design would be projected: say, the outline of a man and woman kissing, filled with one single abstract moving pattern.

And as a filmmaker Van Meter went into the light shows from yet another angle. At first he filmed dancers and sold the film to Tony Martin, who included it in his show the next weekend among the liquid displays and colored slides of faces, flowers, seashells and so forth. Apart from the shock of seeing oneself up on the wall dancing at this same place the week before, the films were disorienting because up to three images were superimposed, as if ghosts were dancing through each other in an arbitrary space. This was not a sophisticated trick accomplished in the developing studio, just the same film run through the camera three times for a triple exposure; Van Meter could afford only one reel of film per weekend. When he did light shows himself, Van Meter used the liquid displays to blend the edges between the several films being projected.

A great blaze of colored imagery seemed to fit right in with a rock and roll dance full of acidheads. When the Grateful Dead returned from Los Angeles and first played in the full-blown dance-hall scene, they had such an unheard-of pile of speakers and amplifiers that it blocked the light-show screen. By the time they next played the Avalon Ballroom, they had painted their equipment white so the light show would be visible on it. By January this kind of psychedelic light show had already reached Austin, Texas, when a Texan named Travis Rivers brought the idea back from San Francisco and founded the Jomo Light Disaster to back the local psychedelic rock band, the Thirteenth Floor Elevators.

The combination of some form of colored light exhibit with rock and roll was such a natural idea in the emerging McLuhan/Mod zeitgeist that gestures of one sort or another were being made in other parts of the country. In the spring of 1966 *Life* ran a story about the new lighting fashions in rock and roll discotheques in the East. The most advanced was the World in Garden City, Long Island, which projected a TV image of the dancers on a screen over their heads with slides of optical illusions on flanking screens. At Le Bison in Chicago, there was a music-operated light box a little like the ones the Red Dog and Mother's had used.

More typical was simply covering a discotheque with colored light bulbs and perhaps turning them on and off, as at the Cheetah or the highly touted Arthur in New York. According to *Life*, the big step in rock dances was being taken at the Cheetah, which had a disc of colored light bulbs *that revolved*. The story mentioned that Andy Warhol was taking his Plastic Exploding Inevitable, with its static movies and colored spotlights, out West. Neither *Life* nor Warhol had a clue what they'd find already going on in San Francisco.

THE BANDS Most of the rock musicians in San Francisco were basically folkies learning how to play electrified instruments. They had a tentative sound at first and played a lot of solemn, chiming chords on the beat. This was just fine with the audience, which had come to dance rather than listen. When it came time for the guitarist to take a solo break, he often noodled up and down the notes of the scale in a way that might owe as much to inexperience in improvisation as it did to the influence of Indian ragas.

The musicians were also stoned a lot of the time, another reason to stick to simple raga-like improvisations. Maybe it was being stoned that led them to play into their loudspeakers and deliberately cause the soul-rattling feedback noises musicians had always tried to avoid; feedback seemed to create itself by magic, as if a new entity had appeared on the stage.

Add the casual stage manner that the musicians had learned as folkies to their technical inexperience and tendency to play stoned, and the result is not what the record industry was looking for. Talent scouts came to the San Francisco dance halls and saw sloppy-looking bands who took forever to tune up and didn't always play on time or in tune. The solos went on too long—one night Jim Gurley of Big Brother played a 45-minute solo—with logicless explorations of the highest or lowest register, sometimes getting hung up on one or two notes forever. The songs themselves sounded a little bluesy, a little folkie, but completely uncommercial with their demented lyrics. One Big Brother song declared the singer to be a series of animals —caterpillar, pterodactyl and so forth—crawling for love, or flying, or whatever mode of locomotion was appropriate for the animal.

The talent scouts saw the garish light show, the curiously blissful or conspiratorial dancers in paint and feathers and antique-shop clothes, and concluded that these were all babes in the woods. Once in a while a record company rep was slipped an acid-dosed cup of coffee and would begin to see an insidious logic in the proceedings. Then he might try to get his superiors to take the San Francisco dance-hall scene seriously, only to realize he couldn't explain why.

Tom Donahue surely understood what was going on, but his Autumn Records label wasn't able to sign up all the bands because of financial trouble. Donahue's psychedelic nightclub was mostly closed, he was getting a divorce and his business partner was mortally ill. He even went back to the Top Forty station where he had worked until the summer of 1965 and asked for his old job, but they didn't want him any more. The only band Autumn signed was the Great Society, which broke up without a record.

On the other hand, a small label named Mainstream did a disproportionate amount of signing. In August Big Brother went to Chicago to play a blues club and at the end of the gig didn't even have carfare back to San Francisco. Mainstream offered to pay their way home if they left a demo tape, and the band—managerless after a split with Chet Helms—reluctantly did it. Wild Flower and the Final Solution ended up on the same label.

The only group with a major label contract was Jefferson Airplane, who were recording their first album for RCA in December 1965, just four months after their debut. When the album, *Jefferson Airplane Takes Off*, finally came out in August, it was disappointing; the sound quality was bad and the band had greatly improved since the recording date. Moreover, any weekend rock dance had a poster more exciting than the Airplane's album cover. But it was a fair selection of the Airplane's repertoire: some blues, some love songs, a song of psychic self-defense ("It's My Life"), all done with the Airplane's earnest romanticism. Ironically, by the time the album was released the female lead singer was too pregnant to perform and was replaced by Grace Slick, star of the recently disbanded Great Society.

The album sold mostly in the San Francisco area, and in the dance halls the Airplane was still top draw. It was the unofficial house band at the Fillmore, where it played more than a dozen weekends in eight months, twice as many as the Grateful Dead, the No. 2 band. The relation with Bill Graham was so warm that the band finally dropped its flamboyant, cape-wearing manager Matthew Katz (pronounced "Cates") and had Graham act as their manager. This move up to the big time had taken place a lot faster than envisioned by the group, which had expected to be the house band at the Matrix and had even considered naming itself Matrix. Balin's old partners started complaining the group wasn't playing the Matrix as often as it should, according to the deal whereby the partners had staked the band for sound equipment.

The Charlatans had moved to Downey Street in the Haight, but they were a little left out of the dance halls. Even the Dead, who were out of town until late April, had played twice as many dances at the Fillmore and the Avalon as the Charlatans had by September. The Charlatans maintained their Edwardian/cowboy style and kept playing a ragtimey, countrified rock that by now sounded positively old-fashioned beside the messianic experimentalism of the Dead, Big Brother and other bands who were playing timeless ragas and experimenting with feedback and other psychedelic effects that re-created revelatory roaring, chills of ecstasy and awestruck wandering. The Charlatans kept a regular gig at a North Beach nightclub where at least one hippie topless dancer refused to work with any other band.

When the Grateful Dead returned from Los Angeles, they moved into Danny Rifkin's apartment building at 710 Ashbury, displacing most of the tenants. They brought with them a version of the sound equipment Owsley had lavished on them, making them the loudest band in town, potentially in the world. Unlike the Airplane, which was already a recording band, they were under no pressure to write original material, and concentrated instead on playing the rhythm and blues dance standards most of the bands had started with—for example, "Love Light" and "In the Midnight Hour," with a fat, solid rhythm underpinned by Phil Lesh's exceptionally melodic bass lines and decorated with Jerry Garcia's rippling guitar runs. They were known as the band most likely to play stoned on acid, and became famous for taking half an hour to tune up or to decide what to play next.

The protest folk-rock record by Country Joe and the Fish was widely distributed to record stores in college towns, and SDS asked Joe McDonald and guitarist Barry Melton to tour colleges in the Northwest. They found that everyone assumed that the Fish was an organized band rather than a spur-of-the-moment jug band, so when they got back to Berkeley they set about organizing a real band. In the spring they put out another small record, this one showing the kind of solemn, chiming guitar band arrangements the Airplane was doing. The cover had the new five-man group slouching like young rockers in front of a Goodwill truck; one member was a conscientious objector working off his alternative service at Goodwill Industries.

With this record under their belts, Melton and McDonald hitched to New York to offer their hot psychedelico-revolutionary act to Albert Grossman, manager of Bob Dylan and Paul Butterfield. Grossman wasn't interested, but they did run into their old friend the *Berkeley Barb*'s folk critic, who had been road-managing the New York folk-rock group called the Blues Project, and he agreed to manage them.

Big Brother and the Holding Company was still putting itself together. They'd gotten a suitable drummer at last, an instructor at the San Francisco Art Institute who had worked in the Catskills nightclubs on drums. And they had developed a following for their weird music: edgy harmony that came from singing at the interval of a fifth, Jim Gurley's attempts to translate John Coltrane's jazz saxophone style to guitar, their rock version of Grieg's "In the Hall of the Mountain King." The final element the band needed was a singer Chet Helms remembered from Texas, a moody little speed freak named Janis Joplin. He had Travis Rivers bring her back from Texas and moved her into an apartment on Pine Street. After less than a week of rehearsals at Mouse's firehouse, the new Big Brother debuted at the Avalon on June 10.

Joplin definitely added something. The original center of the group had been Peter Albin with his surprisingly deep voice, with tall, silent Jim Gurley as the spiritual hero of the large colony of expatriate Detroiters. Now Janis confirmed Big Brother's position in the emerging rogue's gallery of local bands. The Airplane had the slogan "Jefferson Airplane Loves You," which they had even had made into a bumper sticker; the Dead were the eternal Acid Test band, already referred to as the "good ol' Grateful Dead"; Country Joe was antiwar and Quicksilver was shaping up a punk cowboy image. With Janis and her jerky, speed-freak gestures, Big Brother became the dropout band. Janis had bad skin, dull hair and coarse features. Where the Airplane's original soprano had worn miniskirts and Grace Slick, an ex-fashion model, had a striking Mod wardrobe, Janis wore sack dresses and ponchos and made her own funky jewelry out of chicken bones.

But she sang like a banshee. Before her, Big Brother was known for a lurching, unpredictable sound. Janis made them stand out with her electrifyingly overwrought voice.

These bands were the mainstay of the dance halls. Graham and Helms filled out their bills with major out-of-town bands like the Mothers, the Blues Project, Butterfield and the Lovin' Spoonful, plus some Chicago blues bands and a potpourri of lesser-known groups. At the beginning, most of the latter, like the Oxford Circle and the Electric Train, were just teenage rock bands from Northern California, but new avant-garde rock bands were also springing up. The Only Alternative (and His Other Possibilities) included a former Broadway musical comedy singer and her brother, a dropped-out architect. Another was the Sons of Champlin, a Marin County teen band that got turned on to psychedelics in the intense Zen crowd around Alan Watts in Mill Valley.

Every college community in the area had its own psychedelic rock band. The San Francisco Art Institute had the Mystery Trend (the name taken from a misheard line in a Dylan song about a mystery tramp). In Oakland the California College of Arts and Crafts had the Wild Flower. The Final Solution had been around from the beginning, a group of State College students living in the Haight. In the summer of 1966 these last two bands alternated with fellow Mainstream Record Company artists Big Brother and the Holding Company at the nearly forgotten Red Dog Saloon in a now openly hostile Virginia City, which sported a sign reading, "Keep Virginia City Clean—Get a Haircut."

THE HAIGHT-ASHBURY   With its quaint Victorian architecture and the wooded hills of Ashbury Heights behind it, and isolated from the rest of the city, the Haight-Ashbury looked oddly like a quiet town in the Old West. There was even a small-town sense of community among the pre-hippie residents, as they showed in March by defeating a projected freeway that would have eliminated the Panhandle strip of park. Living was still cheap in the Haight, and more aesthetic than ever since the De Young Museum, a comfortable walk away in

Golden Gate Park, had just opened a collection of Asian art with stunning Chinese landscapes and Tibetan religious paintings. Right next to the museum was the lush Japanese Tea Garden. In fact the whole park was full of picturesque nooks, a paradise for getting stoned. The Haight-Ashbury was even blessed with places to go in the dead of night, the twenty-four-hour House of Do-Nuts at Frederick and Stanyan and Bob's Restaurant at the end of Haight Street.

The community that had recognized itself had started to gravitate —"gravitate" was the word they used, in fact—toward this congenial neighborhood. Haight Street had even gotten a sort of hippie headquarters, a better place to hang out in public than the laundromat that had served as a social center by default. The new place had opened on January 3, in time to be mentioned in the Trips Festival handbill: a tiny store near the corner of Haight and Ashbury with the daring name of the Psychedelic Shop.

It was not originally envisioned as a hangout, but the owners didn't discourage socializing. They were Ron and Jay Thelin, natives of the neighborhood whose father had once managed the Woolworth's across the street. As Leary-influenced psychedelic seekers, they found that the books they wanted to read were scattered in occult stores, technical bookstores and newsstands, while incense, records of Indian music and marijuana paraphernalia were in still other places. Their idea was to run a store that would sell everything an acidhead might be interested in. The stock changed all the time; they introduced Indian paisley fabrics, dance posters, imported bells, paste-on "diffraction gratings" that put a spot of prismatic color on your forehead or bamboo flute or whatever. From the day it opened, it was a ticket outlet for the dance concerts.

The Psychedelic Shop seemed like a positive idea to them, but on opening day an anonymous note was slipped under their door denouncing them for selling out the psychedelic revolution.

The Haight was traditionally the San Francisco State student neighborhood, and if it was getting more far out, so was State. In the fall of 1965 a professor there had started the Experimental College, a college within a college where students could decide what they wanted to study, outline a course, get a faculty sponsor and hire a teacher. The courses they chose tended to be in arts, psychology or occult religion, though one of the scholars they invited in the spring of 1966 was an inventor and philosopher of technology referred to in a newspaper interview as "Richard B. Fuller" but better known by his middle name, Buckminster.

At the end of spring more shops appeared on Haight Street to join the Psychedelic Shop and the boutique Mnasidika. The House of Richard moved up from its side-street location near the Panhandle to a storefront right next door to the Psychedelic Shop and directly across from Mnasidika. A little later a health food store opened on Page Street, officially named Far Fetched Foods but commonly referred to as Blind Jerry's. In June Tsvi Strauch, owner of a crafts boutique on Divisadero, opened a Mod clothing store called In Gear a few doors west of Mnasidika. Around the same time another boutique, the Blushing Peony, opened up a block east. A State College instructor started a coffee shop called the I/Thou two blocks west of that central cluster between Clayton and Ashbury.

In July and August a big surge of new psychedelic residents hit the neighborhood. In general the old-timers had nothing against it; the new hippie businesses were beginning to revitalize the Haight Street shopping district, where more than a dozen storefronts had been vacant. In July a group of former SNCC activists started the Haight-Ashbury Settlement House, a grammar school and kindergarten that also taught arts and crafts for adults, in a storefront on Cole Street.

All this was happening rather quietly, except for a bust of twenty-four people at 408 Ashbury in March for marijuana and "suspected heroin"—actually Methedrine. On that occasion, the police captain of Park Station told the newspapers that "the word is out that San Francisco is the place for the far-out crowd," but he did not specify the Haight-Ashbury. To the general public the Haight was known only as the place that had stood up to the freeway builders, unless they remembered the Blue Unicorn stories of a year before.

To the people involved in psychedelics, though, a whole world now revolved around the Haight-Ashbury, and was plainly growing. Sure, there were imperfections. There wasn't much to do on Haight Street itself except meet your friends on the sidewalk—you couldn't go shopping for clothes or roach clips every day—and there was no public drinking fountain or toilet nearer than the Panhandle. Gangs of neighborhood kids occasionally made trouble, to say nothing of the Hell's Angels who had started hanging out. Sure, there had been dubious versions of the psychedelic gatherings, like the various phony Trips Festivals, or the staging of the Open Theater's "Nude Revelations" at a North Beach topless joint (covered by *Playboy*), or a rock and fashion show at the Fillmore organized by a Marin County boutique.

But these were just details. What was happening was so big it would wash such imperfections away, or perhaps engulf them and transform them into unexpected benefits. If you didn't believe it, you could listen to the new Donovan single. Way over in England, Donovan knew of the Airplane. In the last chorus of "Fat Angel" he called on everybody to "fly Jefferson Airplane."

THE DOPE TRADE   The Haight-Ashbury was not only the social and cultural center of the Northern California psychedelic community but also its economic capital in the one business that mattered, the drug market.

Dealing marijuana was the economic base of the Haight-Ashbury hippie community. Nearly every hippie sold a little grass, and many didn't know any other way of making a living. The Beats had smoked grass and dealt it too—since there was no legal distribution system, most potheads had sold as well as bought from time to time—but in their time the grass market was small. Even their language of dealing was diminutive, ten dollars being called a dime and five dollars a nickel.

But in the early sixties marijuana, formerly the drug of working-class blacks and Latins, had rapidly become fashionable on college campuses. In 1966 scores of people were smuggling grass direct from Mexico to San Francisco, but demand, largely on the campuses, still exceeded supply. Meanwhile, college students and the growing number of professional class potheads were not about to take the risk of importing contraband, so the import trade and wholesale dealing fell by default to hippies.

In 1966, lids ("ostensible ounces," as the term was translated in court) of grass were going for $8 to $10 in San Francisco. Kilograms, or keys, ranged from $50 to $75, averaging around $60. Obviously, if there were 20 to 22 honest lids in a key, there was $100 or $150 to be made by breaking a kilogram down and selling it in lids. An attractive proposition, even when the lids actually weighed a full ounce.

In practice, lid dealers smoked a lot of their stock themselves. It was part of the business to smoke with the customers so everybody could "taste" the wares, and a lot of dealers were content to deal no more than necessary to underwrite their own stash of grass. But many started dealing on a larger scale, as Roger the Dealer did. He was a grammar school dropout who had long resigned himself to living a marginal life as a pot-smoking bum. His roommates had a practice of chipping in on a kilo and dealing enough lids to pay their $85 rent, get their money back and end up with a lid or two apiece to last them the month. One day, when it was Roger's turn to score the kilo and deal the lids, he had the inspiration of dealing the *whole* kilo, then buying another with the profits and dealing most of that. His roommates got their money back and their rent paid and their lids, and Roger kept his smoking stash plus $150.

It took a degree of hustle to make big money from dealing lids, because you needed twenty customers or so for every kilo. It meant dealing with strangers and probably hanging around in a coffeehouse or other known dealing spot. It was an easy bust. On the other hand, while dealing kilos was safer because you dealt in private and exclusively with other dealers, a smaller number of people and a group less likely to be infiltrated with narcs, the profit margin in kilos was nowhere near so good. Kilos could be picked up in Los Angeles for $35 to $40, but if you sold one for $60 you were only making as much as a lid dealer was getting for three ounces and risking a longer jail term if you got caught. In Mexico kilos were going for $15 and under, but that meant a major expedition and travel expense, plus the danger of running the border.

The only way to make money dealing kilos without importing them yourself was to move a lot of merchandise. As the Haight-Ashbury became a central drug market, it was possible to do just that.

Somebody would drive in from Denver or Portland with enough money to score twenty or fifty keys for his whole doper community back home, and in an afternoon the wholesale dealer in the Haight would have made as much money as a lid dealer would earn in a week or two.

Eventually a kilo-level dealer was expected to handle a full line of drugs, including psychedelics and even the amphetamines that abruptly fell from fashion late in 1965. But the psychedelic trade was fundamentally different from the marijuana trade. The market was smaller, and those who took LSD didn't use it as often as a pothead smoked grass. And people often found it hard to put a price on something as extraordinary as LSD.

The marijuana trade was high-spirited commerce with a touch of cops and robbers about it, but the LSD trade was more like a heroic conspiracy, particularly for the psychedelic chemists; as they mastered the heady arcana of the laboratory they were playing history like a chess game. The chief figure, without question, was Owsley Stanley. He moved back up to Berkeley from Los Angeles in the spring of 1966 and established a laboratory in a secret rural hideaway, from which new batches of acid emerged from time to time. Originally he had sold LSD in powder form that could be "capped" in gelatin capsules; there was a run on oo size caps whenever a new batch appeared on the market. He had also sold it in liquid form, tinted light blue so the dealer could tell which vitamin pill or sugar cube he had dosed with an eyedropper and which he hadn't. The blue liquid form conveniently resembled Wisk detergent and was usually transported in carefully washed out Wisk bottles, with a bag of dirty laundry in the backseat of the car to complete the disguise.

Narcotics agents began noticing the blue liquid form around December 1965, but Owsley had already moved on from that and invested his profits in a pill press so he could market the first LSD tablets: short, slightly irregular cylinders immediately known as barrels. By August 1966 he had a more professional pill press that made real pharmaceutical tablets with a hairline crack on one side so they could be split in half if desired: his flats. Soon he started coloring every batch of tablets a different color.

In a sense, he was obliged to make these advances in packaging.

His name was already a household word among acidheads as far away as Paris and London in 1966. Dealers handling mediocre and adulterated LSD were trying to sell their stuff as "genuine Owsley," but the counterfeiters couldn't keep up with the latest color.

Even around San Francisco, where Owsley was by far the principal source of LSD, there were other brands on the street. Two or three smaller factories were operating locally and Timothy Leary's personal network was distributing LSD from Czechoslovakia and the remains of the Sandoz production. Owsley's, however, was universally acknowledged as the most powerful. Detractors accused him of spiking it with amphetamines or even strychnine, but Owsley maintained that his acid was simply purer than the rest and that he put an honest 250 micrograms in every tab. In fact he had put a little Methedrine in his early LSD, under the influence of Leary, who claimed amphetamines added "clarity" to an acid trip, but Owsley soon turned against amphetamines in any form.

With his commanding position in the market, Owsley was trying to control prices. He regulated his distribution with the aim of keeping his tabs, which as a premium product might have gone up in price, at a steady $2 retail. He had agents in New York, Los Angeles and a few other cities whose jobs depended on seeing that his price prevailed; and if you didn't do business directly with them, you weren't going to make money dealing LSD because they established the retail price and were the only ones who could offer a wholesale rate.

Owsley's marketing technique included passing out a lot of free samples. A new batch would be announced with people walking up and down Haight Street passing out the Blue Dots, Green Flats or whatever was the latest model. He made a particular point of trying to get his LSD to all the musicians he could, and his intense figure was a familiar sight backstage even at the Fillmore, despite Bill Graham's distaste for dope dealers. At the Avalon he regularly stirred a ripple of awed whispering when he appeared on the dance floor.

OTHER SCENES Since Bill Graham had left in February, the Mime Troupe had mounted a children's puppet show, taken the anti-racist

Minstrel Show on the road, presented a group of sketches satirically called *Traps Festival* for a radical's campaign for mayor of Berkeley, and participated in a benefit for Timothy Leary's legal fund. The giant puppets used in their political skits had continued to show up here and there; for instance, on the trucks the Vietnam Day Committee sent around Berkeley with a rock band in July.

The Mime Troupe's founder, R. G. Davis, had moved his opposition to foundation support from the level of personal example to organized resistance by forming an Artists' Liberation Front (ALF) to circumvent official art presentations, such as those of the San Francisco Cultural Board. A third of the forty-five ALF members were Mime Troupers, the remainder unaffiliated artists and a few allied figures including Bill Graham, Ralph Gleason and Hunter Thompson. The ALF planned a series of street fairs in San Francisco neighborhoods that would use the Mime Troupe, live music, puppet shows, participatory painting and whatever else seemed appropriate to the neighborhood. The ALF benefit held at the Fillmore on July 17 was one of the first shows where the line out front actually went around the block.

But internally the Mime Troupe was more polarized than ever. Davis had always encouraged serious political discussion—such as "rap sessions" about Mao Tse-tung's book of quotations—so open factionalism was nothing new. But the most recent was a particularly deep rift; a group referring to themselves as Diggers after a seventeenth-century English sect of religious communists were in effect advocating throwing all the Mime Troupe's energies into the Haight-Ashbury community as the place of greatest revolutionary potential.

There was one theater in the Haight-Ashbury. The old Haight Theater had failed as a neighborhood cinema, then as a homosexual movie house and finally as an Assembly of God church. Like the rest of the neighborhood it was run-down, with its worn rugs and closets full of dusty old film posters. Previous tenants had pirated much of the electrical wiring and left the basement flooded. But it was the only place large enough to serve as a community center.

In May it was leased by three partners: Luther "Spike" Greene, a movie-star-handsome veteran of the San Francisco/New York/ Mexico psychedelic circuit, and two brothers, Hillel and Bill Resner, a left-wing attorney's sons who had grown up in the Haight and gotten into the same transcontinental doper crowd as Greene. These three had been among the parties bidding for the Fillmore in February. In May they had rented the Avalon for a Wild Flower/Dead concert with a reading by the Beat poet Michael McClure. By that time Bill Resner and a would-be light-show artist friend had rented the vacant theater, renaming it the Straight Theater.

They planned to put in a 4,000-foot dance floor while keeping the balcony seating plus a couple of hundred seats on the floor for a sensorium-theater with a 180-degree movie screen, and there was still room for a film lab, a repertory theater and a dance workshop. As the Fillmore and Avalon hit their stride and psychedelic posters became part of the mix, they projected a poster operation. Their light-show man was already freelancing his show, Straight Lightning.

It looked like a natural. The Straight had a legal capacity greater than the Fillmore and the Avalon combined, and it was in the Haight itself, while the Fillmore was two miles away and the Avalon closer to three. Luther invested his trust fund and they found a young heir who put in $23,000. As word spread about their ambitious plans, more people donated. Quicksilver Messenger Service and Big Brother put in $5,000 apiece. Owsley invested some money and, intrigued by the technological possibilities of the hall, threw in some speakers. Timothy Leary visited and gave his blessing. To the young partners, it seemed as if their good intentions were being rewarded.

On the other hand, it was taking a long time to get anything accomplished. When they started work in May, they expected to open in six weeks. Luther Greene went to Texas to face trial on a marijuana possession charge, and when he was paroled six months later the theater was still being remodeled. Part of the trouble was that no one in San Francisco history had ever petitioned the Central Building Permit Bureau for permission to convert a theater into a dance hall. The other way around was common, but why would anyone tear up money-making theater seats for a dance floor? All the permits were mysteriously hard to get. The building inspectors revealed their requirements piecemeal, often requiring the partners to tear out work that had already been done. When the dance floor was all but complete, the Fire Department announced that it would be declared a hazard unless the space underneath it were divided into compartments four feet square, with walls consisting of three-hour fire wall, each compartment with its own individual fire sprinkler.

In the midst of all this, the Straight Theater School of Performing Arts actually opened. A Martha Graham student was training the Straight Dance Troupe at the abandoned Masonic Hall down the block, which had three large oak-paneled rooms and secret Masonic passageways. Some of the Straight Theater workers were actually living there. Straight Lightning quickly won a reputation as the light show most likely to come to a gig stoned on acid.

The partners faced a mountain of work. But when the day was over, the workers could retire to the office behind the theater marquee, a small chamber which for some reason was lined with mirrors, and space out with some grass in the endless regression of mirrors reflecting mirrors. Their plans were expanding almost by the hour: the rock dances would support other cultural events that might not be self-supporting—Shakespeare productions, for instance, which would presumably look good to the grown-ups downtown. The master plan emerged as the development of the entire block bounded by Haight, Cole, Page and Shrader Streets as a vast cultural complex. Friends and relatives were getting sucked up into this whirlwind.

The whole thing was predicated on income from the dances, which looked like a sure thing because the theater was right in the Haight itself. But Greene and the Resners were among those who still did not know that you needed a city permit to put on a public dance.

Back in January, when the Trips Festival planners had struck it off so well with *Chronicle* music columnist Lou Gottlieb, he had mentioned to them that he had a ranch out in the country, thirty-one acres of land in rural Sonoma County he had bought four years before. It was out in the woods near Occidental, technically in the township of Graton. If they ever wanted to get away from the city,

Gottlieb told them, they could stay there. He was planning to move out there himself and devote eight years to studying piano, with the aim of debuting as a classical pianist at the age of fifty.

It was a tempting offer. Ben and Rain Jacopetti were dissatisfied with the progress of their Open Theater in Berkeley. As for Ramon Sender, he was facing a crisis. His Tape Music Center had been sustained by a small Rockefeller Foundation grant, on the understanding that it would be increased if the Tape Center affiliated with a college. Sender wanted to avoid college affiliation, but the only alternative he had been able to think of was for all the artists involved in the Tape Center to reduce their collective budget by living communally, and the artists hadn't bought it.

So he left the Tape Center on its own and went down to the desert country of the Southwest, visiting the hand-to-mouth Drop City commune that was forming in Colorado near the New Mexico border. He came back to Berkeley talking about sun worship and moving to the country. After Marin County sheriffs rousted him and his girlfriend Joan for bathing nude in the woods, he recalled Gottlieb's offer. In March, Ramon and Joan, the Jacopettis and Stewart and Lois Brand went up to have a look at the farm. It looked good: woods and apple trees and even a stream.

The Brands didn't stay long. Sender had told Brand's old roommate Steve Durkee about the spiritual qualities of the desert, and the Brands soon went down to Sollux, the commune Durkee was building in New Mexico. Later in the spring the Brands went on the road with the USCo light-show exhibition and ended up back in San Francisco.

By April the Jacopettis had tied up their loose ends in Berkeley and moved to the ranch, Gottlieb had moved up to stay, and they were joined by a jeweler-poet friend and the filmmaker Bruce Baillie. They settled into whatever they wanted to do as Gottlieb's guests. Gottlieb was studying piano. The Jacopettis were studying yoga. Sender was sun-worshiping and making regular trips to the San Francisco metaphysical bookstores. Every evening they gathered to read scriptures aloud. They thought of converting the place into a Hindu ashram and affiliating with Sri Aurobindo's Auroville in India.

They even discovered that the place had a spiritual-sounding name when Joan found some old documents showing that it had been known as Morning Star Ranch.

In the tranquillity of the Sonoma County redwoods, the spiritual atmosphere grew into a philosophy of utter acceptance. One day Bruce Baillie asked Gottlieb whether he could rent one of the old ranch sheds as a cutting room for his film work. How much would Gottlieb charge? "Oh, thirty dollars, forty dollars," Gottlieb guessed. Baillie's German shepherd bitch growled at him, and Gottlieb found he felt like forgetting about rent. It worked out okay. In fact it felt fine.

Summer drifted into fall. The name on the mailbox still read "Beecher," and nobody felt any need to update it.

By September 1966 newcomers were showing up in the Haight almost daily. Neighborhood windows had blossomed with all sorts of decorations: curtains made of blankets or Indian print fabrics from the Psych Shop, wind chimes, little glass sculptures, or god's-eyes— wooden crosses strung diagonally with multicolored yarn, a cultural import from the mushroom-eating Indians of southern Mexico. The neighborhood was loose, as people put it. In an apartment at the corner of Stanyan and Alma, tenants sold the coveted buttons that read: "Good Ol' Grateful Dead." If the people were home, you could go in and buy one. If they weren't, you could walk in the front door, find the upended orange crate with the dish of buttons on it, take what you wanted and leave the money on the crate.

But in the outside world, the Vietnam War kept escalating—the big new hit on the radio was "Eve of Destruction," an antiwar song of the bitterest pessimism—and the legal crackdown on drugs was just weeks away. As of the first week of October, it would be a misdemeanor to possess LSD in California and a felony to sell it. The straights were even cracking down on drug references in rock songs. A leading newsletter for radio stations refused to list Dylan's "Rainy

Day Women #12 and #35" at all even though it was one of the best-selling singles in the country.

Between the growth of the Haight and the war and the LSD laws, it seemed time for the psychedelic community to come up with something new.

There had been talk of a newspaper for the Haight-Ashbury psychedelic community, but the project had gotten off to a fitful start. Allen Cohen, a short, bearded poet who was a friend of the Thelins, had had a dream about a newspaper filled with rainbows. As it developed, there were two factions interested in putting out a newspaper: Cohen's arts and psychedelia faction, which had neither journalistic experience nor concrete plans, and a Marxist group that wanted a political paper like the *Berkeley Barb.* The Marxist faction had the upper hand when Ron Thelin, the principal financial backer, declared there had been enough meetings and it was time to put out a newspaper.

The name "Psychedelphic Oracle" had come up in the discussions and lingered on in abbreviated form when *P.O. Frisco* came out at the beginning of September. *P.O. Frisco* was very much like the *Barb,* promoting sexual liberation and appealing to the paranoia of the antiwar movement. The cover stories were on masturbation and the perennial rumor that the government was readying concentration camps for political dissenters.

Masturbation and concentration camps, not exactly the emphasis Ron Thelin had expected in a Haight-Ashbury newspaper. He threw his weight to the psychedelic faction, principally Cohen and Michael Bowen, a collagist from the North Beach–Big Sur circuit. Cohen's program for the new publication, *The City of San Francisco Oracle,* was to "judo the tabloid lowprice anguish propaganda and profit form to confront its readers with a rainbow of beauty and words ringing with truth and transcendence." The first issue was due out September 20.

The day before that first issue, Timothy Leary held a press conference at the Village Theater in New York to announce an evolutionary step of his own. At the moment Leary was out on bail from an LSD and grass bust at Millbrook and was already facing thirty years in jail plus a $30,000 fine on his federal grass bust at the Texas-Mexico border. The subject of his press conference was a new religious organization called the League for Spiritual Discovery. Its fifteen-member board of guides—all of whom, said Leary, "have resigned their jobs and are dedicating their lives to the religion"—would take a psychedelic trip once a week as a religious duty. Leary himself would travel around the country presenting a religious stage show that would reproduce the effects of a psychedelic trip. Leary had already released a phonograph record of his psychedelic philosophy, *The Five Levels of Consciousness,* which was being advertised with the slogan "Does LSD in Sugar Cubes Spoil the Taste of Coffee?"

The following day, as Leary presented his first stage show in New York, the first issue of the *Oracle* appeared in San Francisco. It looked superficially like "underground" newspapers such as the *Barb.* There was a calendar of local events. The cover story was a recent piece of news, the beginning of biweekly community dialogues at the I/Thou between Haight residents and the police Community Relations Unit. One of the editorials would have been at home in any underground paper—"protest has not gained any meaningful change" for blacks or antiwar activists "because we are psychologically and materially dependent on the system we're changing"—except that it quoted Leary's "Turn on, tune in, drop out" slogan. And another editorial described the *Oracle* as "an attempt to create an open voice for those involved in a 'life of art,' as Dr. Timothy Leary calls it."

Elsewhere in the paper a Mime Troupe play, *Search and Seizure,* was reviewed by a Mime Trouper named Kent Minault. The play takes place at a police station where policemen intimidate three archetypal drug offenders: a naive pothead, a commercially oriented Methedrine dealer and an acidhead. The decisive character is the acidhead, who is so stoned he ignores not only his role as a criminal but the policemen's role as authorities. He crosses the invisible line the police have drawn between themselves and the dopers, observed Minault, and threatens their sense of authority.

The playwright—a short blond named Peter Berg who was nicknamed "the Hun" and had been described by a newspaper interviewer as "a bitter young man"—had also written the play that had gotten the Mime Troupe in so much trouble the year before. Like Minault and a tall, verbal ex-folkie named Peter Cohon, he was friendly with the two original members of the Digger faction, a pair of childhood pals from Brooklyn who were relative newcomers to the Mime Troupe. They were quiet, cagey Billy Murcott and flamboyant Eugene Grogan, who claimed to have been an assistant to the Italian filmmaker Fellini. Grogan had recently decided to change his first name to Emmett.

Murcott and Grogan, like Leary and the *Oracle*, felt it was time for the psychedelic community to do something, but they had no use for the passive Learyite tone of the *Oracle*. To present another viewpoint they commandeered the mimeograph machine at the Mime Troupe loft, actually the property of Students for a Democratic Society, and put out a series of broadsides quoting, and at first signed by, a fictitious wise man named "George Metevsky," referring to the famous Mad Bomber who had terrorized New York in the fifties: George Metesky.

The most striking thing about these broadsides was an aggressive sarcasm that was worlds removed from the rather careful and timeless tone of the *Oracle*. The broadsides addressed a sense of dissatisfaction with the psychedelic life for which religious visions were no cure. "Our bowels quake in constipated fear alarms," read a poem in one of the papers, "we are often naked and nameless in boring rooms with tedious records." It ended with "a skinny drab red-haired girl freaking out the gathering/sending everybody to the icebox checking out the Seconal supply."

If such a poem had appeared in an underground newspaper it would have been regarded as a simple denunciation of the drug culture, but the Digger broadsides were committed to a psychedelic quest, in their own way even more poignantly than the first *Oracle* had been. The *Oracle* had not yet dealt with the central problem of psychedelics, what Richard Alpert had called "the problem of how to come down." An early Digger broadside observed that after getting stoned and walking in the woods, we have to return to the world of society and its competitive games—to the "silent-crowded uptight sidewalks with our pockets full of absurdity and compromise between cowardice and illusion."

But "Metevsky" had found the key. All games, he noted, are based on the idea of winning. Even "hipsters" are out for success—the supreme success of combining the pleasures of liberation from middle-class inhibitions with the reassurance of a close community, "the highest material pleasure with a total lack of commitment to middle-class humanism." The way out was to renounce success itself: "To Show Love is to fail. To love to fail is the Ideology of Failure."

On this basis, the *Oracle* and the hip stores in the Haight were the enemy, the very bring-down itself. The broadsides were full of sharp attacks on the stores and even on their attempts at community service. In recent months the Haight, once a cool neighborhood for grass and acid users, had suffered a marked increase in the number of drug busts. Ron Thelin of the Psychedelic Shop, one of the parties behind the dialogues with the police at the I/Thou, argued that the problem was one of misunderstanding and lack of communication. To show the police that hippies were good citizens, religious and nonviolent, and in the hope that hippies would lose their own stereotypes about police, he proposed that both sides get to know each other better. He put up a sign in the Psych Shop window reading "Take a Cop to Dinner," and some of the other merchants did likewise.

But a Digger broadside rudely equated the idea with an invitation to bribe the police and join in the general corruption of society, where everybody was painted as "taking a cop to dinner" in some sense. "And so, if you own anything or you don't, take a cop to dinner this week and feed his power to judge the morality of San Francisco."

The merchants were stung to the quick. They hadn't been talking about *bribery*. And they didn't see themselves as conventional businessmen, anyway. If a craftsman came to a shop with a new item of clothing or drug paraphernalia, the merchant would call the other stores to see whether any of them was already carrying it. If one was, he wouldn't stock the new item; against all conventional business wisdom, they were giving each other voluntary exclusives. The merchants let people hang out at their stores without pressuring them to buy. Some of the stores even had chairs set up for that exact purpose. Many of the merchants thought of their stores as artworks of a sort, pop art sculptures à la Kienholz. They were serving the psychedelic community with desirable goods, presented in a hip and sympathetic way, and here were these mysterious, anonymous Diggers accusing them of being no different from General Motors, and in fact holding them to blame for the slumlike nature of the Haight-Ashbury neighborhood, which if anything had been worse before they opened their doors.

The merchants wanted to talk with the Diggers and asked around about them, but what they they got in reply was a telegram that read, REGARDING INQUIRIES AS TO WHEREABOUTS OF THE DIGGERS. HAPPY TO REPORT THEY ARE NOT THAT. And a new broadside headlined "Beauty Is Carnoby Street."

The powers downtown, however, lumped the merchants with the revolutionists. When the owner of a Berkeley used-book store applied for a permit to sell used books at a storefront he had bought on Haight Street, the Board of Permit Appeals denied it on two grounds, both that his store would fail and simultaneously that it would bring in an undesirable element (book readers, presumably). At the time, the Haight-Ashbury already had two secondhand stores and one used-book store. A few months before, half the storefronts on Haight Street had been vacant. Now there were four clothing boutiques, a coffeehouse, a health food store, even a hippie ice cream store, Quasar's. Craftsmen had opened little storefronts like Peg 'n' Awl Leathers and Silverthings Jewelry.

Bob Stubbs, who had sold the Blue Unicorn a few months before, decided to open up a place on Haight Street and call it the Phoenix. He found he couldn't afford another coffeehouse, so he opened a head shop like the Psychedelic Shop with incense and cigarette papers, only without the books. Another new store owner on Haight Street was Peter Krug, the folksinger who had sung on the B side of the original Country Joe record back in the Oakland March days. At the end of September he and a woman friend opened Wild Colors on the same block as the Blushing Peony. Since the store was planned as an outlet for locally produced crafts, it was subtitled "A Creative Outlet." Momentarily, some people were terrifically excited to think there was going to be a special storefront in the Haight where you could just go and, well, experience a creative outlet.

On September 27, a week after the first *Oracle* and the beginning of the Digger broadsides, a white policeman shot and killed a black youth in the Hunter's Point ghetto where the city rented out apartments in decaying "temporary housing" structures left over from World War II. In the black community, word was that the youth had been shot in the back. A crowd went out into the street throwing rocks and setting fires. It was what white San Francisco had been afraid of since last year's Watts riots, a full-scale race riot in the hot Indian summer weather.

Police and National Guardsmen were mobilized as the rioting spread from Hunter's Point to the Fillmore District, which was not so safely isolated from the rest of the city. Guardsmen rode with the fire trucks during the day; at night they were quartered at Kezar Stadium, just steps away from Haight Street in Golden Gate Park. A curfew was declared for neighborhoods with discernible black populations, which included the Haight. The Students for a Democratic Society staged a march down Haight Street calling on residents to violate the curfew. Some of the hippie merchants put signs in their windows advising people to stay indoors and avoid trouble. The Diggers put up their own signs taking a third position, advising people to ignore the curfew and either walk around or stay indoors as they spontaneously wished. That night 124 people were arrested on Haight Street and the Diggers put out another broadside reminding everybody that the hippie merchants were meeting with the police and trying to make friends.

The rioting went on for six days. Bill Graham's show for the weekend of October 1 was Muddy Waters, Paul Butterfield and Jefferson Airplane, and with a powerhouse bill like that he had originally planned to put on the dance two blocks away from the Fillmore Auditorium at the larger Winterland Auditorium. The threat of rioting made him move it back to the original hall, smaller and located at a prominent intersection, but the show still lost money, with a record low attendance of 400.

A lot of people who might have gone to the Fillmore that night went out to San Francisco State College instead, where Stewart Brand was putting on something called variously the Awareness Festival or Whatever It Is. It showed itself to be a sort of rerun of the Trips Festival without central events: all Side Trips, in effect. Brand was everywhere, running around in an orange jumpsuit and hard hat: out on the lawn tossing around a giant balloon painted like a world globe representing the Whole Earth, for instance.

The Congress of Wonders performed their John Lennon readings in one gallery, the Dead and a band called the Universal Parking Lot played in another where there was an exhibit of electronic art from the Museum of Modern Art. Bill Ham did a light show in the women's gym; in the men's gym there was a novelty called a Sensory Awareness Seminar, conducted by a member of the psychiatric research group in Big Sur calling itself the Esalen Foundation. Ron Boise had assembled probably the largest public display ever of his Thunder Machines. Meanwhile, at the flea market outside, conga drummers played nonstop for fifteen hours.

Around midnight, Brand staged an atomic apocalypse with Don Buchla, the sound synthesizer inventor. They announced to the crowd in the auditorium that Russian missiles, presumably carrying nuclear warheads, had been detected on their way to the West Coast; they had evaded our antiballistic missile defenses; they were now two and one half minutes away; two minutes; one minute; fifteen seconds; ten, nine, eight, seven, six, five, four, three, two, one —and all at once hundreds of flashbulbs went off as the house lights were cut. All good fun among acidheads.

On Saturday, while the Artists' Liberation Front was trying out its first street fair in the mostly Latin Mission District and a hardy few were braving the Fillmore war zone to see Muddy Waters, the Awareness Festival had, unannounced, the biggest star in town. Kesey.

Ken Kesey had returned from Mexico as a wanted fugitive a few days before, holing up in Palo Alto. But he was telling people he'd decided that hiding out was playing the game according to the cops' rules. So instead he was walking around the festival, accompanied by a contingent of Pranksters and a defense squad of Hell's Angels. Probably the police were not terribly concerned about the State College campus, with a riot blazing away in several quarters of the city, but there he was: walking around in his buckskin jacket while the Prankster bus squatted brazenly next to the searchlights that were plumbing the evening fog to give the festival a little supermarket-opening panache.

The plan was for Kesey to broadcast on the campus radio station to the trippers in the women's gym where the Grateful Dead were playing. In the end it wasn't until around four in the morning that his performance finally got organized, with a Hell's Angel named Freewheelin' Frank on harmonica and Kesey's cousin Dale on violin, stretching and doodling while Kesey rapped tales of his nine-month flight in Mexico and crooned an eerie song of his, "Let's Send Me to the Moon."

No matter that hardly anybody heard them; the word was out that Kesey was back. And to the astonishment of the State College sponsors, this particular arts festival, unlike any other they had ever put on, hardly lost any money at all.

On the following Thursday, October 6, the California LSD law went into effect. On the eve of the ominous date (10/6/66 contained 666, the number of the Beast of the Apocalypse, Revelation 13:18), the *Los Angeles Times* recognized the existence of Owsley Stanley in a story headlined "The LSD Millionaire," which portrayed him pulling a wad of bills from his boot and asking a bank teller to change it into $100 bills. The same day the San Francisco newspapers reported Ken Kesey's appearance at State College four days earlier and his announcement that he was planning something called an "LSD Graduation Ceremony" at Winterland, the biggest hall in town, on Halloween.

Three weeks earlier, *Oracle* editors Cohen and Bowen had watched with distress a demonstration by residents of 1090 Page outside Park Police Station. The demonstrators were protesting a recent bust of 1090 by carrying signs reading "Blue Fascism." If this kind of confrontation continued, Cohen and Bowen reasoned, the new community would be trapped in what they called "old forms," a deadlock in which the police always held the physical advantage. The LSD law seemed the natural occasion to try an alternative to protest demonstrations. For October 6 they planned a celebration rather than a protest, a rock and roll party with all the paraphernalia of the psychedelic life. They advertised it with leaflets containing a "Prophecy of a Declaration of Independence":

When in the flow of human events it becomes necessary for the people to cease to recognize the obsolete social patterns which had isolated man from his consciousness and to create with the youthful energies of the world revolutionary communities to which the two-billion-year-old life process entitles them, a decent respect to the opinions of mankind should declare the causes which impel them to this creation.

We hold these experiences to be self-evident, that all is equal, that the creation endows us with certain inalienable rights, that among these are: the freedom of the body, the pursuit of joy, and the expansion of consciousness, and that to secure these rights, we the citizens of the earth declare our love and compassion for all conflicting hate-carrying men and women of the world.

The "first translation of this prophesy into political action," the leaflet went on, would be a "Love-Pageant Rally" at 2:00 P.M. in the Panhandle "to affirm our identity, community and innocence from influence of the fear addiction of the general public as symbolized in this law." At the same hour the mayor of San Francisco, the U.S. attorney general for Northern California and the chief of Park Station would be presented with morning glory plants (of which the seeds are psychedelic) and some mushrooms (which, however, were ordinary grocery-store mushrooms).

The "pageant" part of the title was encouraged in the form of visual motifs. "Bring the color gold," said the leaflet; "bring photos of personal saints and gurus and heroes of the underground . . . bring children . . . flowers . . . flutes . . . drums . . . feathers . . . bands . . . beads . . . banners flags incense chimes gongs cymbals . . . symbols."

It was one of those ideas people had been waiting for, like the Family Dog dances or the Trips Festival: a gathering to bear witness to the psychedelic life, right in the Haight-Ashbury, in the very strip of green park that had always been an aesthetic refuge from the urban grime of the streets. Seven or eight hundred people came to hear Big Brother, the Wild Flower and the Dead, the latter performing their new song "Alice D. Millionaire." Television, radio and newspaper reporters were there as well, five cameras in all, and even Kesey himself was briefly present. The Prankster bus was there for the whole thing, a Prankstress calling herself Prudence Funmaker sitting atop it with a flag bearing the likeness of a giant marijuana leaf, designed by poster artist Mouse. A well-known undercover narcotics agent jumped on the bus at one point and called out hopefully, "Hey, baby, is Ken around?" but to no avail.

Even with the narcs and straight onlookers, the event was judged a success. It had pageantry, music and some really unusual picket signs, such as "The Truly Insane Are Helpless." The *Berkeley Barb* covered the event thoroughly; now that psychedelics were illegal, the *Barb* was even more interested in them. The issue that came out that weekend had two pages of debate about Timothy Leary, and the folk music column written by Country Joe's manager got a new psychedelic-pattern logo.

One day in the week after the Love Pageant, the two original Diggers handed out a simple leaflet on Haight Street:

FREE FOOD   GOOD HOT STEW
RIPE TOMATOES   FRESH FRUIT
BRING A BOWL AND SPOON TO
THE PANHANDLE AT ASHBURY STREET
4 PM 4 PM 4 PM 4 PM
FREE FOOD *EVERYDAY* FREE FOOD
IT'S FREE BECAUSE IT'S YOURS!
the diggers.

There it was, a new step. After baiting the Haight Street merchants for the past two weeks and quoting Dylan's line about how money doesn't talk but swears, they were setting an example: free food, not as a charity but because "it's yours." And they continued it daily.

The food came from a variety of sources about which the Diggers were somewhat mysterious. The meat, most often unsaleable trimmings such as chicken wings and turkey necks, and the vegetables, usually discards starting to wilt, were begged from grocery stores and the city produce market. The bread came day-old from a bakery in North Beach and another on Fillmore Street. Secret donors contributed from time to time and the rest came from quiet theft. The quality of the stew varied, depending on the relative freshness of the ingredients, which was rarely high. All in all, it was a large-scale reworking of the various hustles the Beats had practiced, down to the same day-old free bread from the Ukrainian Bakery.

Grogan and Murcott had hit on a brilliant theatrical-political idea, and friends from the Mime Troupe started helping out. In a short while the cooking chores were taken over by an apartment up the hill on Clayton Street, a group of women from Antioch College doing most of the cooking, while the men concentrated on hustling the ingredients and delivering the twenty-gallon milk cans of soup-stew and the crates of bread or vegetables to a spot about a block from where the Love Pageant had been.

The *Barb* quickly got wind of the free food. Two weeks after the first Digger Feed it published a quasi-journalistic story on the phenomenon by Emmett Grogan (signed "George Metevsky"), which portrayed the free-eaters throwing food in the air with shouts of "Food as medium!" It also quoted one of Grogan's poems, beginning "cool cranberry horsehair mouth cluttered with apple cores" and ending with the "happy to report the Diggers are not that" line.

The free food was a bold and attention-grabbing move, but it gave the Diggers a different tone. The broadsides had been sensitive and intellectual, the work of artists, albeit sarcastic and aggressive ones. With the broad, simple gesture of free food the Diggers' public voice became elemental and preintellectual. For those who had never read the broadsides or met the Diggers—and at first Grogan and Murcott carefully maintained their anonymity, expressing surprise and interest when someone showed them one of the broadsides—the Diggers seemed not the complex intellectuals they were but instead an anonymous group of stubborn moralists, probably stiff-necked primitive Christians in sackcloth. The impression was reinforced in an *Oracle* story about an attempt by the Teamsters to get the Ukrainian Bakery to stop giving the Diggers free bread. The Diggers were quoted as replying, "We'll give them a healthy respect for eternity. . . ."

In the beginning, new arrivals on Haight Street had not been a problem. Old-timers would teach them the ropes, let them set up as dope dealers or find some other scam, and let them work out their adjustments to an unstructured life. In October you could see a breakdown in this pattern of assimilation. Young runaways weren't finding a way to make a living or even a place to stay. Some of them were sleeping in the park and eating at the Digger Feeds, which had quickly gained a regular clientele of fifty to a hundred. Others were begging on the street.

To the old-timers the panhandling was charming at first, another bit of human contact on the streets, like the practice of hugging obviously stoned strangers, that made the Haight such a warm environment. Giving a panhandler your spare change was a way to feel like a Digger on a small scale. There were those who theorized about the holy mendicants of Oriental religions who led a spiritual life of voluntary poverty, though some of these voluntary poor looked voluntarily rich whenever they chose to call back home to Marin County. But apart from the weekend hippies—typically four times as many people showed up for a Digger feed on a Saturday as on a weekday—it soon became obvious that spare-changing was not going to be adequate for the many newcomers.

The hip merchants worried about this. They had opened up their shops with a notion of having a separate community of the hip, self-supporting and independent. As the above-ground members of the community—those whose means of support could bear some public scrutiny, that is—they felt a responsibility to solve the panhandling problem. And besides, the Psychedelic Shop had recently received an eviction notice that specifically charged the Thelins with having a "shabbily dressed clientele" and tolerating "unkempt loiterers." All the shops were open to the same charges.

The shop owners had been meeting informally for some time, socially rather than as a business group. On October 17 they took up the panhandling problem. The Diggers got word of the meetings and painted a picture of the shop owners clearing panhandlers away from their precious shops, but what was actually discussed was a proposal by Peter Krug of Wild Colors to start a job co-op for the indigent hip. The plan was to operate a clearinghouse for any kind of employment available to hippies, similar in a way to hire-the-handicapped programs. Employers would be asked to tolerate long hair and perhaps a little personal untidiness. It was thought of as a "part-time job agency which would hire local artists."

Kesey had been playing an elaborate game of hide-and-seek, giving a newspaper interview, walking around in public several times, and finally appearing in a taped TV interview aired October 20 in which he vowed to remain at large "as salt in J. Edgar Hoover's wounds." Less than half an hour after the interview was broadcast, police spotted him in the rush-hour traffic heading down the Bayshore Freeway to Palo Alto. After an attempt to "flee to the hills in a bright red truck," they reported, and after a brief run on foot, Kesey was nabbed. By this time the story of the fugitive novelist was given national attention, and Kesey told reporters essentially what he had been telling his friends: "Taking acid is not the thing that's happening any more." He said he was still planning to put on his Acid Test Graduation on Halloween.

Once again, here was the idea that it was time for the psychedelic community to evolve to a new stage. But now that Kesey was in the hands of the police, some acidheads wondered whether "moving beyond acid" wasn't simply his ruse to fool his captors. He told the press LSD was "more powerful and dangerous than alcohol," and his lawyers smoothly portrayed him as a penitent sinner eager to recant his heresy. The debate about his motives was further muddled by a news story five days after his arrest, in which Kesey talked about a twenty-seven-man acid trip in the city jail, fueled by LSD painted on one inmate's fingernails. Now the authorities questioned whether Kesey was a sincere penitent, and the Haight-Ashbury wondered whether he was a heretic or a pseudo-heretic turned fink. Was this cagey double-talk artist the utterly fearless man of a year ago? When asked what was going to "replace acid," Kesey's most forthcoming response was: "Leary's supposed to be coming out and he's supposed to know pieces of it. And Jerry Garcia with his music knows pieces of it."

As Halloween drew closer and Kesey, out on bail, went about putting together his Acid Test Graduation, the debate involved more and more people and started taking wild turns. Kesey was using the occasion to catapult himself into politics; hadn't he declared on the day he was caught, "My only chance of getting out of jail is getting myself elected governor and pardoning myself"? He was planning a gigantic bummer; wasn't one of his slogans "Never trust a Prankster"? And the idea of putting on what was expected to be a big LSD party on Halloween . . . well, plenty of people already thought Kesey's game was control, and even from the La Honda days his acid parties had had an aura of danger. Even odds on whether this one was supposed to be a trick or a treat.

Some people were also irritated by the way Kesey traded on his status as an underground hero. For their headquarters the Pranksters were using a warehouse rented by a dance promotion group called the Calliope Company, which was promoting a Halloween dance at California Hall featuring the Grateful Dead. But Kesey said he needed the Dead for his Graduation Party; he insisted. Calliope gave in, despite the contracts they had signed and the posters they had distributed.

Bill Graham had agreed to handle the business end of the Acid Test Graduation at Winterland, the way he had taken care of the Trips Festival nine months before. He had heard the rumors about Kesey's supposed dark plans. Then Ralph Gleason and the managers of two rock bands came to Graham with the scariest story of all. They noted that the day after Halloween the hall was scheduled for a convention of the Democratic party, backing Edmund G. Brown for governor. Kesey had already sort of declared himself for governor, and presumably had no stake in Brown's campaign against the hard-line conservative challenger Ronald Reagan. The story was that Kesey had something bigger planned than just an acid party with "electricity" in the punch. He was going to get the Democrats stoned when they came the next day, maybe by putting LSD in the plumbing or leaving things painted with LSD dissolved in DMSO, the solvent medium that can carry drugs through the skin.

Early the morning of October 30, after an all-night meeting, Graham was convinced. He concluded that there was a risk in letting Kesey have Winterland, and no evidence that Kesey had anything very important to say. If it turned out to be a bummer, it might bring down retaliation. If it turned out positive, maybe it would give Kesey power and create a demagogue. Hadn't Kesey announced he had given up writing? What was left?

With Graham out of the deal, Kesey couldn't get Winterland and the Calliope Company's "Dance of Death" was back on schedule at California Hall with the freed Grateful Dead. Kesey told the press the Commencement Exercise had "grown too big and too hot to handle" and he was now "skittish about the outcome." The word went around that there would be an Acid Test Graduation after all, at the Calliope Company warehouse on Harriet Street, down in the South of Market skid row area, and for the Prankster family only.

The Diggers had announced a Halloween event of their own, so there were three places to go that Monday night, October 31. At California Hall there was the Calliope dance with the Dead, Quicksilver, Mimi Fariña and "six authentic witches." It was agreeably spooky. The balconies of the hall were hung with nets holding plastic baby dolls. A Headless Horseman with a flashlight shining out of his decapitated neck stalked the hall. At midnight a Giant Pumpkin wheeled Death, wearing a red brocade Louis XIV jacket, around the hall in a wheelchair while Quicksilver played "Bo Diddley."

For a faithful few there was the chastened Acid Test Graduation. Pranksters were joined by reporters, including television crews and representatives of *Vogue* and *Women's Wear Daily,* a total of perhaps 200 people under an orange-and-white parachute hanging from the ceiling. In the absence of the Dead, music was provided by the

Anonymous Artists of America, friends from the La Honda days who had inherited the Buchla sound synthesizer and other Acid Test electronic equipment upon dropping out of Stanford University and deciding to learn how to play music.

The event was small enough to take the form of an actual commencement, complete with diplomas for Pranksters and their fellow travelers. Kesey delivered a commencement address with the same message he had been delivering: it was time to "move on; this doesn't mean to stop taking acid"—surprise for the authorities, who were expecting a denunciation of drugs—but to do something besides get stoned and go to rock and roll dances. "The class motto should be Cleanliness Is Next. It's time we did something with our experience."

Much as this fit the current mood, it fell short of being the great answer that had been half promised. The evening had its emotional moments, as when Neal Cassady called up Acid Test veterans and gave them their diplomas with a few comments on each recipient, and when Kesey asked everyone to form a close circle on the floor and brought his wife and children into the center. But there was no breakthrough. Some blamed this on the atmosphere of caution and paranoia that had developed during the last-minute scuffling over Winterland.

Still, those who attended were free to consider themselves graduates. Kesey later revealed that he had consulted the *I Ching* and the verdict of the coin toss was the hexagram Fu: the Turning Point. The commentary chapters of the book declared there would be change, but not brought about by force; societies of people sharing the same views would form publicly and in harmony with the time, so there would be neither separatism nor any mistakes.

The Diggers' event, a Full Moon Public Celebration, had been publicized with 1,500 leaflets passed out in the Haight and another 500 in Berkeley, despite the Diggers' distaste for the grandstanding habits of the Berkeley left. An experiment in psychedelico-political theater and provocation, it started earlier than the other two events and lasted, for some participants, much longer.

At 5:30 everyone in the Mime Troupe who had shown interest in the plans gathered at the corner of Haight and Masonic, where the leaflets, headlined "PUBLIC NONSENSE NUISANCE PUBLIC ESSENCE NEWSENSE PUBLIC NEWS," had announced the "intersection game" was to begin. The Mime Troupers brought the thirteen-foot-square wooden frame, painted yellow, that they called the Frame of Reference and through which people were required to walk before being served at the daily free feeds. They also had the Mime Troupe's eight-foot-high satirical puppets. By six o'clock about 600 people had gathered, including school-age trick-or-treaters as well as hippies.

The Diggers passed out about 75 six-inch replicas of the Frame of Reference to be worn around the neck. They performed a playlet called "Any Fool on the Street" and then started the intersection game, which was, as it were, a lesson in the Digger theory of ownership of the streets. Leaflets gave instructions to walk across the intersection in different directions to form various polygons, relying on the pedestrian's right of way over automobiles: "Don't wait don't walk (umbrella step, stroll, cake walk, sombersault, finger-crawl, squat-jump, pilgrimmage, Phylly dog, etc.)." It was a translation of the civil rights sit-in technique directed against automobiles, and at the same time a terrific goof.

While people were walking in close order around the sidewalks and tying up traffic, an improvised puppet drama was going on around the Frame of Reference. The giant puppets, operated with one man holding the puppet up by a pole and speaking its lines while another manipulated its hands with sticks, were bobbing absurdly around the frame and urging people to walk through it. Police had responded to the traffic jam in progress with five patrol cars and a paddy wagon. While some of the policemen began directing traffic and ordering people to clear the sidewalks, one cop, looking for the perpetrators of the nuisance, somehow decided to address the eight-foot-tall puppets.

"You are creating a public nuisance," he called up to the puppet. "We warn you that if you don't remove yourselves from the area you'll be arrested for blocking a public thoroughfare."

Street theater! Heaven-sent absurdity! The Diggers answered back

through the puppets. "Who is the public?" asked one puppet, bobbing its gawky arms around.

"I couldn't care less," replied the policeman. "I'll take you in. Now
move on."

"I declare myself public—I am a public," insisted the puppet.
"The streets are public, the streets are free." Then the puppets
walked on and the four Diggers operating them, plus the sculptor
who had made them, were arrested as warned. About 200 of the
crowd were still present to boo the proceedings. From inside the
paddy wagon, where the puppets had with difficulty been stuffed
beside their human agents, the Diggers could be heard chanting,
"Public, public," on their way to Park Station.

The intersection game started up again in the meanwhile, and
somebody set up a phonograph for dancing. The police drifted off
about twenty minutes later, the main body of the crowd having
dispersed. At Park Station the Diggers were booked for creating a
public nuisance. They spent part of the night in their cells singing
Mime Troupe warm-up songs such as the Italian Communist anthem "Avanti Popolo," and were released the next morning without
bail.

The bust endeared the Diggers to the Berkeley left even more.
The following week the *Barb* not only reported on the Halloween
event but began listing the daily free food in its entertainment and
events column. It reported that the Diggers were renovating a garage
on Page Street where they would open a "24-hour Frame of Reference exchange" to facilitate community self-help projects, all free.
The Diggers were also going to develop sewing and babysitting
circles, said the *Barb*, and planned to challenge the paramilitary
right-wing Minutemen to a football game. The *Barb* soon reprinted
"The Ideology of Failure" and "In Search of a Frame" from the
Digger broadsides.

In under two months there had been a convulsion of new developments: Leary's League for Spiritual Discovery; the *Oracle;* the Digger broadside critiques; a public rock and roll celebration in the park
instead of a protest; the Diggers' free food and exhilarating street

theater; the planned job co-op. In a way Kesey's admonition to move beyond just getting stoned and going to dances was late. The Haight-Ashbury had already moved into an era of big plans, with battle lines drawn between factions.

The effect was to make the Haight more than ever the center of the Northern California psychedelic community. The *Oracle* was the world's only psychedelic newspaper, the Diggers were the only psychedelic political movement, and the Haight had more hippie business concerns than anyplace else. A new batch had just opened, including Annex 13 Books and a store selling bead stringers' supplies, Chickie P. Garbanza's Bead and Storm Door Co., Ltd. The Haight style was spreading, too. A few weeks after the Diggers' free food started, a group in Berkeley calling itself the Provos began producing cans of stew in a local park, though less regularly than the Diggers and for fewer people.

At what was ostensibly the other end of the social spectrum from the Haight, the fascination of the society avant-garde with hippies was now out in the open. The last week in October a ski shop opened in North Beach with the Grateful Dead and a light show. According to the society page story, it was attended by Hell's Angels as well as post-debs; Joan Baez was there, and so was her sister Mimi Fariña, modeling ski fashions. A few blocks away on another social level, a North Beach topless bar was advertising a show called "The LSD Trip": twelve minutes of flashing images from three film projectors with a soundtrack of rock and roll and heavy breathing, after which the topless girls came back for another set of dancing.

Ronald Reagan was elected governor on November 8 without the benefit of a Halloween prank from Ken Kesey. He had campaigned on a promise to restore capital punishment (Governor Brown had declined to sign execution orders), to punish the rebellious students at Berkeley and to crack down on obscenity. Even though he would not take office for several weeks, government agencies seemed to start implementing his policies immediately. The day after the election the University of California refused to readmit Mario Savio, the firebrand of the 1964 Free Speech movement. On November 15 the Psychedelic Shop was raided for obscene literature, to wit a collection of poems called *The Love Book* by Lenore Kandel. Arrested behind the counter was the *Oracle*'s Allen Cohen, who was working the cash register that day.

Why Kandel's book was singled out as obscene was the subject of much speculation. The poems had already appeared in an anthology called *The Erotic Revolution*, which had been sold nationwide without any trouble. Certainly the poems were about sex, but in a rather romantic and high-minded way for all the four-letter words they contained. They read as if Elizabeth Barrett Browning had taken acid and set about to describe the sex act with relish as a cosmic event, identifying the lovers as the Divine Couple of Hindu mythology. It was virtually a celebration of monogamy, and there was far coarser eroticism available on newsstands and in bookstores all over San Francisco.

So perhaps it was not a real obscenity bust after all, but an attack on the psychedelic culture. Apart from the acidy aura of the poems, the book had psychedelic connections because the publisher taught a course in the State College French department called "Astronauts of Inner Space," in which he gave a mystical interpretation of Dada and surrealism. A brief list of instructions for a psychedelic trip titled "Checklist for Inner Space Astronauts" had appeared anonymously in the third issue of the *Oracle* ("Have an experienced ground crew standing by . . . If it becomes necessary as a last resort to bail out, try a fuel-suppressive such as Niacinamide"). Or maybe the bust was intended as more harassment of the Psychedelic Shop. Or maybe it was directed at the *Oracle*, which Ron Thelin published. In the third issue there had been a story by a man who was busted while tripping on LSD and, he claimed, beaten at Park Station. On November 17, City Lights Bookstore was busted for selling *The Love Book;* City Lights was an advertiser in the *Oracle.*

Or maybe it was all of this, a general attack on drugs, eroticism and the whole avant-garde. *The Beard,* a play by the Beat poet Michael McClure, was already fighting a bust because of a scene that implied cunnilingus, which was deemed obscene in an avant-garde play while topless dancing in North Beach bars were not. A group of State College professors decided to take a stand. They announced they would hold a protest reading of *The Love Book* and the cunnilingus scene of *The Beard* as well on November 23. A little to their disappointment, the police ignored their challenge to arrest them. The three hundred people who attended the protest reading were all civilians.

The Haight Street Merchants' Association had denied membership to the Psychedelic Shop, and the Thelin brothers had fired back a letter warning that the hippie "problem" that the straight merchants saw was going to be vastly greater next year, amounting to a fundamental change in American society. In the somewhat besieged atmosphere that had developed, the hip merchants decided to band together. On November 22 the Thelins, Tsvi Strauch of In Gear and Blind Jerry Sealund of Far Fetched Foods, with the support of the other new merchants, announced the formation of their own merchants' association, the Haight Independent Proprietors (HIP). At a press conference in a tastefully decorated apartment in the former firehouse at 1575 Waller, the merchants pointed out that they were bringing business to a decaying neighborhood, indicated that they had consciously picked the date as the third anniversary of the Kennedy assassination to show that they indeed had a sense of history, denounced the *Love Book* busts and read "A Prophecy of a Declaration of Independence."

Thanksgiving brought out the community's most generous impulses. People made big dinners and went down on Haight Street looking for friends or strangers to invite. Bill Graham, to the puzzlement of the business world, gave a Thanksgiving Eve dinner party to which he invited a couple hundred of his most regular customers. The Diggers celebrated with a "Meatfeast" dinner in their double garage on Page Street.

The garage was officially known as the Free Frame of Reference. The big yellow-painted wooden frame was brought there between Panhandle feeds. Somebody had found a stack of window frames, which the Diggers nailed to the front of the garage. The Free Frame was being used as an experimental store with boxes of clothes and household items free for the taking, "free because it's yours." Some of the younger arrivals to the Haight were nearly completely outfitted from the Free Frame, in styles that one would never have predicted from the Edwardian flash of the original Family Dog dances or the outer-space costuming of the Acid Tests. Beggars can't be choosers. The Digger free clothes were often drab and ill-fitting.

The Free Frame was also an experimental social environment where people were encouraged to ignore all law and custom, much as the acidhead in *Search and Seizure* had. The Diggers called this "assuming freedom." One of their most impressive gestures was a routine they pulled on would-be contributors. Such a victim was Paul Krassner, editor of *The Realist,* who showed up one evening to find out what the Diggers were like. He argued that what they were doing with this free store was excellent but really nothing new, mere "social work." A Digger suggested that he give Emmett Grogan a $10 bill and see what happened. Krassner—as usual, nearly broke—fished out a ten and offered it to Grogan, who took a cigarette lighter and set fire to it.

If anyone asked who was in charge, a Digger would answer vigorously, "You are!" This was theater, this was "assuming freedom"— and also, like the motif of anonymity, it was a shrewd cover. The police couldn't single out anyone as the responsible party in this operation, a useful precaution given the frequent presence of stolen goods in the free boxes. The Diggers had evidently taken care to make their rental arrangement in the name of an untraceable party. As long as the rent was paid—and of course the Diggers did not burn every $10 bill that came their way—the garage could conceivably be used for anything.

The charges against the five Diggers stemming from the Halloween puppet bust were finally dismissed November 27. A *San Francisco Chronicle* photographer asked the group for a photograph as they left the Hall of Justice, and they responded with a range of cocky gestures: upthrust thumb, wild leap, two-finger V sign made with the back of the hand to the viewer. The next day the photo was on page one of the morning edition. The subjects were not identified as Diggers or even Mime Troupe members, but they had shown they were newsworthy. The Diggers then began talking about engineering a media takeover, starting with the two radio stations, in Berkeley and Santa Cruz, that had invited them to speak.

On November 30, as Ken Kesey went to trial for his rooftop dope bust and parole violation, there was a demonstration in Berkeley against the presence of a Navy recruiting table on campus. More than anything it showed the extent of the psychedelic influence on the Berkeley left: the song sung on the picket lines was the Beatles' "Yellow Submarine." Mario Savio, the FSM alumnus, declared that the Beatles' slightly absurd but encouraging vision of life beneath the sea with all one's friends was "an unexpected symbol of our trust in the future and of our longing for a place for us all to live in." According to another story, the "Yellow Submarine Movement" really arose when somebody on a picket line suggested the old left-wing marching song "Solidarity Forever" and found that most people didn't know the words.

The Diggers had sent around a message to "all the seers and prophets of the establishment journals" about an impending destruction of the Haight by police. On the radio they had discussed their notion that money, like God, was dead. The post-scarcity age in America had made it possible for young people to live off society's surplus and divorce themselves from economic counters as units of value. They could create their own units of value: wampum, negotiable only within their community. This sort of thing would of course make life hard on the Haight Street merchants, so far as they depended on wampum-using hippie customers for their revenues. The Diggers scheduled a Death of Money Parade for Saturday, December 3, which was canceled because of rain and rescheduled for December 10.

On December 7 there was a fairly big bust at 69 Carl Street. Not the biggest bust ever made in the Haight, only fifty pounds of grass, but big news because two of those arrested were society kids from Hillsborough, Melinda Moffett and Stuart Erskine. The newspapers identified Melinda as a debutante and an employee of the Straight Theater, and clearly suggested hippie squalor in her living quarters. Also arrested was the black acid dealer who called himself Superspade.

The existence of a drug-abusing debutante might have seemed inevitable, given the lionization of rock musicians, poster artists and their peers that had been going on since spring—there was now a store in the Financial District, Anastasia, which specialized in psychedelic dance posters—but it was a sensational scandal anyway. There had been a few brief stories about teenage runaways before, but these were rich kids who had been given every advantage. Stuart and Melinda told reporters that grass and psychedelics were now commonplace at Burlingame High.

Bill Graham, for one, didn't need any hippie scandals at the moment. He was still fighting the under-eighteen law. The board of supervisors was currently considering a ban on "mixed" (teenage and adult audience) dances while Graham was petitioning to have the age limit dropped to sixteen, or even fourteen for his Sunday afternoon dances.

Timothy Leary was already in town preparing for his psychedelic stage shows in January. On December 12 he held a well-organized press conference at the Fairmont Hotel on Nob Hill and presented a bland and reassuring picture of what he was up to. He was not in town, for instance, to make converts. The congregation of his church, the League for Spiritual Discovery, was limited to an organic "tribe" of personal friends, the sixty people who lived at Millbrook and about four hundred others who had tripped there. It happened that he was touring the country to present a stage show called "A Death of the Mind," to be sure, but this was not proselytization, it was an attempt to demonstrate what his tribe had learned. He could not, he said, defend nonsacramental use of LSD, but on the other hand the spread of psychedelics was inevitable.

This glib and slightly sanctimonious way of talking about LSD was understood in Leary's circle as the appropriate way of "playing the media game"; it evaded the moralistic wrath of the squares, helped avoid busts and freak-outs, and so forth. But although there were some prominent Learyites in the Haight, they were a distinct minority, and the Leary style and philosophy a minority taste. The evening after his press conference Leary visited the Haight with his PR agent and a television camera crew, evidently to get some footage of Leary with "his followers." The front of the Psychedelic Shop must have seemed a good place to look, but the little knot of people sitting there to whom he recited his "Turn on, tune in, drop out" mantra reacted with utter incomprehension.

George Harrison had gone John Lennon one better in heresy. "The religions they have in India," he announced, "I just believe in them more than anything I ever learned in Christianity." On the obscenity front, charges against McClure's play *The Beard* had been thrown out on December 8, and on December 13 the board of supervisors ruled that "bottomless"—totally nude—dancers were legal entertainment in North Beach nightclubs. But as for *The Love Book*, the DA's office was clearly preparing a lengthy prosectuion.

New businesses kept coming into the Haight. The storefront that had been bought for a used-book store was leased to the Print Mint, a poster gallery that had long sold prints of famous paintings for Berkeley students to decorate their walls with and the "personality posters" of movie stars that came in with pop art. Lately it had added San Francisco dance posters and begun commissioning artists to do satirical political posters.

The storefront—actually the former Woolworth's that the Thelin brothers' father had once managed—was more space than the Print Mint needed, so the back of the store was partitioned off. The store's first manager was Travis Rivers, the man who had imported San Francisco light-show techniques to Texas and Janis Joplin to San Francisco. At the beginning of November he put the unused space at the disposal of the *Oracle,* and became its publisher. In December the job co-op moved in from its original office at the back of Wild Colors. A secretary named Camy was promised a 5 percent commission from the salaries of the job applicants she placed.

The most spectacular new business in December was the Drugstore Café at the Haight's busiest intersection, Haight and Masonic. It was handsomely decorated with antique apothecary's paraphernalia, and the tabletops were covered with paisley designs. The police, however, would not tolerate the name "Drugstore," and under pressure the owners changed it to "Drogstore." A lot of the people who had been hanging out at Tracy's Donuts switched to the Drogstore.

But the Drogstore was a new kind of business on the street, and the owners of the successful new café did not bother to socialize with the HIP shop owners.

The fourth issue of the *Oracle* came out November 16. The masthead bowed to reality in describing the publication as "approximately bimonthly." On the average there had been four weeks between issues.

Despite its irregularity and changeable format, the *Oracle* was still a sort of newspaper. The third issue had had a fairly complete entertainment listing which included films, public lectures on the State campus, a dance at Sokol Hall November 12 sponsored by the Hell's Angels, an exhibit of rock posters at the San Francisco Art Institute, and a soft-sell radio evangelist program called "The Transcendental Multilingual Two-Ton Mustard Seed," which played the longer cuts from rock and roll albums that AM rock stations never played. But the listing also included events such as "9:05 P.M., Brains Interchanged. 10:00 P.M., God Dies." In rather essayistic or poetic style, it had covered important events like the Hunter's Point riots, the Love Pageant, the ALF street fairs and the Kesey Graduation. The fourth issue had extensive coverage of the *Love Book* busts, including Allen Cohen's firsthand report on the confusion and revulsion he felt in court and a transcript of the discussion at the protest reading.

Though the Diggers were generally hostile to the *Oracle,* they were represented in it practically from the start, beginning with an ad line for the free food in the second issue and a letter in the third from "a digger" who called it "an old cunt rag of misinformation, outdated 'news,' psychedelic bullshit art and premasticated verbal masturbation about what we already know" and challenged the paper to "let us know what the high incidence of police arrests for nonexistent charges means. Explain exorbitant rents in H-A. Draw parallels between the hippies and others who receive similar treatment from the establishment. Give us some ideas about channels through which to direct our energy, to burn off the guilt of our lethargy."

In the fourth issue the *Oracle* responded with an invitation for reader reports of police harassment to be assembled in a portfolio. It also ran a story on the Diggers' Thanksgiving Feed, in which the reporter wandered into the back room of the Page Street garage to express his enthusiasm about a scene which was "so right 'there was no room for any bad vibrations to get in.' " He said he found a totally different spirit among the Diggers he met in the back room: "It seemed a dark one. . . . I felt I had intruded." He later recovered from this experience and interviewed the Diggers on their philosophy and included in his story a pitch for a heater for the garage.

But news content was receding in the *Oracle*. The emphasis was on poetry, essays (for example, "Yoga and the Psychedelic Mind") and columns. A new column was "The Gossiping Guru," "an open forum for the expression of ideas and notions not having an outlet elsewhere . . . the imaginative and the delightful. Rumors and recipes. Individual voices whispering in the Community's ear." Another was Steve Levine's "Notes from the San Andreas Fault," pastoral meditations from Levine's home near Santa Cruz actually located on that fault, in which he sought in the mystery of nature hope for freedom from war and "history's dream of hysteria and riot."

The Diggers' Death of Money and Rebirth of the Haight Parade had been rained out on December 10, like another gathering planned by the organizers of the Love Pageant. The latter event was rescheduled for January, but on December 16 the Diggers finally staged their parade.

It started at 5:00 P.M. with most of the Mime Troupe silently passing out various paraphernalia on the street: pennywhistles, automobile rearview mirrors, flowers, lollipops, incense, candles, bags of grass (lawn clippings) and signs reading "Now!" Three hooded figures carried a silver dollar sign on a stick. A black-clad modern Diogenes carrying a kerosene lamp preceded a black-draped coffin borne by six pallbearers wearing Egyptianesque animal masks. Other Mime Troupe members, including the Gargoyle Singers—who had recently been arrested for "begging" while singing Christmas carols outside a North Beach topless nightclub, all made up like cripples and dwarves from the Middle Ages—walked down the sidewalk in two groups on either side of the street, chanting "oooh," "aaah," "sssh" or "be cool" as people tootled on the pennywhistles.

Over a thousand people had come for the parade, of which the Diggers had promised, "We will continue until the Diggers feel it beautiful to stop." A lot of the paraders were from outside the Haight, from Potrero Hill, Berkeley or North Beach. The crowd was big enough to overflow the sidewalk and impede traffic. The driver of a 43-Roosevelt line bus, stalled in the traffic jam, alighted for a while and shook hands all around.

At the head of the parade was a file of Hell's Angels on their Harley motorcycles, in the lead "Hairy Henry" Kot with a big "Now!" sign on his handlebars and Phyllis Willner, a prominent Digger woman, wearing a cape made from a bedsheet and carrying a sign reading "Now!" standing in his buddy seat.

After a few blocks a policeman flagged down Hairy Henry and remonstrated with him about letting someone stand in a buddy seat, a violation of the vehicle code. A check revealed that Kot was on parole and the police ordered him back to the Park Station. George Hendricks, an Angel denizen of Tracy's Donut Shop known as "Chocolate George" from his taste for chocolate milk, gave them an argument. Chocolate George was charged with interfering with an arrest and both Angels were taken to the police station.

The Diggers turned the parade around and led it to Park Station, a parade by now rather widely strung out along the sidewalk and reduced to about a third of its original size, with Michael McClure at the head of the march playing his autoharp. At the police station they found scores of patrolmen standing in front of the building. A chant went up: "We want George, we want Hairy Henry." Chocolate was one of the best-known Angels on Haight Street, and had organized the Hell's Angels dance a month before. When bail was announced, the Diggers quickly collected donations in the black-draped Death of Money coffin, but once they had the amount they were told the two Angels had already been taken downtown to the city jail.

The parade turned in that direction and reached the deserted

South of Market neighborhood around 7:00 P.M. Presumably the Diggers themselves could have gotten in trouble for leading a four-mile parade without a permit, but for their cloak of anonymity. Chocolate George was bailed out that night, but Hairy Henry's parole status kept him in jail. The Hell's Angels were nevertheless impressed with the readiness of the hippie paraders to put out money for two of their brothers. They gratefully proposed a party in the Panhandle for New Year's Day.

The newspapers reported on the parade and the Angels' bust but made no mention of the Diggers, who were still unknown to the general public. The first mention of their name in a daily newspaper was in Ralph Gleason's column a few days later, an announcement of a "Christmas Eve for Hippies" being put on cooperatively by the Diggers and Hamilton Methodist Church and publicized through the Free Frame.

Like Thanksgiving, Christmas was a time to invite strangers to dinner, and like Thanksgiving it had its Digger Feed, only in the more comfortable quarters of Hamilton Methodist. After Reverend Andrew Juvinall's sermon on "Jesus the Outcast Beatnik," with an untoward moment when an acid tripper wandered up to the altar, singing loudly but out of sync with the organ, and was kicked out, Christmas Eve dinner was served to 500 people, with turkeys provided by the Diggers in their usual mysterious manner. The fact that it was Christmas Eve had suggested the idea of a mass acid trip, using the free LSD Owsley had been laying on the Diggers. Music was provided by a recently formed band calling itself the Chamber Orkustra, which had a reputation as the Diggers' band. The founder of the band was a brooding nineteen-year-old who affected a top hat and went by the name of Bobby Snofox, or less respectfully, Bummer Bob. He played electric guitar and bouzouki, and the band also included bass, drums, violin and oboe.

On December 27 building inspectors cited the Digger garage for violation of sections 601 and 82 of the Health and Safety Code, using a garage for living purposes (people had been sleeping there) and having improper lighting, ventilation and sanitary facilities. No individuals were available to be cited, but inspectors announced that

© 1980 Gene Anthony

TOP: **Chet Helms (second from left) and Family Dog Staff**

MIDDLE: **The original hippie rock band: the Charlatans**

BOTTOM: **Bill Graham**

© 1980 Gene Anthony

TOP: **Jefferson Airplane**

MIDDLE: **The Grateful Dead one block from home**

BOTTOM: **Big Brother and the Holding Company**

OPPOSITE TOP: **Bobby Beausoleil of the Orkustra, later of the Manson Family**

OPPOSITE BOTTOM: **Stan Mouse, hot-rod artist turned poster artist**

TOP: **The Straight Theater crew in the midst of their handiwork**
BOTTOM LEFT: **Fillmore poster artist Wes Wilson**
BOTTOM RIGHT: **Avalon light-show artist Ben Van Meter**

TOP LEFT: **Stewart Brand**

TOP RIGHT: **Ken Kesey**

BOTTOM: **The Mime Troupe:
commedia dell'arte in a
public park**

**Five Diggers go free, November 27, 1966: Robert La Morticella,
Emmett Grogan, Kent Minault, Peter Berg, Brooks Butcher**

TOP: **The Trips Festival at Longshoremen's Hall: Brand with walkie-talkie**

BOTTOM: **The Trips Festival Acid Test**

TOP: **Allen Cohen, editor of the**
San Francisco Oracle

BOTTOM: **Timothy Leary in**
Millbrook, New York

the place would be boarded up the next day. In frustration the Diggers tore the place apart, even ripping the garage door off its hinges. On December 28 the building inspectors broke up the thirteen-foot Frame of Reference that was leaning against the side of the building, and used the pieces to board the garage up.

The Angels' thank-you party took over the Panhandle at 2:00 P.M. New Year's Day. The Diggers had publicized it both as "New Year's Wail" and "New Year's Whale." The street fliers suggested that people bring whale meat. The Diggers arranged for Big Brother, the Grateful Dead, the Orkustra and John Handy's jazz group to play.

The Angels for their part provided a public address system for the musicians and quantities of free beer. For someone who hadn't been through the preceding year and a half of doper-biker rapprochement, it was a mind-boggling sight: the feared outlaws drinking and dancing with hundreds of mystical acidheads in a foggy San Francisco park.

One person who got his mind boggled that day was Chester Anderson, a veteran of the New York Beat scene, one-time editor of *Beatitude* magazine and author of a science fiction novel set in Greenwich Village. A literary bohemian in his mid-thirties, he was a fountain of quips and bon mots who liked to play Baroque music on his harpsichord and recorder. But he had followed the development of psychedelic culture in various corners of the world for some years and was as shaggy-bearded as the next freak.

Still, he was not prepared for Hell's Angels. He had been visiting Claude Hayward, the young advertising manager of *Sunday Ramparts*, an approximately weekly supplement in tabloid newspaper format that *Ramparts* magazine published. Hayward took Anderson, still high after a night of tripping on LSD, to the Wail and a big Angel came up and handed the astonished Anderson a beer. Noticing that Anderson had another hand free, he handed him another beer. Anderson made plans to move to San Francisco.

On January 8, San Francisco police ordered a hippie named William Pounds to stop decorating the sidewalks with colored chalk. Psychedelic designs in chalk had been showing up since October around Alvord Lake, just west of the corner of Haight and Stanyan in Golden Gate Park and adjoining the rolling stretch of lawn that some referred to as Hippie Hill. The police had put the Alvord Lake area under surveillance, but chalking had spread to the children's playground. The chalkers got around the surveillance by working at night by candlelight. The police order to Pounds had no effect on the chalking.

The straight merchants on Haight Street were complaining more vociferously than ever about the new arrivals in the neighborhood. They were blocking the sidewalks, said the merchants, and lying down in the street to see how close the cars would come to their bodies. They were scaring away customers.

The Diggers' new place was a storefront with a kitchen and a large basement located at 520 Frederick, just around the corner from Park Station. On January 8, when the place first opened, the police moved in immediately. Policemen came to the door three times asking to search the place for drugs and possibly runaway minors, and were told that the place was not open to the public: namely, to policemen.

At six o'clock, when about ninety people were watching Ben Van Meter's *Poon Tang Trilogy*, three squad cars and a paddy wagon showed up and ordered the place cleared because of fire regulations. As it was emptying, an officer named Art Gerrans, who was getting known as the scourge of potheads, entered through a back window and claimed to have found a hypodermic needle. A rough and ready police search of the place left it a shambles. Four people were arrested, including Emmett Grogan, and charged with various offenses, one of them a violation of a turn-of-the-century law outlawing opium dens. The charges were quickly dropped.

The big follow-up to the Love Pageant was now scheduled for January 14, and a number of poets were in town for it. The poets had also heard of the Diggers and had been observing the phenomenon with interest. The Diggers had been imaginative and aggressive, artist-politicians such as the avant-garde had long envisioned. But unlike the alienated Beats, the Diggers were thoroughly enmeshed in a community. And unlike so many in the psychedelic community whose reading never ran beyond religious scriptures and fantasy novels, these underground heroes of the Haight were hip to modern literature. Their handouts quoted Norman Mailer and the Beats admiringly—good friends for these elder statesmen to have in the seething crowds on Haight Street.

All things considered, the poets decided they wanted to thank the Diggers. Gary Snyder, Allen Ginsberg, Lew Welch, David Meltzer, Ron Loewinsohn and George Stanley, plus of course Lenore Kandel and her longshoreman husband Billy Fritsch, himself a poet, organized a Poets' Thank You to the Diggers in a North Beach bar on January 12. The only public mention of the event beforehand was in the *Oracle* and Ralph Gleason's column. About a hundred people came, not all poets and some under the impression that it was a fund-raising party. When money was collected for them, the Diggers showed their anarchist, do-it-now style by recycling it into free drinks for the whole house.

As the new year opened, Youth was declared news. The postwar baby boom, which had peaked in 1947 with a record number of births, was coming of age. *Time* magazine chose for its Fortieth Man of the Year "Twenty-Five and Under"—an entire generation, described as "well educated, affluent, rebellious, responsible, pragmatic, idealistic, brave, 'alienated' and hopeful."

San Francisco police told the *Chronicle* that juvenile drug arrests were up 100 percent over the previous year. In Berkeley, a hillside that high school students had traditionally painted with the name of their school or class year now bore only one sign: the huge letters LSD.

Posters spread the word, in Berkeley, on the Peninsula, in Marin, in the ever-swelling Haight. There was going to be a gathering of all acidheads, and they were reserving the Golden Gate Park Stadium for it.

This community would by now involve an awful lot of people, with everybody turning on their friends and Owsley drenching the Bay Area with acid. A number of people had envisioned another public event to carry on the momentum of the dances, the Trips Festival, the Love Pageant Rally and the New Year's Wail, as *Oracle* editors Allen Cohen and Michael Bowen found. Cohen had discovered a passage in Lewis Mumford's *The City in History* suggesting that there was an occult evil lurking in the very shape and structure of the Pentagon, and he had the idea of organizing an exorcism ceremony in Washington. As a stepping-stone to that, he and Bowen suggested another gathering on the Love Pageant Rally model, with the sole aim of producing a sense of unity. They were quickly deluged with offers of help.

Like the Diggers, who had told the *Barb* their Digger broadsides were aimed at "showing the gap between radicalism and psychedelia," the *Oracle* editors were aware of a disunity between the Berkeley-type radicals and the acidheads. The new gathering would be a way of unifying trips. They approached the principal Berkeley politicos, mostly habitués of a left-wing bar called the Steppenwolf that had once been owned by the editor of the *Berkeley Barb*. The *Barb* had opened its pages to Haight-Ashbury news and most of the politicos had experimented with drugs by this time. The exception was Jerry Rubin, but he was soon turned on.

Still, the politicos did not quite blend with the hippies. They wore proletarian plaid work shirts while the hip planners dressed in furs and brocade and lived in apartments with nothing but pillows for furniture. At the first planning session they told the radicals the event would draw between 20,000 and 50,000 people. "Fine," said a politico. "Now, what are our demands going to be?" They laughed at him. Demands are just words. We aren't going to present *demands*. "But you can't—" he gasped. "It doesn't make any *sense* to get twenty or fifty thousand people together and not make any demands! We *have* to have some demands!"

As one might hand a restless child a toy, they gave him a piece of paper and told him to go in the corner and write down all the demands he wanted. But it was plain that he was not going to get the chance to present his demands in the name of the people who attended the event.

It was just as well the original December date had been rained out. The momentum hadn't really built up yet, and the place they had originally applied for in Golden Gate Park, an outdoor theater with benches called the Music Concourse, was somewhat ugly with its knobby pruned sycamores. Anyway, the Music Concourse was too small, and the Polo Field in the Park Stadium was the only obvious place. The date for the event was January 14, on the advice of an astrologer who had once managed Quicksilver Messenger Service. Eventually a name was decided on, or rather three names: "Powwow," "A Gathering of the Tribes" and "A Human Be-In."

The *Oracle* was going to run a cover that would be identical with the poster Mouse had designed for the Be-In. The *Barb* would play it big and Rubin would star in a press conference. Leary, Snyder,

Ginsberg, Kandel, Watts—all the gurus would be there, as well as the top rock bands. Buddha, the psychedelic ex-Marine drill instructor who was a cult figure in Marin, would be the MC. Michael Bowen knew how to get national media coverage. Musicians, artists, Pranksters, Diggers—everybody seemed to be involved.

On January 12 a press conference was held at the Print Mint. Jerry Rubin told reporters the Be-In would show that hippies and radicals were one, their common aim being to drop out of "games and institutions that oppress and dehumanize" such as napalm, the Pentagon, Governor Reagan and the rat race, and to create communities where "new values and new human relations can grow." Allen Cohen's statement of purpose was read:

"A union of love and activism previously separated by categorical dogma and label mongering will finally occur ecstatically when Berkeley political activists and hip community and San Francisco's spiritual generation and contingents from the emerging revolutionary generation all over California meet for a Gathering of the Tribes for a Human Be-In. . . . Now in the evolving generation of America's young the humanization of the American man and woman can begin in joy and embrace without fear, dogma, suspicion, or dialectical righteousness. A new concert of human relations being developed within the youthful underground must emerge, become conscious, and be shared so that a revolution of form can be filled with a Renaissance of compassion, awareness and love in the Revelation of the unity of all mankind."

The next day the *Barb* went even further: "The spiritual revolution will be manifest and proven. In unity we shall shower the country with waves of ecstasy and purification. Fear will be washed away; ignorance will be exposed to sunlight; profits and empire will lie drying on deserted beaches; violence will be submerged and transmuted in rhythm and dancing."

The *Barb* also reprinted the statement of purpose, and underground papers in other parts of the country, intrigued by the possibility of a hippie-radical fusion, did so as well. The daily newspapers reported on the press conference. The poster for that weekend's Avalon dance had a prominent notice reading, "The Family Dog will be at the Gathering of the Tribes for a Human Be-In" and gave the time and place. At least five different posters were printed to advertise the Be-In, including a drawing of a Plains Indian on horseback clutching a blanket in one hand and an electric guitar in the other, done by Rick Griffin, a cartoonist recently arrived in town, and the poster which was the same as the cover of *Oracle* number five, a photo of a Hindu holy man with a third eye added by Mouse.

The fifth issue of the *Oracle* was abruptly more psychedelic than the previous four. The only newspaper features left were an events column and a report on the New Year's Wail. Everything else was essays, columns, interviews and poetry, including a "Psalm on the Gathering of the Tribes." An essay on "The New Science" (meaning astrology, acupuncture and homeopathic medicine) ended with a plug for Swami Bhaktivedanta of the International Society for Krishna Consciousness. In "Renaissance or Die," an address delivered two months before in Boston, Allen Ginsberg labeled a spectrum of new cultural trends from orgyism to ascetic yoga practices as a new Renaissance, and wholeheartedly recommended LSD to everyone in good health over the age of fourteen. If necessary, he said, we should "have a mass emotional nervous breakdown in these States once and for all."

Most of all, it was the appearance of the *Oracle*'s pages that took a bold psychedelic step. Like the dance posters of the previous summer, the tabloid-format paper began violating the traditional principle that words on paper are primarily there to be read. Now the text of the page was subordinated to its overall design. A few columns were set in widths that varied from line to line, so the margins between columns of type formed slanting patterns leading up to the illustrations. Whole pages of type were printed in purple ink, though most pages were still in straight black-and-white columns. A new style of art based on flaming concentric mandalas, drawn by a Vietnam deserter known only as Dangerfield, supplanted Michael Bowen's collages. The first Dangerfield mandala was purposely used to make the back cover of *Oracle* #5 as striking as the front.

With all the hopes for a union of love and activism, the question was whether the psychedelic revolution truly had a political dimension; whether the figure Steve Levine wrote about, the "Lovebeast" who ignores the mechanized world and looks up at the sky because "it caught his eye," who sits on a wild beach like a Hammurabi considering the politics of haiku, could really be unified with the left in any sense the Berkeley politicos would recognize. Opposite the very page where the *Oracle* printed Cohen's statement of the Be-In's purpose, Richard Alpert—who was scheduled to be on the stage at the Be-In—told an interviewer, "Like, a lot of the papers that come out—a lot of the hip papers—I don't want to have in my home because they bring me down. Now you say, 'Well, the world of reality is a bringdown, man. There's police brutality and there is all this stuff.' Well, to me . . . that is still horizontal game playing. And, man, that's like all institutionalized already. That isn't the individual human being arising above it all."

The night before the Be-In, Alpert was addressing an LSD symposium at the University of California Medical Center, about four blocks from the Diggers' new Free Frame, where he was invited afterward. Immediately his quietistic views ran into conflict with the Diggers' aggressive anarchism. Quizzed about the crime element in the LSD trade, he answered that someday "we" would get the price of LSD down to half a cent per hit, which would remove the attraction for criminals. Until then, acidheads would just have to bear with the intrusion of the Syndicate.

Still, Leary had been associating with the Diggers and had even helped a Digger-associated dancer get studio space at the Straight Theater, and Alpert did not suffer any really hostile questioning.

In the early morning of January 14, a small group of people including Allen Ginsberg and Gary Snyder performed the rite known as *pradakshina*, or circumambulation, around the Polo Field. This ancient Hindu blessing ritual, which consists of walking clockwise around a sacred spot while chanting prayers, was essential for the Be-In to have the proper religious status as a *mela*, or pilgrimage gathering. A wild story reflecting anxiety that the event turn out well soon spread: they had found evidence of a Satanist attempt to undermine the event: pieces of meat and butcher bones impaled on the fence all around the field.

The winter had been one of the rainiest of the decade, but miraculously the morning had dawned bright and clear. The hip stores on Haight Street were closed. Although the Be-In was not supposed to begin until 1:00 P.M., people started showing up at 9:00 A.M., wandering around in the tree-lined meadows that surrounded the 480-by-900-foot field or basking in the sun. The path to the Polo Field led through the park's exotic greenery, a two-and-a-quarter-mile walk from Haight Street that passed the Prayerbook Cross and the Portals of the Past. As the day wore on toward one, the police were busy towing illegally parked cars, and parking places were hard to find even five or six blocks from the 30th Street entrance to the park. But it was easy to find the Polo Field. Wherever you looked, hundreds of people were wending toward it.

The scene that greeted new arrivals as they crested the last rise and looked down on the sunken field was mind-boggling. A seemingly endless sea of people, tens of thousands. And all were present for a purpose too important for words, though a steady stream of words issued from the speakers' platform, at the east end of the field. The Diggers had set up tables to pass out thousands of turkey sandwiches, made from several dozen turkeys donated by Owsley Stanley. Owsley had also donated a lot of his latest LSD, White Lightning, and people were walking around in the crowd handing out these tiny white tablets, the most professional-looking and also the strongest LSD tablets yet.

As at the Love Pageant Rally and the New Year's Wail, there were banners: some showing marijuana leaves, some in paisley patterns or solid colors. A number of people wore robes and exotic clothing, but for the most part dress was student-casual: denim or corduroy trousers and T-shirts for the men, with jackets against the chill of the day, and slacks or long skirts and colorful blouses for the women. The proper ecstatic note in dress was usually provided by a bright shirt or scarf, or nothing more than a string or two of beads or buttons with drug or peace messages. But many people brought fruit, flowers, incense, cymbals and tambourines, suitable for a genuine *mela*.

Many had brought bells, mirrors, feathers or bits of fur, the kind of thing people had long carried around on Haight Street to blow the mind of a passing tripper.

But the event was so much bigger than a stoned meeting on Haight Street that all most people could do was walk around and amaze themselves with all the faces that were present, and then sit down and rest a while. The speakers from the platform were curiously irrelevant, a slightly absurd center to things—if a center was even necessary. In any case the loudspeakers didn't have the power to carry across this whole crowd with all its sound-absorbent flesh and fabric, and the PA system broke down intermittently. At one point the electrical connection to the generator was broken; when power was restored, it was announced that from now on the Hell's Angels were guarding the generator.

One after another speakers and rock bands followed each other on the stage. Ginsberg led a chant of the "Hari Om Namo Shivaya" mantra sacred to Shiva, the hashish-smoking god of yoga. Timothy Leary recited his "Turn on, tune in, drop out" formula. Jerry Rubin was at a loss for words. He had come directly from a night in jail, and in the immediate platform area a hat was passed to subsidize his bail. A comedian recited a parody version of "The Night Before Christmas" in which Santa Claus brought all kinds of dope. Lenore Kandel read from *The Love Book* and proclaimed that the God of the New Age was Love. And the crowd moved in slow random motion, half an ear cocked to the tinny loudspeakers.

The electrical connection had broken during Quicksilver's set. Other bands followed during the afternoon: Big Brother, the Grateful Dead and bands the publicity for the event hadn't even mentioned—the Loading Zone, Sir Douglas Quintet, the Airplane. Some members of Country Joe and the Fish backed a folksinger named Pat Kilroy, but others were too stoned to play at all. Through it all Reverend Suzuki of the San Francisco Zen Temple meditated on the stage.

At the edges of the event a few knots of hostile teenagers from Mission High School and Polytechnic High, Latins and blacks, got into confrontations with trippers. But even the Hell's Angels, usually in the mood for some roughhouse, were basking in the spirit of the incense-laden afternoon. The only policemen attending the event were two park police on horseback who were making no move to enforce the openly violated marijuana laws.

As the Be-In had advertised by its very name, the event was the presence of the people itself. Great things were somehow expected: the *Oracle* had just published a rumor that a flying saucer with good news was going to land near San Francisco around the time of the Be-In. When an airplane appeared over the field during the Dead's set and a figure parachuted out, a large section of the crowd raced over the field to see who—or what—had come out of the sky. Some claimed to have seen a man whose body was entirely swathed in bandages. Others were positive it was Owsley. A few claimed to recognize the proprietor of a parachute school.

The event was scheduled to run from one to five. As the sun began to set, Gary Snyder blew on a conch shell, the ritual instrument of the Yamabushi sect of Japanese Buddhism, which he had joined to the surprise of those who had expected him to become a Zen monk. Then Allen Ginsberg led a chant of "Om Shri Maitreya" to the Coming Buddha of Love. The crowd began to drift off. A number stayed, though, and under Ginsberg's leadership cleaned up the afternoon's accumulation of trash. Afterward they accompanied Ginsberg to the western edge of the park, about a mile away, and straggled across the highway to the Ocean Beach strand, where they built fires and chanted and prayed.

Those who left before the cleanup were greeted by leafleteers proselytizing against LSD. When the Indian holy man Meher Baba had written in the spring of 1966 that LSD was false religion, a Babaite and anti-psychedelic movement had grown up around Dr. Allan Cohen (no relation to the *Oracle* editor Allen Cohen), a former associate of Timothy Leary. The end of the Be-In was surely a quixotic occasion to distribute the message, "If God can be found through the medium of any drug, God is not worthy of being God." The strongest argument against LSD that day seemed to be that it affected your parking. The police towed sixty-nine misparked cars.

Haight Street that evening was less mellow than the Be-In.

Around nine a crowd of trippers on the 1500 block obstructed traffic and a surprisingly swift police raid followed. Nearly fifty people were arrested, including the new manager of the Print Mint, who had merely stepped outside his door to see what was happening. Some people claiming to represent the arrestees showed up at the Fillmore Auditorium, where the Dead and the Doors were playing, and asked to be allowed to collect bail money. Rebuffed by Bill Graham, they went over to the Avalon, where the hot new band Moby Grape was playing, and collected about $50. A lawyer was finally found for the arrestees, Michael Stepanian. By coincidence, he had been playing rugby at the Polo Field that afternoon, down at the west end while the Be-In had been going on at the east end. His Olympic Club teammates had trounced visiting Oregon State University 23–3.

Chester Anderson, the student of psychedelic culture who'd gotten his mind blown at the Angels' New Year's Party, had moved into Claude Hayward's place at 406 Duboce on January 7, still wondering how to get involved. As a McLuhan enthusiast, he immediately thought of print: for this fluid community, an instantaneous newspaper. The *Oracle* was far from that, and getting farther all the time. Still published at intervals of four or five weeks, it was turning into a sort of art object. What the Haight needed, in Anderson's opinion, was a McLuhanite newspaper, up to the second and immediately disposable.

A real printed newspaper was out of the question because of the cost, but with Hayward's *Ramparts* credentials and Anderson's royalty checks for his sci-fi novel, the two got the Gestetner Company to sell them, on time, a Gestetner 366 silk-screen stencil duplicator and a Gestefax justified electronic stencil cutter. Armed with paper, colored ink and an IBM typewriter borrowed from *Ramparts,* they set up at Hayward's apartment, on the other side of Buena Vista Hill from the Haight. On January 10 they distributed a suggestion for hippies to hand out water pistols for the neighborhood school kids to squirt cops with. At the Be-In they introduced themselves as the Communication Company (for short: com/co) with a sheet of recommended tripping places, poems and a statement of purpose that began: "Our Policy: Love is communication."

Com/co's "Plans and Hopes" were "to provide a quick & inexpensive printing service for the hip community . . . to print anything the Diggers want printed . . . to supplement *The Oracle* with a more or less daily paper whenever the Haight news justifies one . . . to be outrageous pamphleteers. . . . to function as a Haight-Ashbury propaganda ministry, free lance if needs be," and among other projects to publish literature originating in the community. They asked for printing orders, writers and Haight Street reporters. Three days later they were swamped with advertising work.

The advertising supplied some money and Anderson had a job as Marin County ad representative for *Sunday Ramparts,* but the economic base of the Communication Company swiftly became donations from dope dealers, largely the ubiquitous Owsley, who was already contributing to the *Oracle* and the Diggers. As a *Ramparts* employee, however, Anderson was also doing research on the Haight for editor Warren Hinckle, who planned a major feature on hippies. One of the first interview sessions was with Emmett Grogan at Mouse's studio on Henry Street, and Grogan had converted Anderson to Diggerdom with the line, "Freedom means everything free." Hence com/co's promise to print anything the Diggers wanted printed, for free. For their part, the Diggers showed they could provide stolen paper for com/co.

On January 16, the Monday after the be-in, charges of interfering with an arrest were finally dropped against Chocolate George, but Hairy Henry was still in trouble for letting Phyllis Willner ride in his buddy seat on Halloween. The HIP merchants, having decided after the post-Be-In busts that dialoguing with cops was not enough, were distributing police whistles on Haight Street. The plan was that whenever an arrest or an instance of police harassment was observed, a chorus of whistles would attract an army of witnesses who would discourage the police from abusing their powers. On the word-of-mouth circuit, though, pothead paranoia converted this plan into the notion that whistles should be blown whenever you saw a cop.

Also on January 16, the International Society for Krishna Consciousness took up residence in the Haight. There had been an ad about him in *Oracle* number four ("Bring Krishna Consciousness

West") and a plug in *Oracle* number five, but Swami Bhaktivedanta claimed on his arrival that he had come to the Haight because the rents were low in the neighborhood, "not to recruit hippies." Dozens of hippies were quickly converted to Krishna with the aid of a testimonial from Allen Ginsberg, who said that the Hare Krishna mantra "brings a state of ecstasy."

By coincidence, the Radha-Krishna Temple was set up at 518 Frederick Street, right next door to the Diggers' Free Frame at 520. Com/co published a broadside giving the words for several Krishna mantras used in *kirtan*s (public song and dance devotions), but the Diggers and the Krishnas were quickly on bad terms. Both groups were recruiting in the Haight and both were offering free food, the Krishnas' variety being a range of sweetish, starchy vegetarian dishes called *prasadam* that were designed, they said, to please without entangling devotees in the "lump of ignorance" known as the material body. So in a sense the Diggers and the Krishnas were rivals, though in practice they attracted different sorts of people. The real conflict between them was philosophical. To the Krishna devotees the senses were "a network of pathways to death." The Diggers were pro-senses, and some talked about going further into their "lump of ignorance" and getting as close as possible to their instincts.

In any case, it didn't look as if they'd be neighbors long. On January 20 a condemned sticker appeared on the building they shared.

There had already been enough news about LSD for Hollywood to chance an exploitation movie, *Hallucination Generation*, but the Be-In took things a quantum leap further. The press found the event riveting evidence of an unexplained, unforeseen mass movement. Newspapers estimated the attendance at 10,000 to 20,000, but even the most conservative stories made it obvious that the actual number was supremely unimportant. The event had been profoundly mysterious. The Hindu, Buddhist and American Indian trappings; the date picked by an astrologer; the stated purpose of unifying hippies and political activists—all clues and ostensible explanations seemed empty in the exalted mood of the afternoon. The fact that the Hell's

Angels—the *Hell's Angels*—had volunteered to protect the sound equipment was a fascinating enigma. The be-in had the air of an immense shared secret, as puzzling as Dylan's notion of carrying a picket sign reading "Microphone." Commentators latched onto the Dylan line, "There's something happening here and you don't know what it is, do you, Mr. Jones?" A burst of reporters, sociologists and religious youth workers headed for the Haight.

The HIP merchants, swimming in enthusiasm, started devising projects to "harness Be-In energy." Perhaps the reverent cleanup of the Polo Field might prove transferrable to Haight Street, where the old-time residents had been complaining of a growing accumulation of litter. So for Sunday, January 22, HIP announced a Clean-In, and with the sidewalks crowded with their now-usual weekend throng, brooms were produced and some of the trash was cleaned up.

On the following Tuesday the Haight Independent Proprietors had a full-scale audience with police chief Thomas Cahill. They read him a statement claiming to represent a hundred merchants and artists, pointing out the appearance of twenty-six new businesses in the area during the preceding nine months and calling on the city to welcome them. They also protested the Be-In night busts. Ron Thelin and Tsvi Strauch described their acid trips to Chief Cahill and explained how they had become better persons because of them. Strauch later said that Chief Cahill "seemed to be turning on" when they talked with him. Thelin affably praised the quality of the San Francisco Police Department during the interview, provoking a sardonic denunciation from the Diggers, published in a flier by com/co.

The HIP reps assured the chief they wanted to prevent trouble with the police and they planned to arrange with Allen Ginsberg to devise a *mantra* (chant) and a *mudra* (finger symbol) that would be signals to disperse when a confrontation threatened. The most amazing consequence of the meeting, though, was a new name for the psychedelic community of the Haight, which the HIP crowd had been thinking of as the "New Community." "You're sort of the Love Generation, aren't you?" asked Chief Cahill.

Gertrude Stein had named the Lost Generation and Jack Kerouac had named the Beat Generation. The Love Generation was such a perfect name, and such a cosmic irony that Thomas M. Cahill should have come up with it.

The Paul Butterfield Blues Band, now settled in Marin County, was losing its popular guitarist Michael Bloomfield. Bill Ham, who had quit doing light shows at the Avalon in November and was replaced there by Van Meter and Hillyard, resurfaced with an improvisational group called Light Sound Dimension, consisting of two jazz musicians and himself. Some promoters were trying to start a dance hall in Berkeley called the Golden Sheaf Bakery. The Monkees, a rock group immensely popular with teenagers due to their transparent Beatles imitation but stung by the contempt of the psychedelic community, were in San Francisco to do a monster show at the Cow Palace. They took the occasion to visit the *Oracle* and secretly contribute money.

The newspapers carried more stories of runaway minors. San Francisco General Hospital reported an average of four victims of bad LSD trips a day, 85 percent of them coming from the Haight. At Park Station a civilian clerk charged that policemen had slipped a dose of LSD into his coffice.

From time to time the Diggers had had doctors present at the Free Frame to treat acid panic and the growing number of ordinary medical problems like skin infections, colds and venereal disease. They had had volunteer lawyers come around to give free legal advice at both the Free Frame and the Print Mint. On January 26 a lawyer from Neighborhood Legal Assistance announced that the Diggers would incorporate as a nonprofit charitable organization, and likewise the Job Co-Op, the Haight-Ashbury Settlement House, the Krishna Temple, the Psychedelic Shop and Haight Independent Proprietors.

And the time had finally come for Dr. Timothy Leary's Psychedelic Celebration, which had been advertised for so long and received such glowing reviews in the East that people figured it might finally demonstrate what Leary had to offer. On Friday night "A Death of the Mind" was at the Berkeley Community Theater. Even the *Barb*, suspicious of Leary because of his apolitical philosophy, said it might be worthwhile because of the famous Woodstock light show of Jackie Cassen and Rudi Stern.

The show consisted of Leary sitting onstage with a light show behind him, accompanied by a musician playing a sarod and occasionally by a rock band called the Outfit as he retold the story of the enlightenment of Gautama Buddha. His recitation featured what was billed as "molecular and cellular phrasing," referring to Leary's theory that LSD put the user in touch with molecular and cellular levels of being. A studied evocation of the trance-like philosophical babble of someone peaking on acid, constantly and serenely losing the thread of what he was saying, it was exalted and slightly silly, as Leary knew. "Some of you," he intoned, "may see me as a . . . radiant Buddha . . . some of you . . . may see me . . . as a whirl of electrons . . . and vibratory energy forms . . . some of you may see me . . . as a foolish old man. . . ."

Much of it had to do with his usual concern of reducing anxiety. "This . . . broad path . . . has been traveled by many . . . millions before you," he assured the audience in one of his many disgressions. "When did we last meet?" he asked, turning conspiratorial. "In the catacombs of . . . Rome?" There was the anti-political message the *Barb* was on the lookout for, and above all there was multiple repetition of the phrase, "Turn on, tune in, drop out." At the end of the show Leary paused dramatically, looked down at the microphone he was holding and remarked that show biz was a ridiculous game. "What am I doing with this . . . electronic gadget in my hand?" he asked, and announced that he was going to drop out of putting on Psychedelic Celebrations.

Unfortunately, the same night Butterfield was at the Fillmore and the Dead were at the Avalon. Despite newspaper publicity and the full backing of the *Oracle*—the cover of the fourth issue was a drawing of Leary so reverent that *Oracle* editors had felt compelled to erase some of the rays streaming from Leary's face—the Berkeley Community Theater was less than half full. This was a bad omen, because Leary was booked the following night at the far larger Winterland Auditorium in San Francisco. Not surprisingly, many free tickets to the Winterland show were passed out on Saturday.

Where the *Barb* had doubts about Leary, com/co was certain he was dead wrong. It handed out a poem by Chester Anderson which denounced Leary's self-granted status as a psychedelic leader and his reassuring picture of harmless hippies. "All manner of straight people are going to have a drugless psychedelic experience tonight—or hope they are, anyway," observed a com/co leaflet which suggested dropping some acid in an unguarded coffee cup.

The art of our thing is Total Experience, Assault, Outrage. Be an
    artist.
Rape every mind and body you can reach.
Put it in their coffee & booze & water. Put it in their cunts. . . .
Because sooner or later somebody's gonna *see* what we're doing down
    here
And you *know* he ain't gonna like it
And he's gonna try and Stop it
And he won't care how he does it. . . .

Inside Winterland Leary was preaching his message of reassurance. A familiar message, because for all the stoned, improvisatory quality of his delivery, his lecture was nearly word for word the same one he had delivered everywhere on his nationwide tour. He even ended up with the identical dramatic pause and the discovery of a distasteful "electronic gadget" in his hand.

At the end of January the Family Dog moved out of its old headquarters at 1725 Pacific Street, in the anonymous flatland at the foot of Russian Hill, into a new place nearer the Haight in the Fillmore District. They had two whole addresses, both slated for urban redevelopment, 639 and 645 Gough. The former became the business office and the latter the poster department, which had turned into a considerable money-maker on its own, selling old posters to head shops and college-town bookstores. Conveniently located around the corner were the McAllister Street secondhand stores, which supplied the office with furnishings.

When they entered 639 Gough, visitors would see a reassuringly conventional-looking secretary at work behind a desk. But when they were directed to Chet Helms's office, they found an Oriental riot of hangings and pillows and no furniture. For a desk, Helms simply cleared away a little space on the floor and put down a desk pad. Visiting music industry businessmen found they often got incense and philosophy with their business deal.

California's new governor began carrying out his campaign promises by firing the president of the University of California, who had resisted using the police against student radicals. Reagan also began cutting the university's budget. It seemed only a matter of time until he got around to doing something about the Haight-Ashbury, now that the Be-In had attracted so much publicity.

Now more young people were moving to the Haight than ever before. Maybe the example of the Haight could divorce the entire younger generation from their parents' ways before the crackdown came. But as a recent com/co handout had put it, it was going to be a race between the psychedelic revolution and the growing reaction.

Certainly a wave of fear was passing through the Haight. Com/co published a storm warning of a super-bust set for February 8. Another com/co handout predicted a no-warrant roust between February 5 and 11 and reported that the *I Ching* had advised, "Get out of town. Come back after seven days. Don't deal. Stay clean. Maintain." On February 5 another flier reported that the police had gone on the radio to deny the rumor, but com/co still suggested that people get out of town, preferably to Los Angeles, where antiwar demonstrations were planned. The wave of paranoia impelled Michael Bowen, on behalf of a group called the Psychedelic Rangers, to counsel nonviolence and equanimity in a com/co handout. "The calm that disperses turbulence emerges from each of us," he wrote.

The Diggers were said to be taking their own steps. They claimed to have a ranch in the mountains near Santa Cruz where runaway minors could stay.

In the midst of the paranoia, the Hell's Angels presented a dance for the benefit of Hairy Henry "and to put a deposit on the Cow Palace for their next dance." When people arrived at California Hall to catch Big Brother and a new band called Blue Cheer, they found a police cordon at the entrance. But it had nothing to do with the Angels. Inside the hall law students were taking bar exams, and the dance had to wait for them.

On February 5 the second Free Frame of Reference was padlocked and the Diggers were homeless again after less than a month on Frederick Street. Three days earlier a group calling itself "pro-hippie squares of the Haight" held a press conference to speak out in defense of the psychedelic crowd, and one of them was Father Leon Harris of all Saints' Episcopal Church at Waller and Masonic. A Digger representative named Arthur Lisch went to Father Harris and asked whether his church had any space the Diggers could use. Yes it did, said the mild gray-haired cleric, a basement room with an entrance of its own right next to his own office. But his one condition ran against the Diggers' grain: someone would have to be in charge and take responsibility for what happened. Lisch was it. Around the same time a frail, bearded Digger named Tobacco rented an apartment at 1775 Haight and started housing the homeless there.

The HIP merchants had held a few meetings "open to anyone who has a stake in the Haight Community," which would presumably include the Diggers, though they did not attend. Now HIP felt there should be meetings with the Diggers. Relations were so uncomfortable that the February 8 public meeting between HIP and the Diggers had to be held on neutral turf, the basement of Glide Memorial Church in the downtown Tenderloin district.

The merchants, inspired with a Be-In glow, were again trying to "dialogue" and "unify trips" with the Diggers, whom they ruefully acknowledged as their collective conscience. By now it was obvious that when school let out for the summer the current stream of new residents to the Haight would become a deluge. The Diggers had already predicted 50,000 newcomers. So far the only provisions HIP had made were the Print Mint's free legal advice and the Job Co-Op, now headed by a saintly, bearlike fellow who had been legally banished from Berkeley for wearing an American flag as a garment.

That wasn't enough, said the Diggers. In the first place they denounced the merchants' ongoing attempt to "dialogue" and "unify trips" with the Police Department. The Job Co-Op, they charged, was getting nothing but low-pay temporary handyman jobs for the men and dollar-an-hour sewing jobs for the women. Sewing dresses that would go for $20 or $30 at the HIP boutiques, in fact. True, it wasn't as if the girls were sewing dresses from scratch. The Haight boutiques mostly sold antique dresses or mass-produced ready-to-wear clothing that had been customized with psychedelic touches.

For the Diggers, that wasn't the point. The point was that the merchants were going to have to get serious about their responsibilities, argued Emmett Grogan, more flamboyant than usual with his aura of New York street gangster and Irish revolutionary. He worked up such a scathing harangue in the increasingly hostile atmosphere of the Glide Memorial basement that both the merchants and the underground press reporters present took it to be a threat of violence if the shops didn't convert to nonprofit cooperatives.

The Thelin brothers agreed that something had to be done. Their idea was to turn the Psych Shop into a meditation room, the kind of Calm Center that Richard Alpert had called for in his *Oracle* interview, "where people just come and sit. They don't turn on, there's no hippie game, it's just *softness* and *thereness.*" Well, this was not at all what the Diggers were calling for, but at least the Thelins were more interested in heeding the Diggers than the rest of the merchants.

Peter Krug, author of the Job Co-Op idea, resented what he considered a demagogic suggestion that the merchants were rich exploiters. The day after the meeting he put up a sign in the window of Wild Colors breaking down the finances of his store: a gross income of $2,000 a month, of which $1,500 went to the craftsmen whose work he sold, $250 to rent, utilities and advertising, and $50 to cover losses to shoplifting. He welcomed suggestions on how to go nonprofit.

A few days later the Diggers responded by spelling out concrete proposals: "The Diggers state simply: their intent as a group is to establish and operate 1) a restaurant service to provide free food 2) productive farms for refuge and crops 3) hostels for shelter and sleep within the city walls 4) a garage to restore broken machines 5) a tentmakers' assemblage to sew the rags of surplus into tepees for those who want to settle into [Mount] Tamalpais [in Marin County] or anywhere 6) the Trip Without a Ticket will be total theatre and offer the store as a social art form." They wanted these proposals to be "functioning rituals" in three months, and they needed supplies, food, talent, tools, space and rent money in order to deal with the 50,000 to 200,000 young people who could be expected that summer.

The idea of seeking farms, for refuge as well as food, made sense. The community was starting to feel real population pressure. Apartment rents had risen and ironically driven out a lot of the lower-income old-time residents who had made the Haight so attractive to the original hip residents. Rents were also going up on storefronts, where six months before there had been vacancies. Furthermore, the publicity was bringing not only young would-be hippies but troublemakers. Haight Street was in any case the corridor that led between the Fillmore District ghetto and Polytechnic High School, and some black teenagers had discovered that hippies were easy to push around. Under all these pressures, a few long-time psychedelic residents of the Haight had already moved out to the country.

Chester Anderson addressed the race question with a "Two-Page Racial Rap" on February 9 in which he called the Haight "the first segregated Bohemia I've ever seen!" He had brought this issue up at the HIP meeting and reported Peter Krug's explanation:

"Spades probably resent us because we have so lightly abandoned exactly what they . . . have worked & fought so long, so hard, with so many dead & wounded, to obtain. We have, if nothing else, cheapened their victory. . . . They resent our dipping so blithely into their ghetto. . . . It's like being locked up for life in jail having somebody in the next cell who's free to come & go as he pleases." Anderson posed the question of what would happen if another Fillmore race riot erupted next summer without brotherhood having been reestablished between hippies and blacks, and "spades who should be our brothers come after us with big muscles, hard fists and clever knives."

News note from the international scene: London now had a psyche-delic nightclub, the Roundhouse. It opened with a big party to which it invited some Americans, Chet Helms of the Family Dog among them. Once again, here was a show "intended to simulate an LSD trip." Fifty-six gallons of jelly were poured on the floor for people to mess around in. A nude man with designs painted on his body crawled down a long piece of paper. Ray Anderson of the Holy See light show introduced the San Francisco liquid projection technique to London, where there had only been a slide show that worked with the Pink Floyd band.

Paul McCartney was there with a tape of electronic music he had composed. Reporters found its effect disconnected. McCartney countered, "Life is such a collection of random things that to orga-nize music seems a bit pointless."

On February 11 a twenty-six-year-old guitarist from Detroit named Larry Miller got married. At midnight he went down to a tiny radio studio at the shabby-industrial foot of Telegraph Hill to start his new job as a rock and roll DJ.

He was going to be a rare kind of DJ, because rock and roll was scarcely ever heard on FM radio, where the music was mostly classi-cal, jazz or easy listening. The station he worked for was an FM station, though, a *failing* FM station. KMPX was a catchall: a "broadcasting school," a station where airtime was in such little demand that any would-be radio personality could buy an hour of time and, if he wanted to, round up his own sponsors. In February, 1967, 60 percent of the week's airtime was marginal-profit foreign language shows. The station's 1966 income tax statement showed a net loss of $20,000. The telephone had been disconnected.

Miller himself wasn't doing too swell at the moment. He'd come out from Detroit to get into a rock band in this San Francisco scene he'd been hearing about and moved into an apartment in Jim Gur-ley's building on Oak Street. Finding the local guitarists far ahead of him, he had to look around for something else to do. Sometimes, he noticed, there was offbeat programming on KMPX-FM: rock and roll album cuts, the kind of music everybody was playing on his phonograph but was never heard on Top-Forty AM or easy-listening FM. But as a one-time folk music DJ, he knew the late-night music programming on KMPX had no direction, Bob Dylan followed by the Supremes, and so forth.

Miller applied for a job at KMPX and was given the midnight to six A.M. slot, Monday through Saturday, at a salary of $45 a week. He would have to sell his own ads. KMPX was not aware how many people had tastes that ran to Dylan's "Sad-Eyed Lady of the Lowlands" followed by a Ravi Shankar raga, but Miller was, and he knew where they were. He publicized his show with a thousand posters given away on Haight Street. They read: "Stereo FM Stereo Turn On Larry Miller Midnight 107."

The new *Oracle* vibrated with color. There had never been a publication like this—they had invented a new printing process for it.

For the last few issues the *Oracle* had been printing on Sundays, at double overtime, in order to have latitude in which to experiment with typography. An Englishwoman on the staff observed that the only reason a newspaper page is printed in black or any single color is that the inkwell, or fountain, that feeds the press rollers is filled with only one color of ink. When printers want more than one color on a page, they run the paper over a second printing roller with its own inkwell. This involves making a color separation and hiring more equipment and more pressmen, and makes multicolor printing more expensive.

She had the idea of putting wooden barriers into the fountain so that several different colors could be used on one roller. When they tried this, it made even more colors than the number of inks used, because as the colors went onto the printing roller they mixed at their boundaries, making the printed matter dazzle with variegated color. From the top of a page down various parts of the printed design would be, say, blue, green, yellow, orange and then red, the distribution of the colors being unrelated to the formal structure of the design, as if the colors were part of some vast pattern that momentarily happened to be moving through the printed design.

The pressmen called this flow-color, or split-fountain inking, but nobody had ever heard of doing this before. Allen Cohen's dream of a newspaper filled with rainbows had come true.

Oracle No. 6 came out February 14, just a month after the Be-In, and the inspiration of that event could be sensed everywhere in it: a photo collage from the Be-In, poems about gatherings, and a poetic report from "The First American Mela." The visionary cover by the new artist in town, Rick Griffin, breathed the Be-In spirit: a bearded prophet pouring out urns of swirling inspiration.

In pride of position was an essay by Chester Anderson, "Notes on the New Geology," which had started out as his review of a Byrds' album but had turned into a McLuhanite essay with a stirring vision of rock revolution. In a section headed "Some Principles," Anderson argued that rock and roll was a legitimate avant-garde music structurally akin to Baroque music, that it was "intensely participational and nontypographic," a tribal art form synthesizing most of the intellectual and artistic movements of the age, and that any artistic activity not allied to rock was doomed to sterility. The New York underground paper Anderson had originally written his essay for had turned it down, but when Ron Thelin came across the manuscript at the com/co offices a few days after the Be-In, he instantly grabbed it for the *Oracle*.

This was also the astrology issue. The *Oracle* interviewed the local astrologer Gavin Arthur, who predicted that in the coming Age of Aquarius people would regard race as merely a spectrum of colors, sex as a smorgasbord of sexual types, physics and metaphysics to be one subject and the physical and the cosmic of equal importance. Arthur saw the Age of Aquarius beginning around the year 2580, but other essays in the same issue dated the beginning of the Age of Aquarius from 1962, 1959 and "the ashes of World War II."

Ambrose Hollingworth, the astrologer who picked the day for the Be-In, addressed both subjects. "Not since the vast empire-armies of old Persia," he wrote, "has there been such an exotic mass gathering for a common purpose. Not in twenty-six thousand years have the aborigines of a new mankind gathered in recognition of their heritage and their gig. It didn't matter that few were up-front hip to either the great humility or the unspeakable splendor of the day. The point was we were there and it was happening. . . . For the next twenty-six thousand years man will work to perfect himself in the patterns set by this primitive prototype generation."

Beside the confidence about the destiny of the new community, there was a sense that the future led out of the Haight into the country. A column titled "Sounds from the Seed-Power Sitar" began: "The return to the land is happening. . . . Land is being made available at a time when many of us in the Haight-Ashbury and elsewhere are voicing our need to return to the soil, to straighten our heads in a natural environment, to straighten our bodies with healthier foods and Pan's work, toe to toe with the physical world, just doing what must be done." It called on anyone who had a farm or the money to buy one, who was wise in the ways of the soil or just wanted to be part of a country community, to call the Diggers' coordinating number. This column also passed on some current rumors: there was a 130-acre ranch for use as a combination farm, ashram, center for human be-ins, country fairs and dances. There was an eighty-acre farm in the Sierras. A co-op food market would be established in the Haight. The Haight would remain a marketplace while the tribes dispersed into the bosom of nature.

The *Oracle* now commanded the attention of underground heroes, for sure. Alan Watts contributed an essay, Michael Murphy of the Esalen Foundation passed on a letter from an ex-Methedrine user, and Paul Krassner gave an interview (striking the only skeptical note in the issue: "I don't believe in the biblical concept, 'Ye shall know the truth and the truth shall make ye free,' " he said, because the truth can always be rationalized). Allen Ginsberg had not come up with a dispersal mantra for use during police troubles as had been hoped, but an *Oracle* contributor suggested one derived from the Japanese word *ikimashō*, which means, "Let's go": "Ikimasho, ikimasho, ikimasho, go, go; ikimasho, go, go, ikimasho, ikimasho."

The traditional format was entirely dead except for a column listing cultural events. About one page in five of the *Oracle* was art with no text, including a full-page portrait of the Grateful Dead, who were at the moment recording their first album. The *Oracle* was no longer exactly a San Francisco paper. The Moscow *Literary Gazette* had subscribed, and the *Oracle* was for sale in many cities of the U.S.

The same date that the multicolored *Oracle* came out, Timothy Leary tried to enter Canada to put on a Psychedelic Celebration in Windsor, Ontario, but was refused admission on grounds that he was a convicted narcotics violator. On return to Detroit he was arrested at the airport for failing to register as a narcotics violator before leaving the country. Now he faced an additional three-year sentence on top of his various pending drug arrests.

Also on February 14, *Ramparts* magazine came out with a blockbuster issue. The story picked up by the newspapers was a documented exposé of CIA infiltration of the National Student Association. But the cover story was "The Hippies." It was the fruit of Chester Anderson's thirty hours of interviews in the Haight, Ralph Gleason's thoughts on what it meant based on his observations since 1965, the galleys of Hunter Thompson's book on the Hell's Angels, and memos on historical background from a *Ramparts* employee named Jann Wenner who had been to most of the big events since the first Family Dog dance.

Most of all, however, it was the fruit of editor Warren Hinckle III's decision to put the Haight-Ashbury down. Hinckle wrote with a snide, knowing tone, though a number of things he wrote so knowingly were false. He thought the "Peyote Indians" were a tribe, rather than a supra-tribal religious affiliation. He was under the impression that Ken Kesey had put on the Trips Festival following the October 1966 law against LSD. His attention to the psychedelic scene was dated by his belief that the conspiratorial magic of LSD would disappear if the drug were legal.

A lot of people got burned for their willingness to help *Ramparts* do a story on the hippie scene, from Anderson with his interviewing to Stan Mouse, who was photographed for the cover as a classic hippie, and Wes Wilson, who contributed a poster-style title page. Ralph Gleason quit the editorial board of *Ramparts* to protest the article's sneering manner and Hinckle's tactic of linking the hippies with Young Republicans, the John Birch Society and Fascism.

Also burned, but in a subtler way, was Emmett Grogan. He had given interviews not only to Anderson but to Hinckle himself. True, Hinckle had referred to him for no discernible reason as Frodo Baggins, the harmless Hobbit hero of *Lord of the Rings.* But on the whole Hinckle approved of Grogan because he was rebellious, while he referred to Ken Kesey, for instance, as "a hippie has-been." It was tainted praise. Worse, Grogan—the apostle of anonymity and purity of purpose—was the only Digger quoted or even referred to, and his photo appeared on a page of "Dramatis Personae" flanked by photos of Savio, Rubin, Leary and others for whom he had no respect.

Now Grogan was open to the charge of being a media whore. In order to restore some of his anonymity, the Diggers informed the newspapers that there was no one person named Emmett Grogan, that Emmett Grogan was merely a name like George Metevsky that any Digger assumed when he wanted to give a name. As for the photo, it was "just an actor with the Mime Troupe."

On February 17 the Diggers put on a crafts class at the still-remodeling Straight Theater. One of the Mime Troupe actresses taught a technique known as tie-dyeing, in which fabrics were knotted in various ways and dipped into dye. The wrinkles and folds not exposed to the dye made abstract patterns like sunbursts.

February 17 was the first anniversary of Chet Helms's Family Dog, so the Avalon dance that weekend was the Second Annual Tribal Stomp. Helms was back from England with an anniversary pronouncement that signaled that the party spirit of the old-time Dog dances was being diluted by nonparticipants. He promised that "dance provocateurs" would wander around the Avalon to break up clusters of coldness and start people dancing. Helms was also going to distribute psychedelic automobile bumper stickers reading, "Where Are You Going, Buddy?" to encourage picking up hitchhikers.

The newspapers were full of new revelations about CIA involvement in supposedly independent organizations like the Newspaper

Guild. In the doper community a scandal at least as big was revealed in the *Barb*. A writer signing himself Silenus, who had written about the Diggers in the past, reported that members of the Lovin' Spoonful band had been arrested in May 1966 for marijuana, and that they had made a deal to get off by setting up an actor in the Committee. Those lovable, goofy musicians had finked on a brother pothead to save their skins.

The Diggers and the Artists' Liberation Front had been conspiring to put on an update of the ALF street fairs of the previous fall, aimed specifically at the psychedelic community. In a way it was a vision of what the Be-In ought to have been. Not a passive stroll around a speakers' platform but a participatory event. Not in the park but downtown in the gritty Tenderloin. Not healthful, peaceful and decorous but smutty, rebellious and possibly dangerous. Not four hours in the afternoon sun but seventy-two hours of nonstop happenings. The name was variously given out as "It's Yours," "It's Here" and "The Invisible Circus—the Right of Spring." Victor Moscoso did a poster for the event showing a human being with what looked like a rubber eraser for a face.

Glide Memorial Church, which had courted hippies before with a Christmas Happening with liturgical jazz, had been the site of one of the ALF street fairs, and the Methodist clergymen were given the impression that the Invisible Circus would be more or less the same thing. What was advertised was an event that would be "not a happening but a total environmental community." The Diggers would provide food and the event would publish its own newspaper, the John Dillinger Computer, edited by the Digger-associated poet Richard Brautigan. You would be able to dial a phone number and hear poets recite poems. Mouse would paint T-shirts. Big Brother and the Holding Company would perform "Amazing Grace," and Pig Pen of the Grateful Dead would play the organ at the 11:00 A.M. Sunday service. Automobiles would collide at low speed in the parking lot. The whole thing would begin with a multimedia invocation at 9:00 P.M. on February 24. The only rules would be no dope, heh heh, and bring your own sleeping bag.

Entry to Glide Memorial was by way of a corridor buried two feet deep in shredded plastic. An elevator, when not commandeered by people singing "Yellow Submarine," gave access to the church itself, where some fifty rooms were ready for happenings.

The Orkustra started playing in the fellowship room at 8:00 P.M. as the com/co Gestetners cranked out the first John Dillinger Computer publication, "I Ching Flash 1," which reported the *I Ching* had declared the pattern of the moment to be "Breakthrough to the Creative." In the sanctuary people were making music on flutes, drums, rams' horns, seaweed trumpets and the church organ. The altar cross was bathed in a light show of pulsing reds and purples while a Christlike face (actually that of a State College professor) flashed on and off on a screen behind it. There were confrontation rooms, quiet rooms, love-making rooms, and forbidden rooms. In one room cloth was being tie-dyed, in another Lenore Kandel read people's feet like a palmist.

At 9:00 P.M. a panel on obscenity convened in the fellowship room, where there was also a "free pulpit" for audience back talk. The John Dillinger Computer publicized the existence of the pulpit with a cartoon of a raging Beat/Old Testament prophet figure, and also turned out a manifesto declaring that the real obscenity was war and everybody on the panel should take off his clothes. At 10:00 P.M. a film of NASA missiles and satellites was shown on a paper screen as a rock background built in intensity until twenty belly dancers, some topless, burst through. Downstairs a dim, ancient pornographic film was shown over and over. Michael McClure and Lenore Kandel read their works in the sanctuary. At 11:00 P.M. the Diggers brought food to supplement the LSD that had been passed out all evening.

The com/co Gestetners were showering the place with poems, *I Ching* readouts, stoned artwork, and announcements: war is based on sexual repression, Emmett Grogan has disappeared ("So what?" the leaflet added), a funeral was being held for the carcasses of the flowers that had died in the hallway. One handout was a fragmented conversation about somebody's reasons for coming to the Invisible Circus, transcribed from a tape recording made in the sanctuary only minutes before it was printed.

Glide Memorial Church had lost its original congregation to the suburbs when its neighborhood transformed into the Tenderloin. Now the Invisible Circus invited the local winos and drag queens, who added to the general atmosphere of blasphemy and desecration; or, as the title "circus" implied, of dramatizing the macabre comedy of life. Around 2:00 A.M. a distraught church vestryman came running into the church offices with the news that someone was performing cunnilingus on the altar. A completely naked man had been walking around in the sanctuary for hours. An event staged in the sanctuary consisted of processions around the pews in two files, with people exchanging candles as they passed . . . spilling wax, dropping candles, waving around their sticks of live fire while stoned out of their wits.

At least 5,000 people came that night and more were expected to show up for the remaining two days. But when the crowd had thinned down at 4:00 A.M., Glide officials announced that they'd had enough. The whole affair was completely out of hand after eight hours and they weren't going to wait to see what had happened after seventy-two. The circus was called off.

Chester Anderson stayed around till noon trying to help wind it down. The John Dillinger Computer sent out a series of announcements about where the circus was going to move. Aquatic Park, between Fisherman's Wharf and the Presidio, didn't pan out because people couldn't figure out how to get there. The Gully Jimson Memorial Happening Experimental Theater was supposed to take place at an industrial district warehouse, but nobody went. Of the people still at the church in the morning, most caught buses out to Ocean Beach, where a few hundred sat around a fire listening as bongo drums and iron trash barrels were beaten.

Glide Foundation officials were so uncomfortable that they did not let Pig Pen play the organ at Sunday's service. A few days later a com/co sheet said the Methodists had objected to: "1. too many people. 2. pornography films in the dining room. 3. burns and candle wax on the red rug of the sanctuary. 4. beings being nude."

The press was making hay out of the new drug news. At the end of January the newspapers had reported how a man had been stopped by Santa Cruz police for driving erratically and when asked his address had replied, "Heaven." On February 26, nineteen-year-old Susan Abshear fell to her death from her third-floor apartment in the Haight, stark naked and holding a tube of toothpaste in her mouth. She had left behind an incomprehensible note in her typewriter which read as if she had been striking keys at random.

Morale was low at the Northern California Unit of the State Narcotics Bureau. The two lab chemists were not allowed paid overtime and they were now weeks behind in their drug analyses. Reports were circulating that some drug cases had been dismissed because of the backlog. The police department said it was making a hundred felony drug arrests per month.

Only last September broadcasters had worried whether coded drug references were being inserted in rock songs without their knowledge. Dylan's "Rainy Day Women #12 & #35" was thought to refer to marijuana cigarettes by the (nonexistent) slang term "rainy day women." As if to make their worst fears come true, a new group called the Rainy Daze now had a hit song—unthinkable a few months back—titled "Acapulco Gold," in transparent reference to the premium grade of Mexican pot.

The Diggers, mostly working out of their own apartments, had been coordinating their activities with a phone number ("Thee Exchange") at an address on Masonic Street two blocks up from Haight. They had turned two of their apartments, 848 Clayton and the recently opened 1775 Haight, into free crash pads for newcomers. On February 27 both places were raided by the cop who specialized in arresting potheads, Art Gerrans, Badge No. 604. A Haight resident told a newspaper reporter, "If 1775 and places like it didn't exist, the streets would be flooded with people at all hours of the night."

The Diggers were already at work setting up communes outside the city, as the *Oracle* had reported. At the beginning of March a small delegation went up to Morning Star Ranch in Sonoma County to talk with Lou Gottlieb.

Morning Star had been drifting along peacefully, with plans of turning the ranch into an ashram. Some of the original people had left, but in November seven young people had come up from the Haight, and four more had come in January. The communal experience had been so fluid and natural that it was an article of faith that Morning Star did not have to enforce any regulations. One of the January newcomers was a young woman from New York who had a habit of standing and screaming for hours on end. Ramon Sender steeled himself and asked her to leave. "Why should I leave?" she countered. "Why don't you leave?" Impressed with her logic, Sender left.

When the Digger delegation arrived to talk with Gottlieb, they stressed the forthcoming influx of 50,000 or more into the Haight. These newcomers would need the Diggers' free food. The Diggers had heard of the Morning Star apple orchard, and they proposed to pick apples and farm a couple of acres of vegetables. Gottlieb thought about it for a couple of days, then decided to trust the flow of events. He said yes.

In the days after the shutdown of the Invisible Circus, a number of Diggers felt like getting out of town. Emmett Grogan flew to New York. Some of the others split to Morning Star, including some of the women who had cooked the free food. On March 6 com/co published a list of things needed by the "Digger Farm": tools, lumber, tar paper, cement, tents, seed, rabbits, tractors, office supplies and "any other materials for homesteading, gardening or farming."

The March 3 weekend offered more rock and roll shows than the Bay Area had ever seen. The Fillmore (Otis Rush, the Mothers, Morning Glory) and the Avalon (the Doors, the Sparrow, Country Joe) had their regular shows, of course, the latter with a "Break On Through to the Other Side" poster by Victor Moscoso that changed from a human face to an abstract pattern under green light, a poster designed to be looked at in the Avalon under the changing colors of the light show. The Matrix also had its usual show (Sopwith Camel, Wild Flower). But there were other shows at Sokol Hall in the Haight (the Charlatans and the Orkustra, presented by a reunion of the original Family Dog people, doing business as the Northern

California Psychedelic Cattlemen's Association), Pauley Ballroom on the Berkeley campus (the Loading Zone), the University of California Medical Center auditorium uphill from the Haight ("Journey to the End of Night," featuring Big Brother and Steve Miller) and Winterland (the Dead, Love, Moby Grape and the Blue Crumb Truck Factory).

The Winterland dance, called the First Annual Love Circus, brought down the wrath of those Diggers who had not left town. They charged that the dance promoters, the Love Conspiracy Commune and High Society Family, were charging an exorbitant rate at $3.50 and they called for picketers. The residents of the Digger crash pad at 1775 Haight charged that a group of people from the Love Conspiracy Commune "broke in" at their place and threatened violence if the Diggers picketed. One of the group, said the Diggers, had admitted that the Love Conspiracy Commune was financed by "some mob." The mob was a group of dealers from the University of North Carolina who jokingly called themselves the "Chapel Hill Mafia."

The Diggers' public image had changed a lot in the six months since the existentialist broadsides of Grogan and Murcott. One Digger flier printed by com/co during the Love Circus controversy, titled "The Diggers Do Not Sell," said, "The Diggers are practicing the Cardinal Virtues, because that's the right thing to do." Already some counterfeit Diggers had come to the Communication Company with a crudely lettered poster (which, if you read it closely, was from the "Diggerers") pleading for food and clothes and rent money. The poster was never passed out, but the illustration—a tousled, bearded man with furrowed brow, set jaw and anguished, slightly crossed eyes—captured the Diggers' current primitive Christian image.

The Diggers lined up about 150 pickets against the Love Circus and distributed leaflets outside Winterland pointing out that the Diggers' film screening, the Birth and Death Ritual, the New Year's Wail, the Invisible Circus and the Be-In had all been free. (Another edition of the leaflet omitted the favorable reference to the Be-In.)

Whose trip are you paying for? How long will you tolerate people (straight or hip) transforming your trip into cash?

Your style is being sold back to you. New style, same shuck, new style, same shuck, new style, same shuck.

The Diggers will not pay for this trip. As you buy a ticket, you kill the Digger in yourself . . . yourself.

The Love Conspiracy Commune went to the Communication Company and got a reply printed up which they handed out to the picketers. It promised that the Conspiracy would give food and drink to the picketers and that their light-show people would carry the picket signs for them when they got tired. The Grateful Dead refused to play that night unless the picketers got into the concert for free, and the door was opened to them. After about thirty people were let in, the doors were closed because the Love Conspiracy Commune said the Diggers were "letting in straights." Both sides took their quarrel to the pages of the *Berkeley Barb*.

The same Friday with all the rock shows, the *Barb* reported amazing drug news. You could get high on bananas.

The story had started when a friend of Country Joe's drummer discovered that banana peel contains small quantities of serotonin and norepinephrine, chemicals occurring naturally in the brain which are involved in the metabolism of psychedelics. He speculated that if a banana peel was oxidized, some of these chemicals might turn into bufotenine, the psychedelic chemical secreted by certain South American toads.

The Fish tried it out and concluded that you could indeed get stoned smoking banana peels. From a scientific standpoint their research was dubious because they were also smoking grass and taking psychedelics all day, but many new drug experiences were infinitesimally subtle the first time you tried them, so they gave the banana effect the benefit of the doubt. For a while Country Joe ran around Berkeley with a bag of toasted banana peel powder and a corncob pipe for turning people on.

The *Barb* announced the "legal turn-on" twice in that March 3 issue. The Folk Scene column by Country Joe's manager gave a recipe for toasting banana peel scrapings in an oven and also suggested soaking marijuana in banana oil. Old-timers who remembered "banana oil" as a euphemism for "bullshit" might have wondered whether he was serious, and the column also had a rather transparent reference to Donovan's recent song "Mellow Yellow," and its line about how "electrical banana" was going to be the next phase.

In the same issue a letter signed "a careful shopper and Co-Op member" gave the same recipe and recommended buying bananas at a chain grocery store rather than the Co-Op stores patronized by radicals, because at Safeway bananas were 2¢ a pound cheaper and you didn't see "suspiciously offbeat gentlemen lurking in the fresh produce section"—as if narcs were already keeping surveillance over bananas. The careful shopper also suggested putting a stick of chewing gum into a sliced banana and waiting a week before chewing it.

That night at the Avalon, Country Joe's guitarist announced the new, legal trip from the stage, lit up a banana joint and passed a trayful around.

The idea spread like wildfire. The *Chronicle* the next day put it on page one and reported that a Haight Street store window was displaying a "mellow yellow" recipe that called for boiling a whole blenderized banana. Jerry Rubin told the *Chronicle* that bananas "work every time." A buckskinned Berkeley acid guru who was coincidentally running for the city council assured reporters that bananas "have been used in some cultures for centuries."

The *Barb* notices had contained a mysterious element of the uncheckable. The Folk Scene column had described the high as "thought to be something like an opium high" and the careful shopper had said, "I am told it is more like a psilocybin than a marijuana high." Both opium and psilocybin were supremely unavailable. On March 5 newspapers reported skepticism in the Haight about the mellow yellow high, but every grocery story on Haight Street was sold out of bananas.

On March 5 the Communication Company put on a benefit for itself at California Hall, Bed Rock #1, involving an incongruous crowd of people. The ascetic Krishna devotees from the Radha Krishna Temple opened the evening with chanting, though the Sexual Freedom League was among the sponsors of the event. Among the other sponsors were the Diggers and, of all people, *Ramparts* editor Warren Hinckle. The poster for the event, showing an idiot kid with a light bulb growing out of his head, was by a young *Ramparts* cartoonist named Robert Crumb.

Meanwhile, two Berkeley students announced a plan to buy a 365-foot steamship on credit and make eight round-trip voyages to Europe that summer carrying up to 1,000 passengers at the extremely reasonable fare of $150 each way. The Lark Shipping Company would offer $1.50-per-hour jobs to passengers on board, thus cutting their expenses even further, but the unique attraction was that the ship would never actually pass through Customs at either end of the trip. Hence, strange substances might be possessed on board with impunity. This plan was advertised in Berkeley by students who blew giant four-foot soap bubbles on Telegraph Avenue.

The Beatles released their first new music since "Yellow Submarine." The hit side of the single was "Penny Lane," a dreamy, disconnected evocation of suburban English life, but the other side, "Strawberry Fields," was unquestionably about LSD. It charted the sort of acid trip in which a breath of escapism swells into a whirlwind of madness, with each chorus of the song descending to a more ominous note. The Beatles' famous Mod dance rhythm had metamorphosed into a heavy flopping beat that suggested the low-level convulsions of a great beast.

Bill Graham announced that he anticipated the arrival of four million young people in San Francisco during the coming summer, and that the Fillmore would be open six nights a week. The music explosion was still going on: current albums were *Buffalo Springfield, The Doors,* the Byrds' *Younger Than Yesterday,* the Rolling Stones' *Between the Buttons.* As Dylan's witty "Rainy Day Women #12 & #35" was followed by "Acapulco Gold," the appeal of which depended solely on its reference to marijuana, likewise the previous year's poetic reflections of psychedelic experience by Dylan and the

Beatles now engendered "I Had Too Much to Dream (Last Night)" by the Electric Prunes.

New businesses on Haight Street: the Weed Patch, which sold cigarette papers and roach holders; the Laughing Raccoon Gallery; BFA Jewelers/Happiness Unlimited. The short-order grill concession at the old Pall Mall bar was leased to a flamboyant red-haired Iranian woman; she had decided on the Haight as a place to do business unaware that there was anything unusual about the neighborhood, but quickly fell into the community and was renamed Love. Naturally, her place was called Love Burgers: a six-stool lunch counter redolent of its maternal proprietor's patchouli oil perfume, selling hamburgers for 25¢—or 10¢, or even free, if you were really broke and Love couldn't bear to see you go hungry. On holidays hamburgers were always free and there were lines up to three blocks long to get them. Love also took it upon herself to put up unwed mothers. Outsiders, however, usually saw no further than the sign reading "Love Burgers" and assumed it was a sleazy rip-off.

On March 9 police busted the Blushing Peony and House of Richard for selling a poster titled "Let's Liberate Posters," a crudely executed orange and blue circle of men and women in *Kama Sutra* sexual positions, drawn by an artist who had also painted psychedelic murals at the Print Mint and Quasar's Ice Cream. The owner of the Blushing Peony maintained that he was singled out because he had complained to Park Station about inadequate police protection. As with the *Love Book* controversy, the effect was to boost sales of the offending item terrifically.

On March 10, the day the Rolling Stones were busted in England for marijuana, the *Barb* printed readers' responses to the banana joint story. A doctor provided the story of bananas' serotonin content. An *Oracle* writer leaked the contents of his upcoming article on bananas: the "peel contains arterenol, a sympatho-mimetic agent that is also found in the human body, in the adrenal medulla, where it affects a balance control factor on the central nervous system and ultimately the heart." In case of banana overdose, he recommended atropine sulfate as an antidote. Another letter claimed that the inner peel of a banana contained "bananadine," which is concentrated there because light and oxygen convert it to the psychologically inactive "bananadone" in other parts of the fruit. "Evidence indicates," the letter continued, "that prior to Dutch colonization a great banana cult stretched across the Indonesian Archipelago. This cult was subsequently eradicated by Dutch trading companies for economic reasons."

A corporation called simply the Corporation announced it would sell $5 bags of "Mellow Yellow." On the following Monday, Berkeley held a mass Banana Turn-On on the steps of Sproul Hall.

Not to be outdone by the *Barb*, the State College newspaper observed that "although the 'banana high' is probably a fraud," you could actually get high smoking hydrangea leaves. "After going up with hydrangea, grass is for the kindergarten set." Chemists immediately cautioned that heated hydrangea leaves might form poisonous hydrocyanic acid. The paper itself acknowledged that the hydrangea high was a hoax.

But once the psychedelic community had tasted the wonder of the idea that "there are turn-ons all around us," experimentation was hard to stop. Morning glory seeds and Hawaiian baby woodrose were already well-known, and genuine, psychedelic highs. Now the *Barb* reported that Scotch broom, a weed abundant in the hills above Berkeley, had psychoactive effects. Those who tried Scotch broom didn't get high, but found an unexpected benefit. In order to make sure you had Scotch broom, you had to distinguish it carefully from a similar plant called common milfoil. Common milfoil turned out to be the native American relative of the mystical and unattainable yarrow plant whose stalks were necessary for the most traditional way of consulting the *I Ching*.

The American Civil Liberties Union had entered the erotic poster dispute, and the police gave up because of a technical error on the part of the arresting officers. They returned the posters to the shops but threatened to come back and make arrests that would stick.

One of Ronald Reagan's campaign promises had been to reinstate the use of the death penalty. Three executions were scheduled at San Quentin State Prison for March 15. The Diggers organized a picket line with rock bands and celebratory motifs in the manner of the Love Pageant Rally, with their own macabre twist: "Bring raw meat," said the leaflets, "fruits, flowers, costumes, eyes taste be flags brooms makeup golfbags bones whatever."

The organizing address was 901 Cole Street, The Trip Without a Ticket: a corner storefront with plate-glass windows on two sides and a mezzanine balcony. The new Free Store was there, and it served as what the Diggers called an "actional theater"—anybody who dropped in off the street might get caught up, willy-nilly, in Digger-improvised drama. The storefront also housed a crafts school, and a child's swing with velvet ropes hung in the window.

The headlines shrieked chromosome damage. An article in the March 16 issue of *Science,* newspapers reported, claimed that LSD-dosed rats had suffered chromosomal changes that could lead to retardation and other abnormalities in their offspring.

No such effects had been shown in human chromosomes, but a shudder passed through the psychedelic community, particularly where people had gone on trips thinking in terms of Timothy Leary's molecular-cellular imagery, exploring "the billions of years old . . . DNA/RNA . . . double helix." Perhaps if LSD really did tune you into your chromosomal energies, you might somehow be disturbing them. Others found this chromosomal damage claim suspiciously neat. Chromosome damage was a ready-made image for the perils of drugs ever since mothers who had taken the sleeping pill Thalido-mide had given birth, in the early Sixties, to pitiful armless monsters.

Easter Week was coming, the trial run for the population deluge expected in summer. Allen Cohen announced a Haight-Ashbury Easter Cosmic Egg Week Human Be-In in the Panhandle, where people would gather "in a pressure pot of irrational confused and mad circumstances until those who see ciphers and zeroes can divine each other's reality." This was the first event staged by Happening House, a sort of academic outreach group for the Haight founded by Professor Leonard Wolf, who had met Cohen and the *Oracle* colum-nist Steve Levine at the *Love Book* protest reading.

The Recreation and Park Commission responded to the various predictions of how many people would flock to the Haight that summer with Resolution No. 7073, adopted just in time for Easter at a special meeting on March 17:

1. No person . . . shall build, construct, erect, put up or maintain any building, structure, tent, facility or other thing that may be used for housing accommodations upon any park, square, avenue, grounds or recreation center;

2. No person shall be allowed to remain between sundown and sunrise in any park, square, avenue or recreation center . . . for purposes of sleeping, resting or any other activity, either singly or in groups;

3. . . . nor shall any person leave in a park, square or recreation center between sundown and sunrise any movable structure or special vehicle to be used, or that could be used, for such purpose, such as a house trailer or camper truck.

In preparation for the Easter crowds, com/co printed up yellow cardboard signs reading "Diggers Welcome" and distributed them to any apartment with available space. It also published an announcement of the formation of a Digger Intelligence Agency to keep track of narcs, and foresaw a Digger Radio Station (KDIG), by April 10.

For Palm Sunday, March 19, the city eased its prosecution of sidewalk chalkers. A Panhandle Chalk-In was legally sanctioned, the city itself providing 144 dozen colored chalks. Some two hundred artists took part, each on his own four-foot square: real artists, psychedelic mandala makers, neighborhood kids and even the Hell's Angels, who executed one square reading "Hell's Angels" and another that said "Mellow Yellow."

The fact was, rain was expected that night and the sidewalks would be washed clean by morning. That night, when the chalk-in was officially over, Officer Gerrans busted four people for chalking the sidewalk in front of Tracy's Donuts.

Rock and roll was the subject of a panel discussion at Mills College. The speakers included Bill Graham, record producer Phil Spector,

Jefferson Airplane founder Marty Balin, Ralph Gleason and Tom Donahue.

Despite being semi-retired after selling Autumn Records and giving up Mother's, Donahue was still a major figure in the local music scene. If they wanted his opinions, he had plenty of them. He had been rethinking radio since his days as "Big Daddy" on KYA. Why did rock radio need the pushy fast talk, the idiotic jingles, the tasteless advertisements, the limited and inflexible playlists? Why, he wondered aloud, did radio ignore songs from an album just because they hadn't been released as 45 rpm singles? The record market had changed in the last few years—people were actually buying more albums than singles—but rock stations ignored songs that weren't available as a 45. Why wasn't rock and roll programmed on an aesthetic, artistic basis, rather than according to a playlist?

After the panel, Gleason told Donahue about a program that had already accomplished what Donahue suggested. It wasn't on AM radio, which was why Donahue had never heard it: Larry Miller's midnight show on KMPX-FM.

Monday, March 20, Easter Week. In England Mick Jagger and Keith Richards were summoned to appear on drug charges. The Navy admitted that LSD was being used at Lemoore Naval Air Station in the San Joaquin Valley; servicemen had painted peace symbols on the jet planes they were supposed to be maintaining. The San Francisco Steamboat Company declared itself a nonprofit cruise ship company and scheduled a Friday trip to Angel Island in San Francisco Bay for picnicking and kite flying.

Spring had been wet and rainy. Already the rainfall was five inches above normal. Being stoned on LSD had taken on an association of shivering in damp clothes. It was drizzling when Happening House began its Easter Cosmic Egg Week with a mass banana turn-on in the Panhandle. Asked by a reporter whether this was a "happening," Allen Cohen replied, toking on a banana joint, that it was "a non-happening; nothing is expected to happen." Cohen, Professor Wolf and Steve Levine passed out cards listing the subjects Happening House hoped to teach, such as yoga, sitar, natural childbirth and weaving. Entertainment for the five hundred people gathered in the Panhandle consisted of poetry readings and folk guitar music. The drizzle turned to rain and the non-happening dispersed.

No question about it, crowds of people were pouring into the Haight for Easter Week. On Tuesday, Father Harris of All Saints brought a pair of Haight-Ashbury spokesmen to a meeting of Episcopalian clergymen: Arthur Lisch of the Digger Office and Roy Ballard, a civil rights activist close to the Diggers who planned a Black Man's Free Store for the Fillmore ghetto. Ballard delivered a fearful warning: "If the Diggers do not receive the help they are asking for, in advance, as far as the black community is concerned, there will be no riot this summer—there will be war!"

By this time Lisch was predicting 100,000 newcomers in the summer as a matter of course. The Diggers had recently appealed to "our straight friends" to "help the Diggers do what Jesus told us all to do." Now the 1775 Haight crash pad was threatening to close its doors because the Love Conspiracy had not answered its call for help in the face of an impending police raid, with the real test of the community's ability to help the 100,000 newcomers still in the future.

The long-awaited seventh issue of the *Oracle*—published on March 21, the day of the spring equinox—greeted the Easter Week arrivals. This issue was intended to provide the most authoritative spiritual guidance in the light of such recent developments as the Be-In, and most of it was given over to a panel discussion by Allen Ginsberg, Alan Watts, Gary Snyder and Timothy Leary.

But not the entire issue. A lengthy essay titled "Bom Bom Mahadev" (from a Hindu hashish mantra which Allen Ginsberg had translated as "boom, boom, great God") discussed marijuana as a harmless, spiritual, politically oppressed substance. There was the promised article on bananas, which also dealt with *Amanita muscaria,* the hallucinogenic toadstool. The Gossiping Guru reported an encouraging *I Ching* reading and a new columnist, the Babbling Bodhisattva, speculated about what form the coming World Teacher would take. "Initiates of the fourth degree," said the Bodhisattva, were working on a new, less selfish economic system, a "system of barter and exchange of which modern money is the travestied symbol."

This time there was no entertainment listing, and the letters section suggested why. The *Oracle* now received letters from all over the country; there was even a letter from Turkey. It was no longer a local newspaper, and there was even less reason than ever to publish "news" or "local" events. The swirling page designs and split-fountain inking effects were more extravagant than ever before; two pages in this issue were full-page illustrations, also available separately as posters.

The post-Be-In exhilaration was now tempered by a sense of responsibility for the newcomers expected in the Haight. The Gossiping Guru wondered, "Will success spoil the Haight-Ashbury?"— postulating a Gray Line bus tour of the Haight, and answered, "Maybe. Probably (I think gloomily). But not if we're very, very good. And careful." The Guru believed with the Diggers that money was the root of all evil, or at least of nearly all hassles, and suggested, "Right at this moment LOVE seems to mean Start Putting Some of That Bread Back in the Community." For prospective newcomers to the Haight the Guru recommended: first, turning on their parents; second, starting a local Haight-Ashbury where they lived, rather than coming to San Francisco.

The twenty-page panel discussion that dominated the issue gathered together four elder statesmen of psychedelia: Alan Watts and Timothy Leary, who had written books on LSD, and Gary Snyder and Allen Ginsberg, experienced bohemians and long-time explorers of the ramifications of psychedelic drugs. The actual discussion was held on Watts's houseboat in Sausalito with *Oracle* staffers and even some Diggers as audience. Watts was in a Zen monk's robe, Snyder in denim and Indian beads, Ginsberg in a nondescript plaid shirt and Leary in a splendid white Hindu tunic with gold trim: four men aware—even several times reminded—of their human limitations, each of whom saw no division between himself and God and who realized the others felt the same. There was the self-conscious jocularity usual in such situations. As a meeting, it was as tedious as any strategy session where a consensus on aims has to be established at the same time as the tactics.

Consensus was the first issue. Watts announced the meeting would begin by discussing the question "whether to drop out," as Leary was endlessly recommending, "or to take over." Each of the panelists gently quizzed Leary about what he meant by dropping out. Leary was vague. Dropping out seemed to mean whatever one started doing after turning on and tuning in, but Leary was adamant that it meant dropping out of school. Ginsberg asked where trained experts would arise without schools, and how dropping out would help to prevent the fascist putsch he expected in America. Leary objected to the idea of taking over and declared himself shocked by the left's desire for power. Snyder admitted he wished leftists had a more profound vision, but still wanted an alliance with them.

Finally even Watts took issue with dropping out, asking Leary how he reconciled dropping out with the fact that LSD shows the Beatific Vision and everyday life to be one and the same. The disharmony between Leary and the rest of the panel was undeniable. At one point Leary said, "I want you to be very loving to me for the rest of . . . and the tape will be witness . . . whether Allen is loving or not to me, for the rest of this evening."

The rift in the psychedelic united front seemed strongest between Leary and Snyder, who between them dominated the evening, Leary with his "turn on, tune in, drop out" program and Snyder with his vision of restoring the neolithic society that had preceded the European invasion of the Americas. Both agreed that modern technology was wrong. Leary had a simple rule of thumb that he said "makes sense to my cells," that metal is a subterranean substance and everything made of metal should remain underground. Snyder had no objection to technology per se; neolithic obsidian flaking, for instance, was okay. He foresaw that in the coming cybernetic leisure society people would leave the cities and devote themselves to, say, hunting and fishing. At first they would do this as if they were on vacation, using modern hunting and fishing equipment. But they would soon abandon modern equipment and start making their own tools out of wood and stone, essentially because they were bored.

Leary and Snyder also agreed that the younger generation was going to abandon its parents' customs and turn to a tribal way of life. To facilitate this, Leary proposed practical steps. One: "tribal landing pads in the city," neighborhoods like the Haight-Ashbury with meditation centers in which the Buddhist scriptures and the *Bhagavad Gita* were chanted. Two: more be-ins. He applauded the idea of another be-in at the summer solstice. Three: acquiring land in the country.

Snyder had a parallel vision. One: Indian technology. Two: meditation centers. Three: group marriage. Four: more tribal gatherings. He and Leary clashed strongly on the group marriage issue, Leary holding that infidelity even within a tribal group was inacceptable and Snyder that the end of monogamy would spell the doom of capitalism. Then Leary took up the numbering again and suggested steps five and six: every tribe to incorporate as a religion in order to beat, respectively, the drug laws and the military draft. Leary and Snyder clashed again, Snyder pointing out that anarchists had disdained to use the capitalist court system. *"You're* the one," he said stingingly, "who said, 'Drop out.' "

"All right, fine," said Leary, "I admire you for dropping out farther than I am. . . . I assure you, Gary, that as soon as I've done this little yoga bit of passing on what I've learned and what I've thought about, I'm dropping out too." When he dropped out, he was going to live by the sea and take LSD once a week and have babies and learn from his babies. The rest of the panel felt obliged to explain what they planned to do when they dropped out.

Then Leary offered another proposal number six: more be-ins, this time in Europe, retracing the steps of the Crusades and winding up in China. Conscious that he had lost track, he proposed step number 42: getting the *Oracle* distributed in more cities; step number 99: reminding the newcomers in the Haight-Ashbury that as dropouts they were engaged in a holy endeavor—indeed, the only holy endeavor; and step number 99a: for all four of the panelists to contribute regularly to the *Oracle*.

So that was the gurus' advice. Meditation centers, such as the Psychedelic Shop had installed and many individuals' homes already were; more be-ins; moving to the country and abandoning modern technology, although Watts and Ginsberg had reservations about this. Group marriage if you followed Snyder and what Leary wanted to call a Children's Crusade in Europe and Asia if you followed Leary. (Snyder had objected that non-Americans, and perhaps even non-Californians, wouldn't understand the point of be-ins; Ginsberg had pointed out that an Indian holy man named Shankara-Deo had tried such a pilgrimage for peace and was stopped at the Chinese border.) Setting up churches to avoid narcs and the Selective Service. Fostering a religious atmosphere in the Haight and, as a sort of afterthought, promulgating the *Oracle.*

As one of the audience noted, "Everything that's been said here tonight is in the air, in Haight-Ashbury, right now. There's a move-ment for people to set up small, organic cooperatives. . . . There is a movement for people to move to the land." More be-ins were planned in any case, the *Oracle*'s distribution was already on the rise and with San Francisco help a *Los Angeles Oracle* was in the works.

At least the panel had voiced many of the psychedelic movement's philosophical concerns, and demonstrated the elder statesmen's re-spect for the Haight. It was one thing when Leary predicted cattle would graze in Times Square within forty years—Leary was always saying things like that when he was "playing the media game." But it was quite another thing when Gary Snyder, protagonist of Ke-rouac's *The Dharma Bums* and hip exemplar of Watts's *Beat Zen, Square Zen and Zen,* gave New York only about seventy more years and predicted that in the new wilderness society there would be no need for laws because people wouldn't *want* to do evil.

Many people, maybe most people, never read the entire article. The transcript was so long, the handsome psychedelic format was so unreadable, and one had so much to do in these psychedelic days anyway. But it was considered an important document, the kind of thing you should save.

In honor of Easter Week, Chet Helms offered rock dances five nights, including, on Easter Sunday, both Quicksilver Messenger Service and the Grateful Dead: "the Quick and the Dead." Mean-while, the Episcopal clergymen, whom the Diggers had warned about trouble this summer, passed a resolution calling on the Recreation and Park Commission to permit camping in Golden Gate Park "on a temporary basis to meet this specific emergency." Regulated housing in the parks would be preferable, they said, to having thousands of homeless young people on the streets.

Police chief Cahill firmly rejected the suggestion: "Any encouragement through the mass media tending to attract still more undesirables to the problem areas of San Francisco is a disservice to the community. They are encouraging kids to expose themselves to health hazards, possible arrest and even injury.

"Law, order and health regulations must prevail."

The next day the mayor asked the board of supervisors to declare that San Francisco did not have facilities for indigent newcomers and therefore a mass hippie invasion would be officially "unwelcome." He suggested stepping up health inspections in the Haight.

March 24, Good Friday. The city's health director announced he would order intensive health inspections in the Haight. Hepatitis and gonorrhea were already reported in the neighborhood, and he considered epidemic meningitis and bubonic plague possibilities as well. The health director with the amazing first name and middle initial was Ellis D. Sox.

The Communication Company immediately urged the hip community to clean up the Haight immediately. The Haight-Ashbury neighborhood council issued a statement denouncing police and Health Department intervention in the neighborhood's business. As for the expected housing problem, "Now that our community is a tourist attraction, we would request that the area be serviced by the Convention and Tourist Bureau using available hotel tax revenues." The mayor did not publicly explain the flaw in their logic.

Confrontation was in the air. A state assemblyman stated that hippies were "potentially the greatest threat to our nation's traditional social structure." Com/co published a demand for the recall of the mayor. As to garbage in the streets, a com/co leaflet charged that the city had irresponsibly put garbage collection in the hands of "a bunch of Sicilian bandits with strong Mafia overtones" instead of running its own garbage service. War on Poverty lawyers protested the mayor's statements and on Saturday he issued a clarification: he intended no "effort to drive the hippies out," only "to make them comply with the rules." Com/co passed out a leaflet asking people in the Haight to devise violent but harmless activities to cool out those among their new tribal brothers who didn't happen to be nonviolent.

On Easter Sunday, celebrations inspired by the Be-In were held in New York and Los Angeles. The New York Be-In at Sheeps Meadow, organized by a Chilean poet and the editor of a new rock criticism magazine named *Crawdaddy!*, seized on the original Be-In's quality of a nonspecific gathering and did without speakers or celebrities. The Los Angeles Love-In followed the San Francisco model and even had its own parachutist. In the Haight, the proprietress of Love Burgers organized an Easter egg hunt.

On Saturday night there had been a protest sleep-in in the park. Something was in the wind for Sunday, the last day of the Easter invasion. Around 5:00 P.M., with the streets and sidewalks bloated with cars and pedestrians, two young men started tossing an empty plastic bleach bottle back and forth across Haight Street. Others walked continuously through the intersections chanting "Streets are for people," a familiar page from the Diggers' book of street theater games. People were handing out com/co leaflets, including its reprint of the neighborhood council's blast against the police and Health Department, to the tourists sitting in their traffic-jammed cars, or calling on them to get out of their cars and join the scene.

Suddenly the police sealed off the street. Com/co instantaneously sent down and circulated a broadside reading, "Stop think peace don't play their game." Allen Cohen counseled prudence over a bullhorn: "People, this is Resurrection Day, but that doesn't mean we have to be crucified!" By 8:00 P.M. police had arrested a dozen people, including one twelve-year-old.

On Monday eight teams of health inspectors descended on the Haight. They visited 691 buildings and issued five-day warnings for sanitary repair to 39. Only 6 of the 39 were hippie pads, but one, the Digger place at 848 Clayton, got fifteen citations for violations ranging from absence of doors on bedrooms—every inside door in the house had been taken down—to dogshit on the floor. The building had housed as many as three hundred people, and showed the signs of Easter Week's heavy use. Arthur Lisch announced it would be up to code in forty-eight hours.

In the backyard of 848 Clayton, health inspectors caught a twenty-eight-year-old named Spider butchering a deer, and the event was reported in the papers as a colorful incident. But a State Fish and Game Department officer saw the newspaper stories and had Spider jailed the next day for possession of venison out of season. A humane officer for the Bird Guardians' League quickly came forward and announced that he was the source of the deer. He had found it on a highway on the Peninsula, killed by a car. He had thought of donating the meat to Veterans Hospital, he said, but rather than face a lot of red tape he'd given it to the Diggers because he'd heard they "helped people."

The Bird Guardians' League came forward to report that this particular humane officer had been kicked out two weeks before and that in any case Bird Guardians were not empowered to pick up deer carcasses. If the Fish and Game Department had checked further, into the matter, it would have found out that the deer-donating humane officer was an old North Beach habitué who had once owned a Beat coffeeshop.

As of Tuesday, March 28, the Health Department had inspected 1,400 buildings in the Haight-Ashbury and passed out notices to 65. Only 16 of the offending buildings housed hippies. Dr. Sox was forced to admit the situation was not as bad as he had thought.

The Public Utilities Commission resolved to reroute two bus lines off Haight Street on weekends and holidays for at least six months for the convenience of commuters, whose buses were suffering long delays.

A com/co leaflet predicted the United States would invade North Vietnam in the summer and, stateside, place black and hippie dissidents in concentration camps. The Beat poet Lew Welch published a manifesto entitled "A Moving Target Is Hard to Hit," in which he suggested living in tribes of fifteen or fewer, five adults and the natural number of children, and keeping on the move. "Choose unfamous forests. Many places won't let you stay longer than two nights. That's a good idea—don't hog, move on."

After last week's brush with the Health Department, the Family Dog and the *Oracle* donated eight large trash bins to clean up the mess left on Haight Street by the Easter Week crowds. A Digger named Big Gene started a Broom Brigade to sweep Haight Street from Central to Shrader on a regular basis.

It was hoped that sweeping would be daily, but the dailiness of free services had become uncertain—even the free food. One day during Easter Week the Diggers had produced a hundred crates of lettuce, but they were more and more involved in projects like the Trip Without a Ticket and "actional theater." Grogan was still in New York and others had moved up to Morning Star, still known in the Haight as the Digger Farm. Altogether, free food had grown rather sporadic since the padlocking of the Frederick Street place.

The Communication Company, however, was still busy. It had picketed an evening of experimental events that included rock bands and the Mime Troupe, put on at Longshoremen's Hall, by the neo-Dadaist Fluxus Group—not because the evening of events was overpriced, but because it was "boring imitative bullshit." Com/co's outrageous pamphleteer duties were served by such leaflets as a photo of a Vietnamese child hideously maimed by napalm, captioned "Poor taste, disgusting," and a cheesecake photo captioned "What? Dope planted in books throughout the San Francisco public libraries?" As a literary publishing house, com/co had printed 500 copies of a 140-page novel, *Informed Sources (Day East Received)*, which depicted an anarchist revolution taking place in a universe of wire-service teletype symbols.

At the beginning of April two men were arrested at Dinosaur, Colorado, for failure to stop at a state port of entry, and a mobile LSD lab was discovered in their car. Santa Cruz's psychedelic dance hall, the Barn, was closed down, and local hippies were trying to improve their image with an art display, guitar lessons and a buying club for wholesale foodstuffs. Com/co fliers called for another sleep-in starting at noon April 1, and an Anti-Rat Demonstration at City Hall at 1:00 P.M. "because the generous and helpful City of San Francisco has decided to help us with our health problem." Nobody, reporters found, actually went to either "demonstration." April fool.

On April 2 there was another disturbance on Haight Street, an "inexplicable walk-in" between Masonic and Ashbury. The *Chronicle* called it apparently spontaneous, but in fact the Diggers had published a flier reading, "Haight Street is ours to play on till we feel it beautiful to stop."

Again traffic was tied up by people walking in the crosswalks chanting, "Streets are for people," "Haight is love" and "We are free," this time accompanied by singing, dancing Krishna devotees. Around 4:00 P.M., with the streets immobilized by a traffic jam, two "Street Closed" signs were rushed down to Haight Street from the Digger office at All Saints. The police appeared, nodded at the crowd and withdrew. A Krishna devotee led a crowd of over a thousand across Masonic Street. A block later, two Diggers turned the procession back the other way and a cry arose, "Let's go to the park!" On the way one of the crowd dashed into India Imports and emerged with handfuls of lit incense sticks which he passed around. The police remained friendly, diverting traffic for the procession at every intersection.

When the crowd reached the stone gate at the Haight Street entrance to Golden Gate Park, it turned around again, reluctant to leave Haight Street. A Digger named Apache began a chant of "We want Market Street!" and the mass of people started the trek toward the city's main artery, about a mile and a half away. Momentum ran out three blocks past Masonic. What now, Market Street or Mayor Shelley's house? In confusion, all retreated to the 1500 block of Haight Street to regroup.

By now it was 6:00 P.M. and the crowd had largely melted away into the sidewalk traffic, leaving a hundred or so clustered around the door of the Print Mint. Traffic in the street was still stalled, particularly since someone had immobilized a trolley by disconnecting its electrical contacts from the overhead power line.

Unexpectedly some forty riot-squad police appeared, greeted by a handful of firecrackers, and they were quickly followed by a hundred patrolmen and five paddy wagons. The crowd was informed it was guilty of unlawful assembly and ordered to disperse. Thereupon the police began an hour of rough discipline with nightsticks, at the end of which thirty-two people had been arrested.

Word filtered back about a bust on April Fool's Day, or rather an attempted bust. Police had sent a kid up to Morning Star in search of dope on the property. By now there were twenty-odd people living there, doing yoga, planting cabbages in the nude, building imaginative living quarters that would never pass a Building and Safety Code inspection, getting stoned. The intended informant liked Morning Star so much, though, that he warned them of the raid and everyone had a good week in which to clean up.

But in the Haight, the Digger pads at 848 Clayton and 1775 Haight were both closed, at least for the time being. Bad weather and lack of materials were blamed for 848's failure to satisfy its five-day Health Department warning; moreover, the place had been vandalized by unknown parties who spilled paint cans and broke doors and furniture. The problem at 1775 was a citation for sleeping an illegal number of people.

Although the Trip Without a Ticket was in operation, Diggers were making ever more use of the office at All Saints Church, running what they described as a "runaway location service and twenty-four-hour counseling" in a basement room that was otherwise unused except for Sunday school one hour a week. But some of the parishioners were not as welcoming as Father Harris. On April 3 the senior warden, the master of acolytes and parishioners representing 5 percent of the church's income resigned from the parish in protest. Father Harris replied that a congregation of God's church "is not a private club that exists to make its members comfortable," and that the Diggers would stay. In gratitude the Diggers organized a party to repaint the church's cracking and peeling undercroft.

The Hilton Inn at San Francisco Airport requested permission from the Public Utilities Commission to install a $13,000 "light-sound contraption" that would, sponsors hoped, compete with the Fillmore and Avalon light shows. The "synesthesia device" for the Hilton's Tiger Room discotheque converted sound frequencies into colors; it was a souped-up version of the nightclub light boxes that had seemed so far out to *Life* magazine a year earlier. The Tiger Room manager told newspaper reporters that the Fillmore show, by comparison, was sensory deprivation. "We're not talking about psychedelic," he said, "but an increased awareness of sight and sound that enhances the entertainment value." He gave a demonstration using a non-rock Mystic Moods Orchestra record and exclaimed, "Man, it's going right through me!"

If there was anything as obvious as the huge crowds invading the Haight, it was the eagerness of businessmen to cash in on the psychedelic market. An advertising executive told the *Washington Post,* "People all of a sudden are becoming aware of a segment of the population having almost a controlling effect on what is bought and not bought—as though it didn't exist last year. Industry is jumping up and down and saying, 'How can we get with it? What can we put in our copy?'" A young Harvard Business School graduate had organized a company called Youth Concepts on the premise that "Youth and only youth can speak to other young people, honestly and creatively." Youth Concepts was talking to appliance manufacturers, whose brand identity had fallen off sharply in the age group from fifteen to twenty-four.

Jackie Cassen and Rudi Stern, who ran Tim Leary's light show, had done a huge window of multimedia stuff for, of all places, Best & Company, the ninety-year-old home of quiet teen taste on Fifth Avenue in New York. Peter Max, an artist with a psychedelic style, was doing consultation on the youth market and designing glassware, wallpaper, fabrics and tile, as well as running a yoga school. Max's art nouveau flower designs and mandalas, all in a soft rainbow of colors with sinuous but curiously static outlines, were expected to be used in a promotion film for the 1968 models of a major automobile manufacturer. Stretch Fabrics Company took a full-color ad in *Women's Wear Daily* with the message: "Horizontals, dots, whirlpools, freedom—that is what psychedelic means, at least when it comes to fabrics."

On April 5 the Gray Line Bus Company did what the Gossiping Guru had predicted in the *Oracle*. It instituted a "San Francisco Haight-Ashbury District 'Hippie Hop' Tour," which it advertised as "the only foreign tour within the continental limits of the United States." Monday through Friday a Gray Line bus piloted by a driver "especially trained in the sociological significance" of the Haight would make a two-hour expedition to the "Hashberry." Explorers were given a "Glossary of Hippie Terms" that contained only a few mistakes: for example, "Speed—combination of heroin and Methedrine."

On the first day of the tours, a TV crew boarded the bus at one stop along with a poster painter living in the Haight who attempted to put the community's best foot forward. He welcomed the tourists in the name of the hippies and explained that he himself was a settled, married man with a job. He asked the tourists to compare the peacefulness they would see on Haight Street with the violence of the beer-drinking college kids at Fort Lauderdale over the Easter holiday.

That same day a press conference announced the formation of the Council for a Summer of Love. At the ostentatiously clean and spacious former firehouse on Waller Street where the Haight Independent Proprietors had held their first press conference, representatives of the new council invoked the name of the pacific saint after whom San Francisco was named and asked the city to welcome the inevitable tide of young people. The council's aim was to serve as a clearinghouse and liaison to the straight world, and to organize art shows and celebratory events. The members were the Family Dog, the Diggers, the Straight Theater (still laboring to fulfill the multiplying building and fire code requirements), the *Oracle*, a church run by a Beat poet and a new organization called the Kiva. This last planned to utilize Be-In energy for a school that would teach rural skills, personal growth and art—in short, "a proposed way of life by which we mean to discover harmony with nature and god and to evolve spiritually through the creative expression of human energies." The Kiva's tribal council was essentially identical to the Council for a Summer of Love itself.

A Summer of Love. Easter had brought crowds, but the stunning fact had been that crowds had again come the week *after* Easter. The widely publicized predictions of 100,000 new arrivals were validating themselves.

Once upon a time, the Haight and its sister scenes had known a mélange of exotic personal styles, with the Edwardian and Old West motifs commanding special prestige. Then came Hell's Angels in leather and Merry Pranksters in Day-Glo paint and superhero costumes, and the Haight Street boutiques with wide-wale corduroy trousers, Mod miniskirts, rough Mexican ponchos and Indian paisley fabrics. Then came the drab and slightly mismatched secondhand store and free store look, and more recently an explosion of sheet-draped Jesuses.

Now the Summer of Love was commencing, and with it a welter of diluted versions of all the original styles, taken by the newcomers from national news media photos. And more and more, Haight Street saw the eager, puzzled faces and the denim and department-store shirts of the nation's high schools.

Haight Street any weekend afternoon, April 1967: Part Old Calcutta with beads and paisley-print fabrics and bare feet, incense and tinkling anklet bells, beggars squatting on the sidewalk. Part football stadium crush, complete with people selling programs—the *Oracle*, the *Barb* and two new papers, the *Haight-Ashbury Tribune* and the *Haight-Ashbury Maverick*. Part Middle Ages, too, with a husband and wife evangelist team haranguing the crowds, and street dealers muttering their traditional street cry: "Acid, speed, lids?" There were conga drummers playing in front of the United California Bank and "sidewalk bikers," who aped the dress and mannerisms of the Hell's Angels and the Gypsy Jokers, hanging out in front of Tracy's Donuts, waiting for the moment when their idols would roar up on their bikes through the traffic jam of tourists' automobiles. Once in a while the latest poem or screed or news flash or *I Ching* reading from the Communication Company would be handed out among the crowds up and down the street.

Things were coming thick and fast. Newcomers found a huge smorgasbord of projects, all somehow related: starting shops or crash pads, planning journeys and rock bands and dope deals, making trippy things to wear or have around the pad, doing yoga, taking steps to create a New Jerusalem, spreading the word. Something absolute was coming into being. Religious scriptures had lost their literary quality and become a sober language for describing everyday life. The rafters above a theater stage or a bush in Golden Gate Park rated as a thoughtful choice of address in the present capsize of conventional wisdom.

To live in the Haight was to meet masses of people all the time, endless masses. If two strangers hit it off, it was not customary to suggest getting together again; they said, "See you around," on the basis that if they didn't see each other on the street or at a dance, they would while hitchhiking in Big Sur, putting together a dope deal in Denver or for that matter, maybe talking to gurus in Nepal. If they were meant to meet again, they would. And in the meantime the waterfall of new people went on and on.

There were some real exotics in the throng these days. A fellow who wore a door knocker strung around his neck and wouldn't speak to you unless you knocked first. Another who wore a poncho with one of his arms sticking out of one sleeve and a plastic baby doll's arm sticking out of the other. As the Straight Theater built its dance floor, it had given away the old theater seats as it tore them out. Most had gone to furnish the vans many people were living in, but the Psychedelic Shop took two and mounted them in its front window so you could sit and watch the passing parade on Haight Street.

The out-of-work DJ Tom Donahue had taken Ralph Gleason's advice. On April 7 he took over the eight-to-midnight slot at KMPX-FM, just before Larry Miller's show, with an option to run the station if it worked out well. As his first act he took the clock out of the studio because he refused to announce the time on the air in Top Forty fashion. Regular listeners to the Chinese language program that had previously filled that time slot heard a steady stream of Dylan, Beatles, Stones, Airplane, Baez, Shankar and Dead—the first Grateful Dead album, which had been released that day.

Donahue's deal with KMPX was to expand his style of radio programming into other time slots as it became economically feasible, with Donahue's North Beach Productions taking one-third of the ad revenues he drummed up. The next morning a fellow jock of Donahue's from his KYA days started a second hip rock show on KMPX. Ironically, the very day Donahue started at KMPX, his old station had decided after a management shakeup that they wanted him back after all.

On the morning of June 8, as the Gray Line bus made its way down Haight Street for the third time, a hippie climbed aboard and commandeered the bus. "You're all free!" he told the startled passengers. "This bus has been taken over by the Diggers!" He directed the bus to the Grateful Dead's house at 715 Ashbury and the Digger Office at All Saints, and handed out avocados to the passengers. Henceforth the Gray Line added the Dead House to its regular itinerary.

Owsley had not operated an LSD lab since December, when he closed down the one in Point Richmond where he'd made the White Lightnings. There was no immediate need for another, as he had stockpiled enough LSD to keep the market satisfied for several months.

But eventually there was going to be a problem. The source for raw lysergic acid had dried up. The president of the Cyclo Chemical Company, whose name was Milan Panic, had informed Bear Research Group that he could no longer fill orders for lysergic acid. There was an alternative, however, or rather a great number of them. Owsley and his partners had the formulas of a number of psychedelic chemicals related to both mescaline and the amphetamines, all invented by Dr. Alexander Shulgin of the Dow Chemical Company. One partner went to scout lab sites in Denver while Owsley continued his program of turning on musicians and conferring with other prominent people in the psychedelic movement.

Early in April, Owsley visited Leary's home in New York. On April 4, as he was driving from Millbrook, he was stopped by police for changing lanes without a proper signal. A search of his car found marijuana, psychedelics and other drugs. But by the time this news reached the Haight-Ashbury, it was pretty obvious to all parties in

Dutchess County that Owsley would be able to beat the case on grounds of improper search and seizure.

For the morning of April 8, Emmett Grogan had organized a sweep-in in Greenwich Village, but New York City had a firmer hand on psychedelic activities than San Francisco did. When the work party showed up with brooms and brushes, they found a Sanitation Department truck had been sent down the street early in the morning and their task had been stolen from them. To add insult to injury, a representative of a soap company was on hand to pass out sample-size bottles of detergent.

Down in Big Sur, police were knocking down lean-tos, abandoned cabins and all other potential shelters around Limekiln Creek. Diggers and other Haight-Ashbury emigrants had lately established whole camps of half-naked flute players in the canyons. Big Sur officials cited the danger of hepatitis, lice and scabies and also claimed that most of the patients in the federal drug program at Lexington had first tried LSD in the Big Sur area.

Com/co denounced the 50¢ minimum established by the Drogstore Café. Like the I/Thou Coffee House, the twenty-four-hour Drogstore now often had a line outside its door. Com/co also charged that the Drogstore's large plate-glass windows made customers sitting ducks for narc photographers. Another thing on Chester Anderson's mind was the Sam Katzman exploitation film *The Love-Ins* being shot in the Haight. Anderson counseled hustling money from the cameramen.

The *Berkeley Barb* had run mysterious messages here and there in its pages reading "Telegraph Avenue April 9." It had published a letter purportedly from Mrs. Martha Graybeal of Poughkeepsie, New York, asking how it was that her grandson had won a T-shirt in his grammar school Fish Pond reading "Telegraph Avenue April 9." The words had appeared as toilet graffiti and on the jungle of public announcements adorning Telegraph Avenue telephone poles.

No other message. The *Barb* was playing street theater to see what would happen.

As in the Haight, the spirit of play waited only to be summoned. On April 9 a crowd formed around 1:00 P.M. and concocted things to do. A game of volleyball was struck up with a milk carton for a ball, a young woman unrolled a big ball of string the length of the street, a banana peel with a stick of incense in it was paraded as a Banana Shrine, a daisy was chalked around a manhole cover. Berkeley being Berkeley, among the body painters and *I Ching* consulters and musicians were militants handing out antiwar leaflets.

In the Haight, the Diggers had promulgated a list of events for that same afternoon, each with the price listed as $0.00. A street-sweeping "event with brooms" at one, a dance with the Grateful Dead at the corner of Haight and Ashbury at two, a "salad bowl" in the Panhandle at three, a "Light Show of Human Auras (mirrors & foil)" at six, and so on. At one o'clock, before any serious brooming could get done, a band (not the Dead) showed up at Haight and Ashbury and plugged in to play for a crowd of about 150. Police immediately swarmed over the intersection. One cop took up a bullhorn and announced: "Now hear this. Now hear this. The action is in the Panhandle with the Grateful Dead."

The Dead were hastily summoned from their house on Ashbury and brought down to the Panhandle, where a crowd of about 2,000 had gathered. Then a good hour and a half passed with hippies and tourists shuffling around in the Panhandle while people tried to locate a generator to power the Dead's equipment. Finally a hundred-foot extension cord was stretched across Fell Street, and the Dead started playing. Twenty minutes into their set, the police surprisingly confiscated the cord. Another cord was found within five minutes and the concert went on.

April 9 was the first day of Angry Arts Week, a week-long series of events organized by the Spring Mobilization Against the War. That night Spring Mobe put on a fund-raising concert at Longshoremen's Hall featuring Quicksilver, Country Joe and the very busy Grateful Dead, who had recently provided soundtrack music for

Sons and Daughters, a film of the October 1965 Oakland peace march.

At one point Spring Mobe had planned such actions as a "constructfully disorderful demonstration" at the offices of the Internal Revenue Service to frustrate the final day for filing income tax returns, which this year had a special surtax for Vietnam expenses, and flooding the draft boards with males of all ages demanding reclassification. These plans had now boiled down to a non-judged art show, a free poetry reading and a rock concert in the Panhandle, six fund-raising concerts and a big march at the end of the week.

One thing was clear: they wanted the hippies. The march had originally been scheduled to run from Marina Green to the Army Presidio up at the north end of town, but now it was going to go through the Panhandle and wind up at Kezar Stadium, right beside the old Krishna-Digger building. Publicity spoke of a Peace Fair at Kezar, featuring Moby Grape, Quicksilver and Big Brother.

Monday, April 10.   The board of supervisors finally voted to lower the age limit in dance halls to sixteen, over objections of police, parent groups and the Juvenile Justice Commission. Effective in thirty days, sixteen-year-olds could attend the Fillmore and stay until 2:00 A.M.

In the Haight, the thrill of having a Gray Line bus touring the neighborhood was wearing thin. Some Haight residents had taken to walking alongside the bus with mirrors in their hands, showing the tourists their own faces. On Tuesday the bus was pelted with tomatoes.

The Mime Troupe had recently been busted for marijuana in the notoriously tough town of Calgary, Alberta. Bill Graham put on a benefit for the Mime Troupe's legal fund at the Fillmore on April 12: Appeal IV, as it were. Mouse Studios designed a poster and the old Appeal bands donated their services: the Airplane, the Dead, Quicksilver, the Loading Zone.

The most successful Mime Troupe benefit ever, it contributed $6,000. But what a difference sixteen months had made. In the old loft on Howard Street, the Mime Troupe was famous, and the bands were the big surprise. At the Fillmore in April, the audience showed hardly any sign of knowing who R. G. Davis was.

In his column publicizing the Mime Troupe benefit, Ralph Gleason mentioned that he'd been listening to KMPX a lot. The Gray Line tour added the KMPX studio at 50 Green Street to its itinerary.

April 13.   Three buildings were condemned: 848 Clayton, 1773-1775-1777 Haight, 728-730-732 Ashbury. The last-minute cleanup campaign for 848 Clayton had fizzled. Apart from the buildings condemned, two others were ordered to clean up, but Ellis D. Sox acknowledged that some other parts of the city were "as bad or worse" than the Haight.

The board of supervisors voted to delay taking action on the summer's impending hippie influx. The Haight-Ashbury Neighborhood Council voted to debate a proposal to turn Haight Street into a mall. Park Station reported having picked up 114 juvenile runaways since the first of the year and having arrested 87 minors and 184 adults.

April 15.   The Spring Mobe march assembled downtown on Market Street at 10:00 A.M. Three hundred and fifty police officers were on hand "to protect the marchers," and Market Street buses were running on only one side of the street in order to accommodate the march. Lest anyone get the wrong idea, however, Mayor Shelley proclaimed this U.S. Serviceman Appreciation Week.

Earlier in the week, the Spring Mobe leadership had divided bitterly on the issue of allowing marchers to carry pro-Vietcong banners and signs. The Committee for a Sane Nuclear Policy withdrew, demanding recognition that there were "*two* armed ideologies in Vietnam" and arguing for the slogan "Negotiation Now!" A story in the *San Francisco Examiner* dwelt on the presence of highly placed Trotskyists in Spring Mobe, and noted that the Northern California chairman of the Communist party had contributed a hundred dollars. In the end virtually the entire San Francisco Council of Churches decided to boycott the march.

But as the march proceeded up Fell Street, it was obvious the VC flag issue had meant nothing to the Haight. On its last leg the march doubled in size and the final crowd that overflowed the 62,000-capacity stadium was at least three-quarters young people. During an early speech, a parachutist landed in the parking lot, be-in style.

What speeches they were. Labored speeches about what the march meant and what the crowd should feel, pacifists pushing their brand of pacifism and trade unionists talking solidarity. The young majority grew restless, as if thinking: You're *talking* peace, we *are* peace.

Also thinking, Where's the *music*? Despite the promise of rock bands, only seven minutes of music were scheduled, tame humanitarian stuff: Judy Collins and Jon Hendricks. Down at the stadium field gates some Diggers were gnashing their teeth at the politicos, who were, the Diggers thought, going to drive the whole younger generation away from the peace movement. They broke the lock on the gates and let Country Joe's flatbed truck out on the field for the only rock and roll of the afternoon, but the truck was quickly bundled off.

When the speakers had built up to the star of the afternoon, Mrs. Martin Luther King, the stadium was less than half full and emptying fast.

Printed by the Communication Company, April 16:

Returning Returning Returning
Your Brothers and Sisters are returning
Tribes of Love and Peace returning to nature for a
Human Be-In beginning on April 22
in the Malakoff Diggings State Park just north of Nevada City, California
Continuing through the Summer
Continuing through the Fall
and continuing. . . .

Also printed by the Communication Company, April 16:

Pretty little sixteen-year-old middle-class chick comes to the Haight to see what it's all about & gets picked up by a seventeen-year-old street dealer who spends all day shooting her full of speed again & again, then feeds her 3000 mikes [micrograms of LSD, 12 times the standard dose] & raffles off her temporarily unemployed body for the biggest Haight Street gang bang since the night before last.

The politics & ethics of ecstasy.

Rape is as common as bullshit on Haight Street.

A shudder passed through the Haight. Nobody, not the Diggers, not even the cops, had publicly claimed anything as bad as this was going on.

Three months after the Be-In, three weeks after the beginning of the post-Easter deluge, Chester Anderson was describing the Haight as a ghastly trap with no escape. "Are you aware that Haight Street is just as bad as the squares say it is?" he asked, with the perspective of having spent a few mornings giving first aid at the All Saints Digger office and having heard about a lot of drug burns and beatings as a com/co editor.

His impulse was to blame the *Oracle,* the HIP merchants and Timothy Leary (the broadside was titled "Uncle Tim'$ Children") for luring young people to the Haight for their own profit. The psychedelic spokesmen believed that LSD would provide answers to all problems in good time, but this belief, said Anderson, merely allowed them to ignore the problems and shirk their responsibilities. The *Oracle* hired some kids to sell papers; not good enough. The Council for a Summer of Love was merely interested in polishing the hippie image. The Kiva, the council's practical arm, might be operational by September, but in any case it was only an answer to the merchants' own problems.

Not good enough, none of it good enough. The merchants were criminals, honorable thieves, murderers. The Diggers alone were selflessly working for the community's good. If the merchants wanted to talk to Anderson about his charges, they would first have to show good faith by feeding the hungry, clothing the naked, sheltering the homeless and comforting the sick. He did not address the problem of sixteen-year-old girls falling into the hands of rape-minded street dealers.

Neither did the HIP merchants, though they protested that Anderson wrongly blamed them for everything that was wrong with Haight Street. The next day Anderson conceded that the HIP merchants were not to blame for bringing kids to the Haight-Ashbury, but insisted they still had a responsibility to help them. He himself had just inaugurated a series of survival school classes at the Trip Without a Ticket, lecturing on how to use drugs safely.

But the original lurid anecdote of "Uncle Tim'$ Children" left its flavor. Some people were nudged the last inch toward a decision to move to the country. Even those who were merely irritated by Anderson's presumption in lecturing the Haight when he had scarcely heard about the place until January could no longer ignore the presence of evil in the psychedelic swarm.

At the beginning com/co had exulted in McLuhanesque moment-to-moment effects, like someone at an Acid Test playing with the multiple-interfaced video systems, but Anderson's street raps had taken on a flavor of crisis. Now he even made an urgent demand for gurus to make themselves available: "Go now to the kids and teach The Way. Now."

April 17.   Two doctors from the University of California Medical Center reported to the California Medical Association that loud rock and roll can irreparably damage the ear. KMPX-FM, for its part, was doing so well it needed a second telephone. Listeners had sent flowers, posters and boxes full of other decor, as Donahue had invited. One advertiser was astonished to have over a dozen people drop in his shop at one time or another to say how pleased they were that he was advertising on KMPX.

April 18.   The poster obscenity trial barely avoided a guilty verdict with a jury hung eleven to one. Apartments on Ashbury and Haight that had been closed by the Health Department were raided, and eleven squatters were arrested for trespassing. Newspapers reported that the French were working on an auditory weapon, a sound that could kill. Twenty-five evangelists descended on the Haight, and to their chagrin found the hippies trying to convert them to Oriental mysticism.

April 19. New Jersey Representative Frank Thompson, Jr., proposed two new acts to Congress: the Banana Labeling Act of 1967 and the Banana and Other Odd Fruit Disclosure and Reporting Act of 1967. They were aimed, he said, at "those banana-smoking beatniks who seek a make-believe land described in the peel-puffers' secret psychedelic marching song, 'Puff, the Magic Dragon.' "

He was kidding, of course. Among other things, he was making fun of a government-sponsored study to discover the contents of peyote, which had taken four years to complete.

April 20. Chester Anderson had acknowledged the Diggers' "messy imperfections." Now Emmett Grogan, back from New York, was anonymously addressing some other problems.

"Turner was going to have Tobacco killed and Apache wanted to confront the cops and nobody cared any more," he wrote. "1775 is now a closed shop complete with tenure and seniority. 848 was abandoned to the selfishness of sidewalk bike riders." Signing himself X, he dated the decline of true Diggerism from the acceptance of offices at All Saints. At that point, he wrote, the two original free-food Diggers had faded away and suddenly money had become a necessity: rent money, bail money, lawyer money. Now a "new breed" in the All Saints Digger office was getting $16 a head for turning in runaways, he said, and free food hadn't happened for a long time.

In the beginning the Diggers had had lots of fun with the nonexclusiveness motif: "Am I a Digger? Who told you I'm a Digger? You're a Digger!" It was a "street theater" device that threw a would-be observer on stage—where as trained actors the original Diggers had an edge. It was also a smoke screen against the police and a reproach to the cliques that had grown up around various shops, rock bands and other institutions. Together with contempt for money, nonexclusiveness had made the Diggers a moral and political force in the Haight.

Of course it was never intended as simple we-don't-care-who nonexclusiveness. If you wanted to call yourself a Digger, you were expected to be on the Digger wavelength. But the influx into the Haight, the work to be done, and of course the Diggers' publicity had swelled the ranks of Diggers. By now nonexclusiveness had led to the growth of factions. One of the old-line Diggers told the *Barb* he had been "verbally ejected" from the All Saints office and that henceforth it should be known not as the Digger office but the Clearing House.

Some people saw the difference. But the All Saints Diggers, busy with their first aid and housing services, saw no reason to stop calling themselves Diggers. And Tobacco, originator of the Digger pads, was now accusing Emmett Grogan of lusting for publicity and of being on a violence trip.

April 22. Police Chief Cahill announced a series of orders to implement the Recreation and Park Department resolution. No tents in any park after 10:00 P.M. No musical instruments to be played in any park from 9:00 P.M. to 7:00 A.M.

The hottest rumor of the moment concerned Bob Dylan, who was known to have suffered a motorcycle accident after recording *Blonde on Blonde* in 1966: He had died, but the fact was being covered up.

April 23. The rainfall was already seven inches above the usual total for the entire July-to-June rain-measurement year, but the weekend crowds demanded an event on Sunday, and the result was an impromptu Rain Festival. Five guitarists set up in a second-floor apartment at 609 Ashbury, near the corner of Haight, and played for a rainy sidewalk dance of about four hundred strong, with what were said to be three ex-nuns dancing naked in the window. When police arrived to unplug the band, the crowd pelted them with vegetables and raw eggs. The cops retaliated with a sweep of the street by a phalanx six men abreast and made fifty arrests. They were delayed in transporting the arrestees to Park Station because the crowd immobilized the lead wagon by cutting the valve stems on three of its tires.

That same Sunday, the Berkeley city government permitted a dance in the park where the Provos were accustomed to giving out free food, in hope of avoiding another quixotic event on Telegraph Avenue like the one April 9, at which no arrests had been made.

April 25.   A *San Francisco Chronicle* reporter visited the be-inners at the old gold rush site of Malakoff Diggings and found only three hippies staking claim to an abandoned mine. They were sure crowds would come later, though. They had seen a flying saucer on their drive from San Francisco.

William McGlothlin, a research psychiatrist at UCLA who had studied LSD for six years, declared the LSD cult to be "in a vital stage much like the early days of Christianity."

In San Francisco, ninety socialites held a "hippie party" at the airport cocktail lounge as a send-off for their trip to Hawaii. Buttons with hippie slogans were distributed while they sipped their ramos fizzes.

April 27.   The state dropped charges of possession and sale of marijuana and LSD against Superspade dating from the December debutante bust. His attorney promised the judge, "We won't be back again."

April 28.   The board of supervisors, still wrestling with the mayor's request for a statement of non-welcome to hippies, voted to support such a statement *in principle*.

April 29.   In Los Angeles a love-in drew four thousand people. In London, the Fluxus Group artist Yoko Ono put on a fund-raising Twenty-Four-Hour Dream event for the *International Times*, a London underground paper fighting obscenity charges. The Dream featured thirty rock groups, San Francisco-style light shows and Warhol movies. In Berkeley, the Mime Troupe and the Cleanliness and Godliness Skiffle Band performed at a dance benefiting . . . Country Joe and the Fish, who suspected they couldn't make a living because the San Francisco dance halls were snubbing them for being from Berkeley.

In Santa Fe, New Mexico, a group of people from Los Angeles and San Francisco conferred with the Hopi Indians about a grand be-in they wanted to hold on the summer solstice, June 21. Even before they could address such questions as how feasible it was to gather an expected 15,000 people on Hopi land six miles north of the Grand Canyon—remote, waterless, ecologically fragile—they had to face the Hopis' doubts about their white admirers. The Californians made a bad impression. Some had tried to turn Indian children on to grass and Hare Krishna mantras. Some had shocked the Indians' sense of sexual propriety with their nudity and outdoor lovemaking. Worst, for these self-styled white reincarnations of Indian souls, some had invaded Hopi shrines and taken the groovy kachina masks.

Richard Alpert argued that a Grand Canyon be-in would publicize the injustice that Indians had suffered on their reservations, and cited a prophecy of reconciliation between red man and white man. The Hopis' doubts were not assuaged. It didn't sound truly tribal to them, this community of elective, voluntary tribes. "You are a tribe of strangers to yourselves," one of them said. "You gather and disperse. You are not together."

Emmett Grogan took a firm position against the be-in, and Allen Cohen of the *Oracle* and others sided with him. The Thelin brothers, Alpert and the *Los Angeles Free Press* were still for it, but with both the *Oracle* and the Diggers opposed, the event was dead. Alpert declared he still wanted to do something at the Grand Canyon on the solstice, with or without Indians.

April 30.   United Fruit Company, the principal importer of bananas, had asked the drug expert Dr. Sidney Cohen to research the hallucinogenic properties of their produce. The author of *LSD: The Beyond Within* reported that bananas gave "a mild sort of high."

May 1.   The news told of the Expo 1967 fair in Montreal, the marriage of Elvis Presley, a new organization in Oakland's black ghetto called the Black Panther party. President Johnson declared that he admired the skeptical nature of the younger generation, and San Francisco sported the fourth highest rate of venereal disease in the country. Other San Francisco news: Jefferson Airplane had a best-selling album and a single, "Somebody to Love," at No. 31 on the charts.

In the preceding four weeks some fifteen storefronts in the Haight-Ashbury had changed name, owner or nature of business. The Print Mint was turning its back room into a coffeehouse, and the displaced Job Co-Op was moving back to Wild Colors. The Golden Cask, an old neighborhood bar, installed a pizza oven and put up a sign reading "Lee, Sam and Dick" with the very prominent initial letters L, S, D. Storefronts on Haight Street were renting for up to $40,000 a year.

In a low-rent section of Haight Street six blocks east of Masonic, a new venture served vegetarian food, mountain spring water and flying saucer information from 8:00 A.M. to 9:00 P.M. The Here and Now Air Research Club was sponsored by Universal Millennium Groups, a cult from Southern California that had moved up to the Haight in December. Its leader, a former sign painter named Allen Noonan, was Supreme Officer of the Galactic Command and in contact with Higher Intelligences, as well as being World Messiah.

Noonan had called for a May Day rally, but his rhetoric was not the sort to inspire be-ins: "The buildup in the Haight Ashbury district of San Francisco is accomplished by craft of the Galactic Command, which are broadcasting a high frequency aura the turned-on youth are struggling with to gain control of their higher mental faculties. . . . We are in the last 1,335 days now. You shall either deliver yourselves into a New Age by cooperating with the Messiah's Plan or cut your hearts out."

Another reason why the Messiah's rally didn't draw great crowds might have been the scuttlebutt about him. "Everything is groovy," wrote the editor of *The Electric Garden of Eden's Orifice,* a mild *Oracle* parody occasionally published by com/co, "but if he asks for your money (if you have it, he will ask you), and you want to keep it or use it for your own thing, run like hell—he'll get it if it takes half the acid in town."

A fireplug on Nob Hill was painted in psychedelic patterns with six colors. The Psychedelic Rangers, who had invited the press to watch them paste the word "Love" over the word "Haight" on the street sign at Haight and Ashbury a few weeks before, took credit. The Fire Department immediately repainted the fireplug white.

The board of supervisors, having finally voted in principle to declare hippies unwelcome, again delayed making the actual declaration. One supervisor pointed out that during the Depression, Los Angeles' attempt to bar indigent migrants from the Dust Bowl states had been ruled unconstitutional.

May 2.   After two hung-jury trials, Ken Kesey was allowed to plead nolo contendere to a lesser charge of "knowingly being in a place where marijuana was kept," which carried a penalty of only ninety days in jail.

Levi Strauss & Company, the San Francisco-based manufacturer of denim clothes, had always kept in touch with youth trends, and it was not ignoring what was going on in its own town. In December Wes Wilson was hired to design a special Fillmore-style poster to honor fifteen retiring employees. And now Jefferson Airplane was singing a radio commercial for the company's new line, White Levis.

Naturally, a debate ensued. To some people, the Airplane was simply doing its thing, even pushing a subliminal love message at Levi Strauss's expense. But a sizable number condemned it as "merchandising love." The *Barb* charged that Levi Strauss followed racially discriminatory hiring policies, and on that basis Country Joe and the Fish decided against recording a White Levis ad, which they had planned to do in exchange for 30,000 pairs of factory seconds to be donated to the Diggers.

May 3.   Eight persons were arrested at an address on Baker Street in Pacific Heights on various charges of manufacture and sale of

Methedrine. It was a lab associated with the Love Conspiracy Commune, which had been manufacturing four pounds a week of Methedrine plus quantities of the "half-hour psychedelic" DMT.

The grapevine reported a new psychedelic on the market, the one being made in the Denver lab set up by Owsley's whiz-kid friend Tim Scully. It kept you stoned for three days, and with LSD going for $2.50 a hit, this new stuff was a bargain at $4.00. It was being called DNA or ZNA, but a hanger-on at the Straight Theater dubbed it STP and the name caught on.

May 4.   A group of Diggers appeared on the steps of City Hall at noon and began offering free spaghetti to office workers. Wondering whether this had something to do with the city's shabby treatment of the Haight, a reporter asked a Digger named Cowboy, "What do you want City Hall to do?" He replied, "Eat."

The Psychedelic Shop announced that it planned to incorporate and sell shares on the street for next to nothing, possibly giving some shares away. Ultimately it intended to be nonprofit as well as cooperative, but first, the store manager said, it would have to clear $6,000 in outstanding debts attributed to "poor management and speculation."

One reason for the store's decline in profits, despite its fame and the number of potential customers on the street, was that half the shop had been given over to the Calm Center. That not only cut into sales space but also reduced the hours the Psych Shop could be open. Some people came to the Calm Center for its original purpose, to meditate or perhaps to pull out of an acid bummer, but others came to smoke grass, deal drugs or sleep. The Thelin brothers could either close the store earlier in the day or run what was essentially a bustable crash pad at the most highly publicized address on Haight Street. Closing the Calm Center, of course, was out of the question.

The state of Nevada had only 90,000 registered voters, and its residency requirement was only six months. Underground papers in various parts of the country printed a proposal for young people to take the state over. If only 90,001 hippies moved there, went the reasoning, they could vote heavy taxes on the gambling casinos and live for free in the holy land of the Washoe and Paiute nations.

In the San Francisco area, the *Barb* publicized the idea. For all its fun with banana joints, the *Barb* was aboard for the psychedelic revolution. The May 5 cover was a trippy drawing of a bearded neo-primitive clutching a god's-eye, the work of an artist named John Thompson. The *Barb* had already published art by the official Country Joe and the Fish artist, Tom Weller, who specialized in broad-shouldered, Wes Wilson–derived female nudes with huge masses of hair and heads slightly too small for their bodies. Both Thompson and Weller gave their figures a uniquely Berkeleyite expression, at once tranced-out and militant.

Months and months behind the times, the Federal Drug Abuse Control Agency suddenly reported finding LSD in "well-made tablet form," the work of Owsley's pill press.

From time to time Ralph Gleason had mentioned in his column a rock and roll music festival planned for the city of Monterey, eighty miles to the south. He had heard rumors that Paul McCartney and Donovan would perform at the Monterey International Pop Festival.

Early on, the original promoters of Monterey Pop had been bought out by a group of Los Angeles music biz people, principally record producer Lou Adler and John Phillips of the folk-rock group the Mamas and the Papas. They changed it into a nonprofitmaking festival. Monterey Pop started sending out a stream of publicity notices, one of which gave the impression that the festival's profits would be used to help feed newcomers in the Haight-Ashbury.

May 5 saw Wes Wilson's last weekly poster for the Fillmore. Wilson had improved his graphic technique prodigiously in sixteen months, and his posters were on college dormitory walls all over the country. His style had been imitated in Los Angeles and Austin and London, and the Grande Ballroom in Detroit had slavishly followed every phase of his development.

But Bill Graham had already slipped in an occasional poster by another artist, so Wilson decided to demand a raise from Graham while his iron was hot. No deal. Wilson's last poster showed a serpent with a bold dollar sign in its mouth.

May 8.   The board of supervisors finally reached a decision on the mayor's resolution to declare hippies unwelcome in San Francisco. They voted to support it with reservations.

New bands on the scene: Mad River, Frumious Bandersnatch, West Coast Natural Gas, Freedom Highway, the Vast Minority, Baltimore Steam Packet, Pacific Gas & Electric, the Salvation Army Band, the CIA (Citizens for Interplanetary Activities). New shops in the Haight: the Hobbit Hole, the Bead Freak, New Reflections, Xanadu Clothes, the Garuda Coffee Shop. This last had a floor strewn with pillows, which soon made it one of the few coffee shops where you could regularly hear snoring. At 1837 Fell Street, a Summerhill-type elementary school was organized as the Shire School.

May 11.   The board of supervisors voted to adopt yet another formula for dance licenses. A general license would permit dancing until 2:00 A.M. for an audience eighteen years old or older. A special license could be used for dances lasting only till midnight for an audience sixteen to twenty years old, no older and no younger.

Country Joe and the Fish celebrated their first album on Vanguard Records with a free party at the Fillmore. Five kilos' worth of joints were distributed.

May 13.   On Saturday, the Haight had its usual weekend invasion and Panhandle concert. The police arrested one couple for indecent exposure and a young man for spitting on an officer, but there was no violence. Diggers provided a game of Capture the Flag in the Park ("The Game of Breath and Clouds") for harmless physical exertion. Anyway, the police were busy elsewhere; the nonpsychedelic youth of the city were having a riot with race-war overtones at Playland, a beach amusement park.

Free concerts in the Panhandle were regular events, though unscheduled and unannounced: something between a rehearsal, a community service and a little free exposure for the bands.

The Council for a Summer of Love released the following announcement:

This summer, the youth of the world are making a holy pilgrimage to our city, to affirm and celebrate a new spiritual dawn. . . . The activity of the youth of the nation which has given birth to Haight-Ashbury is a small part of a worldwide spiritual awakening. Our city has become the momentary focus of this awakening. The reasons for this do not matter. It is a gift from God which we may take, nourish and treasure. . . .

These are facts I give you. Already, individuals and groups who have seen deeply into the situation are making preparations. Kitchens are being made ready. Food is being gathered. Hotels and houses are being prepared to supply free lodging. The Council for a Summer of Love expects to receive a huge tent, larger than a football field, which will be put up by the Haight-Ashbury community, and will be open all summer. It will contain a field kitchen, sleeping facilities, educational programs, concerts, art shows, lectures and similar activities.

The announcement also promised small meditation centers and large festivals: a Summer Solstice Festival, a Tolkien Festival of Elves and Hobbits, festivals of Christ, of Krishna, of the young and of the old. "There is a beautiful statue of Saint Francis," it concluded, "located in Marin County, and carved from a holy California Redwood Tree. We are now collecting the money to buy this statue. It will be brought by hand or cart across the Golden Gate Bridge in a mighty procession of children and it will be given to the city to be placed in Golden Gate Park at the foot of Haight Street facing East toward the place of Dawn."

That evening the local educational TV station broadcast a panel discussion by members of the city government and representatives from the Haight. A member of the Haight-Ashbury neighborhood council got an ovation when he complained that the "new community" failed to understand the supposedly repressive middle class. But the biggest hand went to Peter Cohon, when he blamed the restlessness of youth on the American Empire's materialistic orientation. "The hippies are the fruit of the middle class," said Cohon, "and they are telling the middle class they don't like what's been given them. As things are shaping up now, we are really heading toward a revolution of violence."

May 14.   The Army unveiled a new secret weapon—an oil-based spray containing a mind drug called BZ, which was intended not to kill the enemy but to render him harmless with confusion. The military had experimented with LSD for the same purpose, but found it too erratic for use as an "incapacitating agent."

The city's chief gardener complained that hippies were tearing up the flowers in Golden Gate Park. What irritated him most was their serene claim that "flowers belong to God, not to the city."

   Meanwhile, the city had already removed six times as much refuse and garbage from the Panhandle as in all of 1966.

Monday, May 15.   "I Was a Hippie," a week-long series of front-page feature stories on the Haight, began running in the *San Francisco Chronicle*.

   The reporter, a thirty-four-year-old nonhippie, had spent a month in the Haight wearing a black turtleneck sweater, a navy pea jacket and white Levis with a Mod belt. By the end of the month he was sympathetic to the Haight community, and wanted to avoid writing the story. Finally, with the help of a fellow *Chronicle* writer (himself an ex-Beat poet), he concocted a story with imaginary or safely disguised characters that presented the Haight in a relatively favorable light. On Monday, for instance, he wrote that the unwritten code of the hippies was, "Get high and stay high, closer to God and the real you. . . . Hate is a hangup, they say, that robs you of energies and others—like the Vietcong—of life."

May 15.   The Hippie Hop bus tour was canceled. The Gray Line cited the congested traffic in the neighborhood as the reason, not hostile reactions from hippies. In just over five weeks the tour had grown so popular as to have expanded to two trips a day.

May 16.   *Look* published a photo article about Jefferson Airplane with fervent prose by John Luce: "The name itself is a riddle. Like a Zen Buddhist koan, it traps your mind, jerks you into feeling. . . . The Airplane must share itself. It cannot take off until you do. Jefferson Airplane *must* love you. Can you love Jefferson Airplane?"

Arnold Toynbee had visited the Haight and published his observations in the *London Observer*. The historian was fascinated by the hippie challenge to conformism and "the American religion of the State," and by the Diggers' search for "jobs that are not meaningless."

In San Francisco a dress manufacturer named Alvin Duskin introduced a simple shirtwaist dress covered with peace symbols. A drug factory was uncovered just a few steps down an alley directly across the street from the Hall of Justice.

May 22.   The board of supervisors voted 8–2 to endorse the seventh draft of the dance hall ordinance, using the two-license formula with the proviso that sixteen-year-olds could attend the over-eighteen dances if accompanied by parent or guardian. The Jefferson Airplane album *Surrealistic Pillow* was No. 10 on the charts, and "Somebody to Love" was the seventeenth best-selling single. The news reported that John Lennon had, over the formal protest of the Rolls-Royce Company, painted his Rolls with bright colored flowers, leaves and scrollwork.

Five midshipmen at the U.S. Naval Academy were restricted to quarters for smoking marijuana. Captain Howard B. Levy, court-martialed for refusing to train Green Beret medical aid men for Vietnam, defended himself on the article of the Geneva Convention that requires noncombatants to refuse to be parties to the commission of war crimes; he lost. May was shaping up as the bloodiest month of the war so far for the Marines.

May 26.   The HIP Job Co-Op held a press conference at its new address, 842 Cole. The director announced, "We're telling people,

'If you see violence start, flow to the park. When the heat hits, split! Go to the parks! Go to the sea!' "

The Federal Food and Drug Administration reported that it had found "no detectable quantities of known hallucinogens" in either banana peels or banana juice. It was the end of a three-month golden age for potheads, when police were reluctant to stop cars in which people were sucking away on hand-rolled cigarettes for fear of the embarrassment of finding they were smoking banana.

May 28.   Two days after a jury unanimously declared *The Love Book* obscene and without redeeming social value, Lenore Kandel announced she would donate 1 percent of the profits from her book to the Police Retirement Association. This was her way, she said, of thanking the police for bringing *The Love Book* to public attention. Before the obscenity bust, the Psychedelic Shop had sold only about fifty copies, but since then over twenty thousand.

May 29.   Monday night there was a benefit show—separate concerts on two floors of California Hall—for the Haight-Ashbury Karmic Bail Fund. Fifteen bands played, including relative old-timers like the Orkustra and newer bands such as the Notes from the Underground and the Flying Circus. On Tuesday a benefit was held at Winterland for another legal group, the Haight-Ashbury Legalization Organization (HALO), which essentially consisted of two lawyers, Brian Rohan and Michael Stepanian. Their office was at 715 Ashbury, a Victorian building directly across the street from the Dead house, though in the current fluidity of life you might easily see the Dead hanging out at 715 and Hell's Angels frying eggs in the kitchen of 710.

May 30.   The general manager of the Municipal Railway proposed rerouting buses off Haight Street "as a temporary expedient because of so-called new residents and tourists." Some bus commuters had been getting home to the Sunset District an hour or two late because of congestion in the Haight.

Haight residents were still doing their best. In the last week there had been two sweep-ins, a rock concert put on by the Summer of Love council (the Park and Recreation department had forced it off the Panhandle onto a little triangular meadow on the other side of Kezar Stadium) and a public forum on the neighborhood's problems at Hippie Hill. This last event, the World's First Idea-In, had bogged down in irreconcilable viewpoints, though everybody admired the Thelin brothers' Oriental gong that called the meeting to order.

Even though school was not yet out and the real invasion was presumably still to come, every institution in the Haight was already swamped. The Haight Independent Proprietors had not met in weeks because they were either too busy running their shops or planning to get out of the city. The old-time Diggers who hadn't gone off to Morning Star Ranch were working at the Trip Without a Ticket, running occasional street-theater provocations in the Panhandle and getting involved with the Black Panthers; the Digger Pads were closed at the moment and the Digger Feeds in the park had mostly stopped. In their absence a number of people in the Haight were spontaneously trying to help out newcomers. The director of Howard Presbyterian Church's coffee shop put up dozens of people in his basement and many others were feeding and housing whoever they could. Even the *Oracle* office always had a pot of vegetables and brown rice on the stove for any hungry person who staggered in off the street.

The output of the Communication Company shrank by more than half during May, largely because the offices moved out of the Haight at the end of April and the new address, 742 Arguello Street in the Richmond District, was not made public. This was not Chester Anderson's McLuhanite vision at all, but Anderson was now on the outs at com/co. The old-line Diggers had demanded that com/co put its Gestetner machines primarily at their service, and Anderson's partners had sided with them. In May the com/co output ran a high proportion of Digger broadsides and announcements of free events and donated printing for the Black Panther Party. The artsy stuff Anderson liked (he had once printed some Baroque harpsichord music on a flier) and the personal commentary he had sometimes appended to Digger announcements, such as "none of the above appears worth getting busted for," were absent.

The marijuana supply was drying up, a normal seasonal shortage, and the use of amphetamines was on the rise. The latest newcomers weren't using much grass or LSD at all. Amphetamines were popular because they guaranteed a positive mood and enough aggressiveness to deal with any amount of hassle on the crowded street. The result was to make the neighborhood even more tense and hassled: the more people took speed to deal with the street, the more crazy speed freaks there were on the street. Bob Stubbs no longer kept his shop open till midnight, because there were too many manic weirdos at large after 8:00 P.M.

The Diggers, like a number of people in the Haight these days, had taken to carrying guns. Com/co published a broadside reading, "An Armed Man Is a Free Man."

The Diggers reacted with the gravest skepticism to the Monterey Pop press release that suggested the festival might donate part of its proceeds to the Diggers. They informed the *Barb* they would not accept this "guilt money," and that they preferred a half-price or free event to charity. No one had actually contacted the Diggers, and no money had in fact been offered. It was all a misunderstanding caused by an abortive scheme to get local Monterey restaurants to offer free food during the festival.

The Diggers charged that the promoters of Monterey Pop were well aware their publicity would draw as many as 100,000 people while the Monterey Fairgrounds held only 20,000 and the arena itself sat only 5,000. The Diggers suspected they were being called in to participate in the festival for riot control purposes. But their fundamental criticism was the "old star/manager/booking agent syndrome." Monterey Pop, they predicted, would be "a rich man's festival. They will not turn people on to the fact that the San Francisco bands, the Dead in particular, don't look on themselves as separated from the community, but live in the streets."

June 1. "The Flower Children," sung by Marcia Strassman, was No. 115 on the charts. A writer in the *East Village Other* reported to New Yorkers that the "gropings and fumblings" in the Haight "may not reach the fruition of a true utopia, which the world has never seen, but one leaves San Francisco with the feeling that it is here and now where the new world, a human world of the twenty-first century, is being constructed."

The long-awaited new Beatles album was out: *Sgt. Pepper's Lonely Hearts Club Band.*

The cover was a collage of famous faces, largely film stars but also Bob Dylan, Edgar Allan Poe, Karl Marx, Lenny Bruce, Oscar Wilde, the English satanist Aleister Crowley and E. W. Evans-Wentz, the translator of the *Tibetan Book of the Dead.* The mustachioed Beatles stood in front of this mob dressed in brightly colored marching band uniforms adorned with braid and frogging and epaulets. Next to them were wax museum statues of the callow 1964 Beatles in their dark Mod suits.

Inside the album cover—a folding album cover with room for lots of artwork, rather than a simple cardboard sleeve to hold the record —was a sheet of stiff paper printed with various bits of material such as a cut-out mustache, two embroidered uniform stripes and a badge showing the face of "Sgt. Pepper," the fictive leader of the variety show presented on the album. Apparently you were supposed to cut them out and do things with them, though most people reverently kept the sheet intact with the album cover.

So this was what they'd been up to for all these months. The music had only a faint resemblance to the bright pop tunes that had made the Beatles famous. Instead of clean and simple arrangements, the music was a rich, dense texture of overdubbed voices and orchestral sounds. The lyrics were printed on the back cover, a novelty in a rock and roll record but a necessity now, because it was no longer easy to make out the words as they were sung. The music had more of the lurching rhythms and ominous, bittersweet tone of "Strawberry Fields," more sitar, more curious sound effects.

There was no denying it—the Beatles were taking psychedelics, just as everyone had been half daring to hope. What's more, they were talking about them as if they knew what to do about them. Fixing a hole (in the mind?) where the rain gets in—was this some kind of Beatle yoga? With our love (or was it theirs?), we (they?)

could change the world? And at the very beginning of the Summer of Love, the most popular musical group in the world was recording the story of a teenage runaway, "She's Leaving Home."

A *San Francisco Chronicle* column that outlined walking tours of the city visited Hippie Hill. The poet Richard Brautigan guided the columnist around, asking her to point out the quietness and color of the scene.

One of the busiest institutions in the Haight was the newest, founded in May. The twenty-four-hour Haight-Ashbury Switchboard was getting a hundred calls a day, mostly from people asking where they could find a place to stay or begging for help on a bad drug trip. Switchboard operators also had to be ready for the occasional trivia calls, such as "What was Gandhi's sign?"

June 5.   Moby Grape's first album was released with an unprecedented publicity splash. Columbia Records rented the Avalon Ballroom for a press party and pointed out that it was releasing not one but five single records simultaneously with the album, to publicize the fact that all five members of the band were songwriters.

The Grape's manager was the same Matthew Katz who had once managed Jefferson Airplane, and there was talk that Columbia wanted to buy him out of the Grape. He was suing the Airplane for $2.5 million, and his original demand for cover art on the Grape album would have identified the group as "Matthew Katz's Moby Grape."

There was a hip fashion show ("fash-in") on the Berkeley campus featuring designers who had made costumes for rock musicians. The daily papers had stories about the new drug STP and stressed that "no known antagonist" could bring you down from a bum trip.

June 7.   Three members of Moby Grape were arrested for contributing to the delinquency of minors. They had been found parked on a fire trail in the hills above Sausalito with three seventeen-year-old girls.

Buses were rerouted off Haight Street. The Juvenile Justice Commission was returning two hundred minors a month to their families from the Haight-Ashbury.

June 8.   A half-million-dollar mescaline factory was busted in the Marin County suburb of Fairfax.

Tom Donahue's operation at KMPX-FM had become a roaring success. The second week on the air, disc jockeys at his old AM station KYA had told him their listeners were asking them for records he was playing. KYA had successfully overcome its scruples about playing hippie music, to the extent that it announced a Big Brother single as "a KYA exclusive!"

KMPX had already acquired a full-time ad salesman, a veteran of the Red Dog Saloon named Milan Melvin. When KMPX came on the air, Melvin offered his services to Donahue, saying he'd even sweep the floors.

He started selling radio time in May, using a sales technique perfectly attuned to the new breed of potential advertisers. With a gold earring in one ear and wearing a purple cape, a top hat and a buckskin shirt, he would descend on a boutique with an FM radio and demonstrate the sound of KMPX on the air. Once he left his radio at Mnasidika and ran to the radio station to get Donahue to mention the store; he made the sale. On another occasion he offered an instrument store a cut rate on a radio spot in exchange for a violin case he figured would make a good briefcase.

KMPX was the only station in town with female sound engineers, because one of the DJs had fallen in love with a waitress at a North Beach vegetarian restaurant and cagily suggested to Donahue that the station hire some female engineers rather than those ugly old male engineers. The waitress got her third-class license in May and on June 5 the station hired a second female engineer.

June 9.   A twenty-four-hour free medical clinic opened at 558 Clayton, right at the corner of Haight Street.

The free doctor occasionally available at the Digger Office had proved entirely inadequate for the Haight Street crowds. The new

Haight-Ashbury Free Medical Clinic had thirty doctors donating part of their time and scores of volunteers doing nonmedical jobs, all unpaid (except that some of the volunteers used the clinic as a place to sleep).

The founder was David Smith, a medical student who had lived in the Haight while doing his internship at San Francisco General Hospital. When bad drug reactions and ordinary medical problems afflicting hippies started showing up at General, he tried to get the hospital to put aside two hippie beds. But the drift of city policy toward the Haight community during the spring, particularly the firing of the head of the Alcohol and Drug Screening Unit, had convinced Smith that the city was going to deny hippies medical care for political reasons, despite the physician's oath to help the afflicted. And coincidentally, the Haight was the perfect place for Smith to study his medical specialty, clinical toxicology, which is the study of ailments caused by medicines.

The idea of a free clinic for the Haight occurred to him after the University of California Medical Center symposium on "Psychedelic Drugs and the Law" that Leary and Alpert had addressed in January. By the time the clinic opened in June—prepared to treat venereal disease, drug reactions and foot ailments as well as to give out first aid—there was a crying need. It was immediately crowded with patients and, by the natural evolution of things, also became the center of a network that arranged floor space for people without a place to sleep.

"San Francisco (Be Sure to Wear Flowers in Your Hair)," a song predicting a "love-in" in San Francisco that summer, was a new single record on the sales charts. The songwriter was John Phillips, the Mamas and the Papas' leader and a director of Monterey Pop, and the singer was his friend Scott McKenzie. *Royal's World Countdown*, a pop music magazine that had joined the Underground Press Syndicate, put McKenzie on its cover and reported that he had worn daisies while recording "San Francisco" and that two of his friends had meditated hour upon hour in the recording studio.

The Diggers printed a sardonic response: wear a flower in your hair "and if San Francisco doesn't work out we can always do it in London, sings John Phillips."

Ads appeared in underground papers for "The Hip Tourist Agency," which would take small groups on guided tours of the Haight-Ashbury. The ads were obviously aimed at straights who might buy a souvenir copy of the *Barb* or the *Oracle* from one of the importunate magazine salesmen who stood on street corners in the Haight and even knocked on the windows of the cars stuck in traffic. Vendors were hawking underground papers on Broadway and even downtown in the Financial District.

June 10. An AM rock station sponsored a music festival on Mount Tamalpais in Marin County that had the makings of a be-in. There was an Indian tipi, a geodesic dome with a light show inside, a nine-foot-high statue of the Buddha (originally projected at forty feet), and various games to play among the redwoods, like a toboggan slide on pieces of cardboard down a straw-covered slope, a set of automobile tire swings arranged so that the motion of each swing affected the others. The Mount Tamalpais road was closed to automobiles for the two days of the Magic Mountain Fantasy Fair, and ticket holders were transported ten miles up the hill in a hundred "Trans-Love" buses. Radio station KFRC promised to donate part of the profits to the Hunters Point Child Care Center.

Some 15,000 came on Saturday to see major second-line bands like the Sons of Champlin and the Morning Glory, and another 21,000 on Sunday to see the Airplane, the Doors, Country Joe and the Steve Miller Blues Band. But this was no be-in. Hardly anyone danced in the Valley of Dance a hundred yards from the amphitheater. The swings were half-occupied. Business was slack at the booths, even the one selling "Acid Shakes" for 50¢. The owner of Far Fetched Foods in the Haight did such poor business at his health food booth that he tried to give away his vegetables while they were still ripe. The parachute motif showed signs of becoming a cliché as three parachutists landed each day.

June 11.   Bill Graham married Bonnie MacLean, a Fillmore em-
ployee who had been doing posters for him since Wes Wilson quit.
Her style was Wilsonesque but sweeter and less muscular, without
Wilson's sense of crisis and exhilaration.

STP's bad publicity, both in the newspapers and through the dope
grapevine had driven the price down to $1 a hit, then 10¢, then
nothing. *Inner Space* magazine, however, praised STP as "pure molecular energy, beyond mysticism, beyond love, beyond Maya: IT."
But the writer acknowledged that in addition to raising the mystical
kundalini serpent from the base of one's spine, making the vocal
chords vibrate mantrically and causing the body to arrange itself into
spontaneous yoga postures, STP also "shakes you clean like a dust-
rag" and that the freak-out ratio was said to be 60 percent.

The cover of the eighth issue of the *Oracle* showed a mountain with
the words "San Francisco" on its snowy peak, over which three flying
saucers hovered. An op art pattern of purple rays on a flow-color
background of turquoise shading into violet formed the face of Chief
Joseph of the Nez Percé, which loomed over the mountain. Inside,
swirling patterns were everywhere, and only a third of the pages ran
text in conventional straight columns. As the issue was being printed,
Oracle workers squirted the press rollers at random with colored inks
from catsup dispensers, giving each copy of the *Oracle* a unique color
scheme. The entire press run of 100,000 copies was scented with
Jasmine Mist perfume.

   This was the Indian issue, with articles on Indian mythology,
native Indian psychedelics, Indian rights, the Indian style of living
on the land. The real theme of the issue, though, was spiritual
development in accordance with prophecies that Western material-
ism would collapse. Both spiritual development and Western collapse implied living in the country, but what should be done about
the great wave of youth rolling toward the Haight-Ashbury now that
school was out? All the *Oracle* could suggest was the Exchange, the
old Digger phone number, which was soliciting and providing information about rural areas and communal living, and the Kiva, by now

virtually synonymous with the Exchange. The Kiva's ultimate goal was to assist "the thousands of seekers coming to San Francisco in finding their way back to nature." At the moment the Kiva was located on a vacant lot on Hayes Street north of the Panhandle, between Ashbury and Clayton, where building projects were planned.

The *Oracle* editors warned that their best efforts had so far failed to gather civic support and material resources for the flood of visitors to come. "We feel," they wrote, "that every community in America must practice the warless way and communicate among its races and between young and old; celebrate, commune together, practice free giving and receiving in your own cities and countrysides."

In other words, please don't come to the Haight. For those who insisted on coming, they recommended bringing ("in addition to flowers and bananas") money for food and rent, sleeping bags and camping equipment, food (hundred-pound sacks of brown rice cost $12), warm clothing for San Francisco's foggy summer weather, and proper ID.

On the facing page was the Council for a Summer of Love's optimistic May 13 statement about the summer's holy pilgrimage. A boldface headline had been added: "It All Depends On . . ."

Shortly after the Be-In, when predictions of 50,000 to 100,000 new residents in the Haight were first tossed around, certain church groups began to worry. One result was the Regional Young Adult Project, sponsored by the Methodist Church, the Glide Foundation, the United Church of Christ and the San Francisco Council of Churches. With backing from a charitable foundation they were able to announce that on June 18 they would open a clearinghouse for runaways at 42 Broderick Street in the Haight, with the reassuring name of Huckleberry's for Runaways.

Word seeped back to the Haight that the Digger farm had a name of its own—Morning Star, Morningside or something. Population pressure there had gradually built. So far, most people who had taken advantage of Lou Gottlieb's nonexclusive policy had fit right in, though some had drifted away. Now the place was troubled by five or six alcoholics, mainly winos from the Sixth Street skid row in San Francisco who had first panhandled tourists in the Haight and then moved to Morning Star. They had rugged names like Nevada and Bad Annie and abrasive personalities to match; the parking lot at Morning Star was their turf, and they hit all visitors for wine money. All the psychedelic people agreed they were bringdowns, even though they contributed generously to the Morning Star brown rice fund.

One day the winos went down to the Russian River for the day, and the acidheads decided that when they returned they would be asked to leave. The winos took their expulsion with good grace and said they'd be gone in a couple of days. But the next day one of them came to Gottlieb and begged to stay. At first Gottlieb was firm, but he started to develop headaches, cold sweats, nausea and uncontrollable fits of weeping. He took this as a sign of God's will that he never order anyone off his ranch. The winos stayed.

Jefferson Airplane's "Somebody to Love" was the No. 3 song in the nation.

June 16, the first day of Monterey Pop. Friday was the festival's pop mainstream night, and apart from the English blues band Eric Burdon and the Animals and an unknown English folksinger named Beverly, it was all soft rock and crooners: the Association, the Paupers, Johnny Rivers, Simon and Garfunkel.

Already the crowd numbered 30,000 and John Phillips was predicting 100,000 or even 200,000. As it turned out, the arena held more than the Diggers had charged, but not much more—a total of 7,500. Activities were provided, however, for people outside the arena; a playground, a projection room, a stage for impromptu acts, demonstrations of closed-circuit TV and the Moog synthesizer, and about forty shops and booths, many of them recycled from the Magic Mountain Festival (including the three-headed Buddha statue). Rooms had been set aside for meditators in the Seminar Building, which later in the weekend featured a music industry colloquium moderated by Ralph Gleason and a guitar workshop with Jim McGuinn of the Byrds and Michael Bloomfield, recently of the Butterfield Blues Band.

But this was obviously no solution to the problem of 100,000 people. Led by the Dead's manager Rock Scully, who knew the ins and outs of the Monterey bureaucracy from having once worked for a local state senator, a delegation approached the right people with prophecies of riot and catastrophe if something wasn't done— namely, unless the football field and the Home Economics Building at Monterey Peninsula College were put at the disposal of campers. A stage was erected on the football field for jam sessions, and sheets were tied to the goalposts to serve as screens for animated cartoons. Word about these facilities was spread at the festival by mimeoed fliers.

Saturday morning, June 17, the number of people at the festival nearly doubled, and the main event was walking around in the high-spirited crowd, which included Brian Jones of the Rolling Stones (Mick Jagger was denied a work permit in the United States because of his pending drug case, so the Stones were not scheduled to play). A group of Los Angeles Diggers gave away free fruit and Hell's Angels were said to be guarding the fences, despite the city of Monterey's horror of the gang. A souvenir program carried messages from various bands, including a mind-blowing direct communication from the Beatles: "Love to Monterey from Sgt. Pepper's Lonely Hearts Club Band." Above all, there was a special batch of LSD from Owsley's Denver lab, the Monterey Purple or Purple Haze tabs.

Sunday afternoon was essentially San Franciscan, MCed by Chet Helms. Apart from Canned Heat from Los Angeles and a group of East Coast musicians led by Al Kooper, all the bands were living in the Bay Area: Big Brother, Country Joe, Paul Butterfield, Quicksilver, Steve Miller and the new band Mike Bloomfield had put together, Electric Flag.

But before anybody could go on stage, trouble developed. Donn Pennebaker, who had filmed the Bob Dylan documentary *Don't Look Back*, was going to shoot the festival for an ABC television special that was going to help finance the festival. For this reason no other cameras were allowed on the stage. At the last minute festival organizer Lou Adler asked all the bands to sign a release form that granted all worldwide rights for any use of the film "to the Festival." The San Francisco bands thought they smelled a rat, a slick L.A. show-biz rat. They also wanted to know why, if this was a charity event, all the bands had been paid expenses, particularly a couple of acts that seemed to be nothing more than friends or clients of Adler and Phillips.

Eventually most of the bands signed the form, once they'd been given the proper assurances. The TV show was apparently down the drain and a movie of Monterey Pop was the only way to recoup the vast expenses already incurred. But the Grateful Dead didn't sign and were not filmed. Big Brother's manager also refused to sign, but Albert Grossman, the big-time manager of Dylan and Butterfield, advised Janis Joplin to sign and she finally overruled her manager. In order to get Big Brother in the film, though, the band had to be rescheduled for a second set on Sunday night, Superstar Night.

Another band that didn't sign was Country Joe and the Fish. The reason, for at least a couple of them, was simple: STP. They were filmed anyway.

Saturday evening's show combined San Francisco and soul: Moby Grape, the L.A. jazz musician Hugh Masekela, another set by Butterfield, Laura Nyro, Jefferson Airplane, Booker T. and the MGs, and Otis Redding, whose set was cut short because Masekela had gone over his time. Redding was a big hit with his good-humored reference to the audience as the "love crowd" and his soul version of the Rolling Stones' "Satisfaction."

By now the necessity of the football field and home ec building for camping was plain. Campers already covered every available square foot of the fairground, including the parking lot, and a local property owner was renting out his field as a "sleep-in" for a dollar a night. Some of those camping at the football field weren't even troubling to visit the fairground, though, since they had already seen free all-day jam sessions with the Dead, Country Joe, Steve Miller and others.

Sunday, June 18, was Paul McCartney's birthday. To celebrate, he told the press that in the past year he had taken LSD four times and it had made him "a better, more honest, more tolerant member of society, brought closer to God." He was not advocating LSD, he said; he didn't "want to 'turn the world on'" (despite the fact that the final words on the *Sgt. Pepper* album seemed to say just that), but if the leaders of the world's nations were to take LSD even once, they would be ready to "banish war, poverty and famine."

At Monterey on Sunday afternoon, Ravi Shankar performed a lengthy raga on sitar despite threatening rain. Thousands of orchids were thrown into the audience. Before he performed, Shankar complimented the audience on its selection of incense, which accorded with Indian custom, and afterwards he remarked on the religious and inspirational atmosphere of the afternoon.

That evening's show, the psychedelic superstar lineup, began with the Blues Project, Big Brother, an L.A. group called the Group with No Name (making possibly its first and last performance) and the Byrds. This was Big Brother's second set of the festival, which the announcer mistakenly attributed to "popular demand," creating an instant mystique about the band. Janis Joplin was fully equal to it, wearing a gold lamé dress rather than the beatnik clothes she'd worn on Saturday.

This was the show, all right, that everybody'd been waiting for. The Who played a dramatic set that ended with Pete Townshend's ritual destruction of his guitar. Then the Grateful Dead came on, upholding the San Francisco style. Rhythm guitarist Bob Weir told the audience, "You know what folding chairs are for, don't you? They're for folding up and dancing on." Between numbers the MC, Peter Tork of the Monkees, bantered with bassist Phil Lesh and heard Lesh suggest to him, over the microphones, that since this was the last night and there were a lot of people outside the stadium, it made sense to open the gates and let them in. All of a sudden it didn't feel like banter but something backed up with crowd menace. Tork nervously asked that the gates be opened, and a huge mass of people from outside joined the stadium audience. After the Dead came the Jimi Hendrix Experience in its first American appearance, showing off the titanic, roaring effects of Hendrix's guitar. At the end of his set Hendrix knelt in front of his guitar and set it on fire.

Inevitably the final act was a letdown, though the Mamas and the Papas apparently expected their appearance with Scott McKenzie would generate mass hysteria. Half an hour before they went on in their long medieval robes, security precautions had been doubled around the stage, and a limousine readied for their exit.

As of midnight on Sunday, the crowd at the Monterey Fair Grounds had been estimated at between 55,000 and 90,000. Monterey Pop was similar to the Be-In not only because it, too, was a huge, exhilarated gathering, but also because it was uncharacteristically peaceful for its size and density. At a press conference on Sunday, Monterey police chief Frank Marinello announced that he had already sent half his security force home. "I feel the hippies are my friends," he told the press, "and I am asking one of them to take me to the Haight-Ashbury." Festival director Lou Adler and publicist Derek Taylor gave him a glass and leather necklace imprinted with a peace symbol, and Taylor told him, "Now you're one of us."

June 20.   On Tuesday, the Fillmore Auditorium began putting on shows six nights a week, with an opening bill of the Airplane and Jimi Hendrix.

When the Grand Canyon be-in scheme collapsed, the planners had proposed that local summer solstice celebrations be held all over the country instead. Allen Cohen sent a message to all the Underground Press Syndicate papers recommending "indigenous native tribal celebrations in every urban center or natural surrounding countryside of America." He included a dignified prayer written by the medicine man Black Elk, and a letter of witchcraft lore from the English witch Sybil Leek that called for ox roasts, maypoles, jugglers and other medieval trappings.

In San Francisco, the Diggers took a leading part in solstice plans. Emmett Grogan wrote that while the Be-In in January had been a shuck, at the summer solstice the people would "build their courage and leave be-ins to the college students, ad men and news medea. They will look to their brothers and not men who claim to be their leaders. And they will never tell anyone what they saw." The solstice was planned as another "do-in" like the Invisible Circus.

By 4:30 on the morning of June 21, the official beginning of the solstice and consequently of the Summer of Love, a thousand people had gathered on Twin Peaks to watch the dawn from the highest point in San Francisco. A *Chronicle* reporter found a nineteen-year-old "rock promoter" who was dressed in robes for the occasion and eager to talk. "I don't think anybody thought the sun was really going to rise," he said, "but I stood up here and I pointed to where I knew it was and I said, 'Get bright, get bright.' And everyone looked and there were chants and drums and incense and bells and flares and red smoke bombs and somebody even brought a portable record player and some Beatles records."

From Twin Peaks the sunrise watchers eventually wandered down to the Haight, a mile or so to the north, and joined the crowds moving in the direction of Golden Gate Park. The solstice celebration was scheduled for Speedway Meadow, a long, tree-lined meadow adjoining the Polo Field.

As announced, the style of the solstice was in conscious opposition to that of the nominally centralized Be-In. Wooden stages were set up at the sides of the meadow, and a flatbed truck served as a third stage at one end. Over to one side Diggers were barbecuing a lamb and frying hamburgers in shovels. Paper flowers decorated the park shrubbery. A lady in a tent painted people's faces. An eight-foot canvas globe was bounced around above the crowd to shouts of "Turn on the world!" There were archers, magicians, jugglers and many freelancers playing whistles, flutes and guitars and even a Tibetan liturgical orchestra complete with conch shells, Chinese oboes and six-foot-long trumpets. The Dead, Big Brother, Quicksilver and other bands played, using Fender speakers and amps surreptitiously borrowed by the musicians from Monterey Pop. And there were no speeches. When the sun was setting, many of those who remained marched toward the sea, as at the Be-In.

The solstice was over. A beautiful day, but was there a kind of unease?

It was generally agreed that the spirit of the solstice didn't compare with that of the Be-In. Maybe it was because of the more confined space of Speedway, or because the crowd was smaller than the Be-In's and *much* smaller than that at the Monterey Pop just three days before. Some people blamed it on the decentralization of the event, which perhaps dissipated the sense of unity.

But there was no comparing the Be-In and the solstice celebration. The Be-In was the beginning of something unknown, while the solstice was the official beginning of the Summer of Love. Until now the failures and conflicts in the Haight-Ashbury enterprise might be regarded as mere eddies in the current that the cosmic flow would untangle. But now, with its political rifts unhealed, thousands of newcomers pouring in and the tribal elders urging people to get out of the Haight, the community had officially entered its self-proclaimed Summer of Love, for better or worse. Now it would succeed or fail.

June 22. Again the police ordered a crowd on Haight Street to disperse and made some arrests. The Juvenile Authority tentatively decided to equip the Polytechnic High School gymnasium with Civil Defense cots if the influx reached emergency proportions. This was not intended to subsidize a new tribal way of life, for it would be policed. The avowed purpose was to return children to their parents.

Chief Kiely of Park Station withstood the recent tide of civic concern for the Haight. *He* didn't see any exploding hippie population, and estimated the number of hippies in the Haight at a fairly stable 3,000 to 4,000—an astonishingly low figure, about half as many as most observers had estimated in January and a quarter as many as Father Harris of All Saints estimated now. True, said Chief Kiely, there were about 300 new arrivals every day, but "the outflow is just about the same as the inflow" because San Francisco's summer weather was too chilly for camping and there was a great shortage of women.

Chief Kiely was right about the fast turnover, but he didn't mention another reason: the housing shortage. While a lot of newcomers were returning home, either disappointed with the Haight or easily satisfied with their adventure, the rest were moving into communes in other parts of San Francisco, or Berkeley, or going straight into the country: Sonoma County, the New Mexico desert or beyond.

"I pulled out my magic stone and asked myself if this was the right thing to do. I flipped my stone and it said it was. So I said, 'What the hell,' and jumped." Wanting to "save his soul," a nineteen-year-old New Yorker suffered fractured vertebrae and a broken right ankle when he jumped thirty-five feet off a pedestrian overpass within sight of the Fillmore Auditorium.

"San Francisco (Be Sure to Wear Flowers in Your Hair)" was the No. 5 single in the country. Bookstores offered a book entitled *Sexual Paradise of LSD;* a bargain-basement import store sold a package of printed optical effects as a "Trip Kit." Ken Kesey began a six-month jail term for his original marijuana conviction and told a reporter, "We're all preparing for the big earthquake."

June 24.   John Lennon and George Harrison announced that they too had tried LSD and felt the same about it as Paul McCartney did. Brian Epstein, their manager, said he had a bad experience and doubted he'd take it again.

A Palo Alto electronics engineer who had taught bread-making under Happening House auspices brought 400 pounds of flour to All Saints Church and baked 166 loaves of whole-grain bread in coffee cans, working from early morning to early evening. Father Harris invited divinity students to pitch in; friends and passersby also helped.

The Diggers announced that there would be another bread bake the following Saturday. This was tantamount to an admission that free food in the park had collapsed, and the *Berkeley Barb* canceled the standing notice of daily Digger Free Food in its events column.

TOP: **Newcomers in the Summer of Love**

MIDDLE: **The Diggers' free store after the Death of Money parade: Take anything you like, officers**

BOTTOM: **The "Death of Money and Rebirth of the Haight" parade, December 16, 1966**

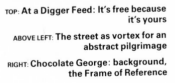

TOP: **At a Digger Feed: It's free because it's yours**

ABOVE LEFT: **The street as vortex for an abstract pilgrimage**

RIGHT: **Chocolate George: background, the Frame of Reference**

OPPOSITE: **The Panhandle during a Digger Feed**

TOP: **The Human Be-In, January 14, 1967**

LEFT: **George Harrison on Hippie Hill, August 7, 1967**

Hippie Hill

TOP LEFT: **Inside the Print Mint on Haight Street**

TOP RIGHT: **Dance posters: advertising art for acid's sake**

LEFT: **The lobby of the Fillmore Auditorium**

TOP LEFT: **The capsize of conventional wisdom**

TOP RIGHT: **Selling the *Oracle* across from the Straight Theater**

RIGHT: **Lou Gottlieb of the Morning Star Ranch**

The author at home, 1967

"Flickout" premiered at the Mission Drive-In:

"Three Awareness Levels—6 Hours! 1. 1,000-speaker psychedelic sound show 2. 50-foot-high Beatles for visual stimulation 3. millions of electronic frequencies—live and in person Country Joe and the Fish bathed in spectrums by Head Lights." Admission was free to members of the American Airlines Youth Plan, membership cards $3.

June 25.   A party of old-time Diggers left for the SDS convention in Denton, Michigan.

June 26.   More scare stories about STP, 10,000 doses of which were said to have been distributed free. The danger: convulsions could result if the tranquilizer Thorazine were administered during the "maniacal period," which could last three days. This warning was necessary, said Dr. Smith of the Free Clinic, because street hippies were carrying LSD in one pocket and Thorazine in the other for bad trips.

The press speculated that STP was "similar" to BZ, the military chemical weapon that had recently been in the news. The original stories about BZ in its warfare context had referred to it as an incapacitating agent. In the stories about STP tablets, BZ was regularly called a nerve gas.

June 27.   A new dance hall opened at the corner of Polk and O'Farrell, four blocks from the Avalon. The Western Front, as it was called, planned to be open six nights a week and offer food and crafts shops as well as a dance floor. The proprietors were the four pre–Chet Helms members of the Family Dog, doing business as the Northern California Psychedelic Cattlemen's Association, as one might have guessed from the first week's lineup: the Charlatans and Bill Ham's jazz and light show group, Light Sound Dimension. A dance permit was on appeal.

Eric Hodgeman, announcer at the Avalon and also at events in the Panhandle, quit the Council for a Summer of Love and accused it of being establishment. He charged the council was cutting down its concert program to six hours of music and chanting a week, 11:30 A.M. to 5:30 P.M. on Sundays in the little triangle west of Kezar Stadium, when they should be going 24 hours a day every day.

June 29.   In London, Mick Jagger was found guilty of possessing four amphetamine pills and given three months in jail. Keith Richards was found guilty of allowing hashish to be smoked at his house and given one year.

The Avalon Ballroom added Thursday night audition shows to its schedule, so it was now open four nights a week. "Crowds bug you?" read the ads; "The Avalon Thursdays."

Thursday became known not only as quiet night but as the "Dealers' Convention," from the great number of young men wearing long bulky pea jackets who clustered around the stage.

June 30.   Vietnamese strongman Nguyen Cao Ky bowed out in favor of Vietnamese strongman Nguyen Van Thieu. Mario Savio and two other Free Speech Movement celebrities went to jail thirty months after their arrests. Ken Kesey received a ninety-day sentence for the rooftop bust to run concurrently with the six-month sentence for his first grass bust. President Johnson's popularity rose from 42 percent to 58 percent.

End of the year's rain season. The Springtime of Love had been the third rainiest in twenty-five years.

On Haight Street fun-loving hippies were calling in false fire alarms almost daily. There was a new drug on the street, an animal tranquilizer named phencyclidine or PCP, although the dealer thought it was tetrahydrocannabinol, the main psychoactive ingredient of marijuana. Every morning he parked his bus on Haight Street and lectured on the benefits of "THC" from the hood while a partner stealthily sold it from the back of the bus. For a brief while he even hired a man to walk around Haight Street wearing a sandwich board reading, "Ask Me about THC."

The *Haight-Ashbury Maverick,* a direct imitation of the *Oracle* with a less taxing format that was aimed largely at tourists, published a "Survival Manual" written by Peter Krug of the Wild Colors store. Krug had originally planned to publish the compendium of handy hints and lists of free or cheap necessities via com/co, but com/co was no longer in business for outside contributions. Chester Anderson was back in New York, either raising money for his own Communication Company or simply making his getaway from the highly charged scene back on Arguello Street.

July 1.   Another rock festival on Mount Tamalpais, the Festival of Growing Things. Virtually all the major San Francisco bands were on the bill except the Airplane and the Dead. All who attended were given free packets of flower seeds.

Ads appeared in underground papers for the Haight-Ashbury Models Society "for serious artists and photographers." Sidewalk vendors of underground papers complained of police harassment. The Digger heavies came back from Michigan.

July 2.   The Straight Theater announced that it would soon open. Plans had expanded to develop the Straight's block as "Red Mountain Square," and the *Barb* reported paranoia among shop owners on the block. The owner of the Garuda Coffee Shop was certain that the owner of a North Beach topless nightclub was an investor in the Straight.

July 4.   The *Santa Rosa Press-Democrat* had published a series of articles on Morning Star Ranch, and local hostility resulted in a petition against it. On July 4, Lou Gottlieb was given a cease and desist order, signed by the Health Department, that gave him twenty-four hours to cease operations as an "organized camp." Of all things.

At All Saints a Housing Office opened, listing cheap or free places to crash.

July 5.   The Digger known as Billy Batman, who ran an art gallery on Fillmore Street, became a father, and the home birth was celebrated in a poem, "The Birth of Digger Batman," by the poet, novelist and sometime *Oracle* writer Kirby Doyle. Digger was the child's given name, and from this time forward the original Mime Troupe axis of the Diggers stopped using the name Diggers and started calling themselves the Free City Collective.

July 7.   *Time* did a cover story on "The Hippies" in which it called Morning Star "perhaps the most encouraging development of the hippie philosophy to date" because of the neat rows of cabbages, turnips, lettuce and onions in its garden.

July 9.   The tourist season was at its height and on Sunday it was hard to walk down the sidewalk on Haight Street, much less drive in the dead-crawl traffic. The tourists whose presence was making life even more difficult in an already difficult situation had obviously come to gawk at what they despised. The ones who deigned to get out of their cars walked around insulting the people and the merchandise in the stores. They rarely bought anything but *The Love Book* or the photo poster of the street sign at Haight and Ashbury.

This Sunday, there were run-ins all day long between tourists and hippies, the majority of whom by this time were Haight residents of under four months' standing. At one point somebody poured paint out of a window onto the sidewalk. In front of Tracy's Donuts—on the shadowy south side of Haight Street, where the bikers hung out and eerier things happened than on the north side—a crowd gathered in an ugly mood and occasionally tried to tear off tourists' neckties. Around 7:30 some unidentified young men stopped their cars in the intersection of Haight and Ashbury, the second attempt that day to stop traffic altogether. Hippies goofed around among the stalled tourists' cars, jumping on the bumpers and pretending to take photographs. When the police showed up, somebody threw a bottle that missed the police and hit a hippie girl. There followed shouts of "Fascist bastards! Police brutality!"

Twenty police patrol cars arrived, and in the hour-long melee that followed, nine people were arrested and four badly injured. A girl who had shouted, "Revolution! Revolution! Get the cops!" had her jaw broken in two places with a three-foot riot stick. In the scuffle that ensued when a man walking his sheepdog was arrested, an officer killed the dog with a riot stick.

July 11.   At 3:30 in the morning, eighteen people were arrested at 42 Belvedere Street for possession of twelve marijuana cigarettes, two tablets of an unknown substance and two rolls of suspected pornographic film. The police had come on a noise complaint, but when they decided it was a drug arrest a lithe figure swung into the room from the roof where he'd been hiding and announced, "It's not a party if I'm not here." It was the ballet dancer Rudolf Nureyev. Police flashlights easily picked out the figure of his dance partner, Dame Margot Fonteyn, cowering on the roof in her white mink coat.

Stories differed on how they had come to visit 42 Belvedere in the wee hours of the morning. Some said Nureyev, Fonteyn and a party of friends had decided to drive through the Haight-Ashbury after a midnight dinner and were attracted by the sounds of a party. Others said fans had left the address backstage at the Opera House. In any case, charges were quickly dropped against all eighteen people, including the Nureyev-Fonteyn party, which included the assistant manager of the Seattle Symphony and two hairdressers. At 5:45 that afternoon the assistant district attorney declared the evidence was insufficient to show who was contributing to disturbance of the peace or who had possession of the drugs. As he read the news on the air, a KMPX DJ commented, "I guess there's a lesson here. If you're going to take a fall, do it with a name."

Dame Margot was overheard saying on the telephone, "As if we could smoke marijuana! We don't even smoke cigarettes!" Nevertheless, that night two hundred hippies joyfully snake-danced in front of the Opera House where Nureyev and Fonteyn were performing.

In Sonoma County, Lou Gottlieb pleaded innocent to running Morning Star without the sanitary facilities required by law for an organized camp. "Morning Star is not an organized camp," he said.

"I hope it will be in the future." The people staying there were not campers but his personal guests.

The move to the country had affected musicians as well as street people. While the Grateful Dead was on tour, the members' old ladies were in New Mexico scouting out rural commune sites. With 710 Ashbury largely empty, a bunch of Pranksters had moved in.

July 14.   Summer race riots materialized in Newark, New Jersey, and spread quickly to ghettos in other cities. In the Haight-Ashbury, tension between the races had been growing. It was generally ascribed to blacks "coming up from the Fillmore" by newcomers who were unaware that blacks had lived in the neighborhood before hippies. The Fillmore threatened to erupt like Newark.

The University of California ruled that students who took, distributed or possessed drugs would be "subject to disciplinary action, including dismissal from the university." The original proposal had called for mandatory dismissal.

July 16.   There were two or three Free Buses, not counting the yellow-painted Digger Bus, running up and down Haight Street from time to time, picking up anybody who seemed to need a ride. The owner of the Provo Free Store in Berkeley ran a Provo Bus from his store to Telegraph Avenue every afternoon, then sometimes to the woodsy bohemian community of Canyon in the Berkeley hills but more often to Haight Street and back. The driver told the *San Francisco Chronicle,* "There may be five hundred meth freaks in the Haight who'll get on a bus going anywhere."

July 17.   A full-scale exhibition of dance-poster artists' work opened at a San Francisco gallery. It was not the first recognition the poster artists had gotten from the art world: the Oakland Art Museum had collected posters since early 1966, and shows had already been held at the San Francisco Art Institute and another art gallery. What made "The Joint Show" at the Moore Gallery significant was the direct involvement of the artists, who did a series of original posters to advertise it.

The show seemed designed to demonstrate that there was more to these artists than posters. The souvenir program was an exact 5½-by-10-inch blowup of a Zig-Zag cigarette paper packet containing samples of their art, statements of philosophy and even astrological charts. In addition to the posters on display (for sale at $2.50), there were oil paintings by Kelly, Mouse, Moscoso, Griffin and Wilson at considerably higher prices.

The opening brought out more than the usual number of society people, some wearing love beads, to drink champagne and listen to Country Joe and the Fish. The artists themselves delighted in going out on the roof with their old ladies and smoking grass fairly openly, confident that the police would not trouble this upper-crust assembly.

The Western Front appeared before the Board of Permit Appeals for its dance permit. Police had banned dancing at the club and Lieutenant Leo Hayes denounced it as a "den of iniquity." The board rejected the permit appeal.

The Fillmore ghetto hadn't exploded yet, but Newark was in the papers every day. In the Haight people debated whether to stay indoors like good Hobbits when the riot came or whether to get guns and stand their ground.

July 19.   A Digger and Mime Troupe actor named David Simpson appeared in court on a routine bust for obstructing traffic. To the court's surprise, the young actor refused the services of a public defender and demanded to act as his own lawyer. His unexpectedly vigorous and acute defense included an attack on the constitutionality of the public nuisance law, P.C. 320, which had long been used against hippies as a general-principles bust.

The judge denied that particular petition and cautioned the courtroom audience of hippies against partisan displays, but Simpson's strong personality and persuasive arguments (prepared with the help of his roommate, one of the Free Store lawyers) eventually got him a hung jury. He argued that because he was not blocking traffic when arrested for handing leaflets to people in cars, he had not been a nuisance. The leaflets read, "Middle-class brothers! Loosen up, let God flow through you. Remember, we are with you as you drive through the valley of the shadow of death."

An attorney petitioned that Nureyev, Fonteyn et al. be prosecuted. Otherwise, he argued, they were receiving preferential treatment. The D.A. answered that marijuana was not being smoked in the room when they were arrested, and the attorney immediately countered that it would be "of some value" if that criterion were adopted as a basis of whether or not to convict.

Riots in Cairo, Illinois.

July 21.   An LSD lab was uncovered in the conservative city of San Diego; it was run by a lab technician at the Salk Institute research labs and the owner of a surfboard shop.

July 23.   The Beatles were among fifty-five signers of a petition to legalize marijuana in England that was reproduced in a full-page London *Times* ad. The next day the Beatles were said to be vacationing on a Greek island far from the enraged public reaction to their signings. They were getting it from both left and right, from those who were infuriated that they should have signed such a petition (including their titles as Members of the Order of the British Empire) and from leftists who attacked them for running off to Greece, where three months before a right-wing military junta had staged a coup.

The U.S. Army was ordered into Detroit to put down rioting. In New York, riots broke out in Spanish Harlem.

July 25.   Peter Cohon told reporters that the Diggers had begun work on the Reno Hotel at 272 Sixth Street in order to make it a free hotel, with the owner's permission. "We want a free theater, free movies, a hospital," he said. The place was big, with 482 rooms —indeed, part of the building was the old Calliope Company loft where the Acid Test Graduation had been staged. The Reno had one big drawback: it was in the heart of skid row.

"Hungry?" read a com/co sheet. "Turn on to food at All Saints." The sheet was advertising a class in nutrition put on by Happening House, but it drew a lot of people expecting free food.

Headlines: "Rioters Rout Cops." "State Guard Called Out in Toledo."

July 26.   The world premiere was held for *The Love-Ins,* the Haight-Ashbury movie from the producer of *Twist Around the Clock, Hootenanny Hoot* and other exploitation films. "The hippies and diggers are here!" read the ads for the film, which was set on a college campus with a sinister Leary-type acid messiah professor as villain; "with the way-out excitement that's turning on America today!" The Diggers protested the use of their name and the admission fee, and called the film "mind death."

But producer Sam Katzman was proud of his film. His writer had spent a full six weeks in the Haight doing research. "I think," said Katzman, "that half the kids who see this film are going to lay off LSD." Presumably they would do so after the modern dance scene where Susan Oliver freaks out on acid and thinks she's meeting the White Rabbit, the Caterpillar, Tweedledum, Tweedledee and the Red Queen.

Emmett Grogan visits London to address a Conference on the Dialectics of Liberation.

Tanks employed in Detroit. State Guard called out in South Bend, Indiana. Firebombing in Detroit, Oakland, the Fillmore. Black gangs from Harlem doing early-hours hit-and-run raids on Manhattan stores.

In the Haight-Ashbury a rumor spread that the riot would start at 6:30. Bikers passed the word that so far as they were concerned,

nobody had better make trouble. The jeweler's at Haight and Ashbury removed its window displays and many of the HIP stores did
likewise.

Still the streets didn't clear. Six-thirty came, and eight-thirty, ten,
and there were still a number of people in the street watching for
the riot, some even stoned on acid to get the most out of the
experience. Down around Haight and Fillmore, nine blocks east of
Ashbury, firebombs were thrown and police sealed off a twelve-block
area of the black neighborhood, but the apocalyptic race war did not
erupt.

Around midnight a truck drove up Haight Street after a tour of
Fillmore Street. It was full of Job Co-Op volunteers and members
of a group pushing a marijuana legalization referendum, all shouting
"Love and peace!" and handing out the remainder of their load of
100,000 carnations.

July 27.   After a false alarm on July 21, the Straight Theater finally
opened with a performance of a play called *The Dossier*. In Cuba,
Stokeley Carmichael called for a Vietnam-type war of resistance in
the black ghettos.

July 28.   A com/co bulletin appeared with a warning about "that
riot—if it hasn't happened yet," and suggested moving uphill or
westward through Golden Gate Park in case of a breakout. "Remember," it said, "San Francisco is a city made of wood. The other cities
have been mostly brick and stone. Once San Francisco gets started,
it'll burn like a crate of matches. . . . There exists the possibility of
firestorm. If this starts to happen (flames & smoke towering high in
the sky, strong winds blowing *toward* the flames), head for the
beach."

Actually, on July 28 the other riots ended and the Army began to
withdraw from Detroit. By coincidence, in usual com/co style the
bulletin provided the advice of the *I Ching* as consulted at the time
of writing, and the oracle had given Hexagram 38, K'uei (Opposition), changing to Hexagram 11, T'ai (Peace).

July 30.   The Cheetah nightclub in New York was held up for $15,000. A Methedrine lab worth $100,000 was busted in Santa Cruz. The Gallup poll showed that less than a majority now believed it was a good idea to have gotten involved in Vietnam, while the number considering it a mistake had gone up by nearly 10 percent. In any case, the public opposed President Johnson's proposal to send 100,000 more soldiers, 49 percent to 40 percent.

Food and Drug Administration commissioner James L. Goddard visited the Haight-Ashbury Free Clinic and the I/Thou Coffee House, where Ron Thelin met him and tried to convince him of the worth of the macrobiotic diet. And Owsley's latest drug on the market had been christened FDA.

July 31.   The Free Clinic held a benefit concert at the Fillmore, featuring Big Brother, the Charlatans, Blue Cheer and the Anonymous Artists of America. The comedian Bill Cosby, who was living on a houseboat in Sausalito, turned up and drummed for a while with the Charlatans.

This was the first fund-raising event the clinic had been allowed. Originally Dr. Smith had set the clinic up as a private practice, David E. Smith & Associates, in order to sidestep the health code restrictions that apply to a charity clinic, but as such it could not legally accept donations. By now he had found a licensed nonprofit corporation willing to merge with the clinic, leaving Smith as the director. Besides holding benefit shows, the clinic could legally place a donation can in its office to collect the spare change of patients or visitors.

Mick Jagger and Keith Richards were freed by a London court. The lower court had erred, a judge ruled, in telling the jury that the nude girl wrapped up in a rug at the time of the bust had been smoking hashish.

August 1.   The Straight Theater's appeal for a dance permit was opposed by police chief Nelder, who cited a "high instance of crime" near folk rock dances. By this point the backers of the Straight had spent around $65,000 satisfying the building, health and safety and fire code inspectors in order to open as a dance hall.

Hans Raj Gupta, mayor of Delhi, India, visited the Haight. One of his aides compared hippies to the Hindu wandering ascetics known as sadhus, but noted that sadhus did not use drugs.

Not LSD, maybe, but Haight Street shops—all of which, from head shops like the Psych Shop to clothing boutiques, sold basic marijuana paraphernalia such as rolling papers and roach clips—had already discovered a stemless clay pipe called a *chilam,* which was used by the ganja-smoking sadhus of Benares.

August 2.   Another clean-in on Haight Street. The *Barb* reported that LSD Rescue, a bum-trip talkdown service that had made extravagant claims of talking down four hundred people a week in December, was being revived and was now claiming thirty calls a week. No reason was given for its lapse, but the organization had been accused of talking bum trips into worse ones. One young woman said she called when she was stoned on acid and worrying about whether LSD had damaged her chromosomes and deformed the child she was carrying. "Don't worry," she said the LSD Rescue operator told her, "LSD kills babies."

August 3.   Dr. Ellis D. Sox pronounced Haight-Ashbury restaurants the likeliest in town to have hair or bacteria in their food. Eight were ordered to hearings on the revocation of their food permits: the Garuda, the Drogstore, Love Burgers and five straight-owned places.

A man named John Kent Carter, also known as Jacob King or Shob, was found dead in his apartment just a few blocks outside the Haight. He had been stabbed twelve times, once through the heart. His right arm had been cut off cleanly above the elbow and removed. His girlfriend told newspapers that Shob had been carrying $3,000 in cash two days before.

Carter had been one of the best-known acid dealers in the Haight, and the community chewed over the story with horrified fascination.

The Mob did it, the CIA, did it, sinister forces from the nether world, a karmic debt. Some fellow dealers recalled Shob Carter having a paranoid habit of handcuffing the briefcase he kept his money in onto his wrist to prevent theft—his right wrist.

No matter which way you turned it, though, somebody had actually been killed in the Haight. An acid dealer had been killed.

August 5.   The No. 1 song in both England and the United States was the new Beatles single "All You Need Is Love." In England, the No. 2 song was "San Francisco (Be Sure to Wear Flowers in Your Hair)"; in the United States, the No. 7 song was the Airplane's psychedelic reading of *Alice in Wonderland,* "White Rabbit." In San Francisco, three or four thousand people attended an unharassed marijuana smoke-in at the Polo Field. Owners of topless nightclubs on Broadway complained that the Haight-Ashbury was cutting into their share of the tourists.

Eric Frank Dahlstrom, twenty-three, a well-known motorcycle racer, was stopped by sheriff's deputies in the Sonoma County town of Sebastopol. He was driving Shob Carter's car and carrying $2,600 and Shob's pistol. In the back of the car was a severed arm wrapped up in a black and red suede cloth bag.

August 6.   KMPX-FM went rock and roll twenty-four hours a day.

A bearded black man was found dead in a sleeping bag near Point Reyes Lighthouse in coastal Marin County. The first news reports did not identify him, but he was the famous acid dealer Superspade. He had suffered a puncture wound in the left chest and a bullet was lodged in the base of his skull. He had apparently been thrown over a 250-foot cliff, but the sleeping bag had snagged on rocks and undergrowth 40 feet down. When found he had been dead about three days.

Since his legal troubles in the spring, when he gave his address as 848 Clayton, Superspade had lived in the quiet Richmond District with an eighteen-year-old woman who reported him missing on August 5. When found he had only $15 in his wallet, but friends claimed he was carrying between $30,000 and $55,000 three days before he disappeared. Rumor had it that Shob Carter had planned to front Superspade $3,000 for part of the three ounces of LSD Superspade was going to buy—until they both died, within a day of each other.

August 7.   At three this Monday afternoon, about two hundred people attended a meeting on Hippie Hill at the behest of a new organization calling itself the Flame, symbolized by banners with a design of a phoenix arising from flames.

Like the other sporadic public meetings since spring, it quickly bogged down in an inconclusive exchange of irreconcilable viewpoints—quietists proposing that everyone get his head in the right place and Diggers demanding that everything be free, with endless variations in between. The sole plan that emerged was for a nightly torch parade, inspired by the recent cross-country peace-torch walk, starting at the Calm Center and proceeding to Alvord Lake near Hippie Hill.

The leadership of the Flame, another shuffle of the Council for a Summer of Love, inclined to the vision of the earliest generation of HIP shop owners: a self-sufficient community that lived on the sales of its creative output. Besides having torch parades, the Flame was using money collected from tourists to serve meals to indigent hippies, since the All Saints bread-baking was only twice a week and the Diggers/Free City Collective was confining its food activities to a free food-delivery service that provided groceries to a couple of dozen communes and families.

At 6:00 P.M. a car parked at Haight and Masonic, and several people emerged: a man with long hair and a mustache who wore flowered bell-bottom trousers, a denim jacket with a button reading "I'm the Head of My Community," and dark glasses shaped like hearts; a blond woman wearing a long dress and rimless grannie glasses; and a couple of reporters and photographers. They strolled up Haight Street to the park and Hippie Hill, attracting no particular attention until the man borrowed a guitar and started playing a Beatles song.

He was George Harrison, and the blonde was his girlfriend Patti Boyd.

A crowd quickly gathered and the "mystical" member of the Beatles said, "Let's go for a walk." A couple of hundred people paraded down Haight Street with George in the lead strumming the guitar. "What do you think of the Haight-Ashbury?" someone asked. "Wow," said George, "if it's all like this, it's too much." When they reached the car he excused himself to catch a 7:30 plane to Los Angeles for his sitar lesson with Ravi Shankar.

Eric Frank Dahlstrom told police he had killed Shob Carter in self-defense during an argument over bad LSD he said he'd bought from Carter. As for the severed arm: "I'm very, very hazy about that arm. The principal reason I'm in jail is LSD."

The next day his lawyer entered a plea of innocent, on the ground that Dahlstrom had lost his mind on LSD. For eighteen months, Dahlstrom said, "I tried never to come off. I had a lot of bad trips. When you voyage alone for any length of time, you're going a real hard pattern."

Acid dealers *killing* each other? This was what the New Age promised?

The vague disharmony between vision and reality had become a wrenching torture. Horror and ecstasy, two sides of a coin; a great drama being played out in these few city blocks, with good and evil changing faces any moment. Would the experiment fail? The nation, if not the world, was watching via TV, daily newspapers, *Life, Look, Time, Newsweek,* even *Playboy* and the *National Review.* George Harrison had come to visit in a season of murder. Was it best to stay in this God-fingered neighborhood and ride the drama wherever it lead, or to start anew in the country? For much of the original Haight crowd, the drama was now in Sonoma County or northern New Mexico. Perhaps it was time to get a gun of your own.

While marijuana was still in its seasonal short supply, there was more LSD than anybody wanted. The price of a tab of acid had fallen to $1 and under as demand dried up. Haight Street was speed street now, with half the hippies in the neighborhood shooting Methedrine. One out of five had tried heroin, which they used as freely as tranquilizers or barbiturates to overcome the feeling of depression that followed a week-long sleepless "speed run" of Methedrine-fueled activity. If they became junkies they became thieves, but as speeders they were physically dangerous. After a couple of days without sleep they started to "space," to fall into moments of unconsciousness while physiologically awake. Speed freaks developed hallucinations, as if the mind were struggling to dream in the absence of sleep. These hallucinations tended to be paranoid and violent.

August 10.   About 500 joined the Flame's parade and chanted "Om" on Hippie Hill.

August 11.   A New Jersey public health administrator declared that there was a new psychedelic on the market named "68" or "sex juice." Thirty hippies and twenty members of the Gypsy Jokers bike gang demonstrated against police brutality at the San Francisco Hall of Justice. Thirty-seven illegal squatters were arrested in an apartment at 474 Frederick, ranging in age from fifteen to twenty-seven; the females were all under eighteen.

A story in the *Village Voice* reported that Emmett Grogan was back in New York after his visit to Europe, talking up his plans for a "trip without a ticket" expedition of 150 San Francisco figures: the Dead, Big Brother, Steve Miller, half a dozen Beat poets, a couple of jazz musicians, the Mime Troupe, the Pranksters, the Communication Company, Mouse, some underground filmmakers, Paul Krassner. The itinerary was Harlem and the Lower East Side, London, Stonehenge, Scandinavia, Spain, Eastern Europe. "Some people will leave in Italy and become farmers," Grogan mused in the story. "Some people will die on this trip. Some will fall in love; some will fall out of love. No one knows where this trip will begin or where it will end." Grogan was said to be seeking "free money" for the enterprise.

President Johnson approved the bombing of the North Vietnamese port of Haiphong. The U.S. military admitted to having bombed Laos daily for the preceding three years without informing the American public.

August 12.   Jeffrey Allen Sacks, a Haight Street habitué who wore straight clothes and a button reading "Supersex," came into the Free Clinic saying he was freaking out. Early in the morning hours he left the clinic's twenty-four-hour Calm Center, heading for the Panhandle with the words "You'll never get me back in that institution." Then it was discovered that he had stolen penicillin tablets, a couple of disposable syringes and a bottle of tablets used to test urine samples for sugar. A couple of hours later he was seen at the corner of Haight and Ashbury handing out the latter, blue-speckled tablets that contained a highly poisonous mixture of copper sulfide and caustic soda.

Communication Company broadsides reading "Stay clean today" were passed out and police began an all-points search for Sacks. Discovered in the East Bay suburb El Cerrito, he escaped. The following day he was caught on Hippie Hill. He denied everything, and occasionally even denied that he was Supersex. Twenty-five pills were as yet unaccounted for.

Morning Star called Sonoma County sheriffs to deal with a biker problem. A group of Gypsy Jokers had moved onto the ranch, and three of them had just ordered everybody out of the Big House. Of course at Morning Star they believed the Gypsy Jokers had moved in only after sheriffs had rousted them for camping on public land and recommended that they go to Morning Star, where the rule was that nobody could get kicked out.

August 15.   Happening House tried to put on a Sam Katzman Memorial Fair in the Panhandle with crafts displays, hoping to make the Haight economically self-sufficient. Fourteen rock bands had been scheduled, but police informed Happening House that they had received complaints about concerts from people who claimed the music could be heard three blocks away. So no music. The director of the Switchboard charged the city with "trying to subdue a culture." The bands performed after all, but at tiny Sokol Hall on Page Street.

Chester Anderson published a six-page bulletin to the underground press, "Hippie Siamese Twins Split," announcing the final break between him and the Diggers at com/co. His last street rap had been published on June 8. After that date the Gestetners were taken to the basement of the Trip Without a Ticket, and he was permanently barred. Writing from Florida, he outlined plans for his own Communication Company, which he expected to operate out of the Happening House building when he got back to San Francisco.

August 17. The Flame held a press conference at All Saints to protest the ban on amplified music in the parks. The Provo Bus was sabotaged by persons unknown.

August 18. U.S. senators had threatened to withdraw American troops from Vietnam unless the upcoming Vietnamese elections were open and honest. A vocal group in the Senate had also criticized the bombing of Haiphong. President Johnson's response was to dare Congress to rescind its Gulf of Tonkin Resolution, which had given him a free hand to direct military actions in Vietnam. In July alone, the war had cost $6.51 billion.

August 20. The Flame gathered again in the Panhandle. On Mount Tamalpais there was a separate gathering called either the Summer of Love Festival of Lights or the Om Festival. Some 2,500 came to hear the Grateful Dead and then chant Om on the mountain. The Dead's generator burned out and a rhythm chorus on garbage cans completed the musical part of the evening.

As night fell, the Om chanting began on an outcropping that overlooked the north end of the Bay. At 10:30, as some people lit candles, rangers ordered the whole crowd off the state park grounds. Apart from the fire hazard, the problem was that Om Festival organizers had made the mistake of notifying the fire marshal of their event while neglecting to obtain a permit.

Happening House was informed that no rock and roll bands would ever be allowed to play in the Panhandle again. Once more the ongoing Sam Katzman Memorial Festival had its bands play at Sokol Hall. On August 20 Sam Katzman was "reincarnated" by Happening House magicians as a eucalyptus tree.

San Francisco General Hospital reported the number of drug abuse victims showing up at its clinic had gone from 150 in February to 750 in July. For weeks, half the 100 inpatient psychiatric beds had been occupied by "toxic drug reaction" cases.

August 22.   At last, about two months behind schedule, the new *Oracle* was out. The design of No. 9 was more psychedelic and unreadable than ever. Part of an essay on "Programming the Psychedelic Experience" was printed in white letters on an orange background.

Among the various occult writings included, two recognized the subtranscendental reality of Haight Street. "A Flower from the Street" gave a picture of the life lived among young people for whom Haight Street had turned from a shopping district to "an abstract vortex for an indefinable pilgrimage." It concluded, "Is community and brotherhood being built here? Is Haight Street going to take off before it is absorbed into the grade B movie of the American Mainstream, which is likely to turn into another bad Nazi flick?"

Allen Cohen's "In Memoriam for Superspade and John Carter" blamed the recent killings on a "state of mind called Mafia" and called for the removal of drugs from the context of buying and selling. "Chanting Om or Hare Krishna or Peace in America, Peace in Vietnam, or staring with attention at a candle or water coloring or beading or reading or writing poetry or painting or building or studying ancient or new scriptures or practicing yoga will keep you high until you can receive alchemical turn-on for FREE from a friend or magician or guru."

The rest was art, articles on the Buddha Mind and on Cosmic Consciousness, and poetry such as Stephen Levine's "Notes from the Genetic Journal": "As Song Master of the Phylums / I ascend the multitonic scale of evolution to the tune hummed by / the Genetic Host beaming in my chromosomes."

August 23. Happening House finally opened its promised headquarters at 409 Clayton. The building had actually been purchased by a group of doctors known to Dr. Smith of the Free Clinic. They incorporated as Happening House Venture and bought the building, because many landlords had refused to rent Smith space for psychological counseling; purchase seemed the only solution. The upper floor was for the clinic's use, and the original Happening House—not the Venture—took twelve rooms downstairs for arts and crafts classrooms.

August 24. At one in the morning, a man died in General Hospital of a skull fracture sustained when an automobile collided with his motorcycle at Haight and Shrader. He was Chocolate George, the popular Hell's Angel who ran Angel dances.

Two hundred fifty people marched on McLaren Lodge, the office of the Park and Recreation Department located just a few hundred yards north of Hippie Hill, to protest the ban on amplified music. The hippies were joined by a hundred Methodist Youth Fellowship members who, when not attending meetings of their convention, had been visiting the Haight. The department lifted the ban on music, but insisted that the march had not influenced its decision.

In Washington, D.C., a group calling itself Flower Parents Anonymous announced its formation "to help parents understand the problems and ideals of runaway youth."

In New York, the new left activists Abbie Hoffman and Jerry Rubin threw money onto the floor of the New York Stock Exchange from a balcony. Identifying themselves to the press as Diggers, they claimed that a thousand dollars had been thrown away to dramatize the meaninglessness of money. Reporters saw them tear up some ones and burn a five.

August 26. The Beatles and the Rolling Stones were photographed in Bangor, Wales, at a lecture by an Indian holy man known as the Maharishi Mahesh Yogi. This was said to be "one of his last lectures before he retires to a 'life of silence.' "

August 27. Beatles manager Brian Epstein was found dead of an accidental drug overdose at his home in London.

August 28. The decision on the Straight Theater's dance permit was postponed. Opponents of the theater bused sixty-odd neighbors to the hearing to testify that they didn't like rock and roll.

A series of daily dances began at the Muir Beach Lodge, scene of the long-ago Muir Beach Acid Test. The afternoon beach dances were free, but the evening dances inside the tavern were fund-raisers for the Vietnam Summer peace organization.

One hundred motorcycles promenaded down Dolores Street in the Mission District, a funeral cortege four blocks long for Chocolate George. Two hundred mourners attended services at the Daphne Funeral Home. Reporters covering the funeral learned to their surprise that the deceased Hell's Angel had worked for the previous twelve years at the Recreation Center for the Handicapped, handing out volleyballs to children.

After the service some 1,500 people attended a riotous wake in Lindley Meadow in Golden Gate Park, with the Angels' old favorite bands Big Brother and the Grateful Dead. Chocolate's hippie friends didn't socialize with the assembled Hell's Angels, Gypsy Jokers, Nomads, Vagabonds, Satan Slaves, Cossacks, Misfits, or Saints Executioners until the music showed up and the bikers stopped the snowball fights they were having with ice from the beer truck. When the wake was over, only four hippies had been stomped.

August 29.   Cream, the hot new English rock trio, debuted at the Fillmore for the first of six straight jam-packed, sold-out nights. The Soviet magazine *Izvestia* published an article portraying hippies as a side effect of the Vietnam war and as rebels against a machinelike and unemotional way of life. In the classified section of daily newspapers, ads appeared for Hire-a-Hippie Unlimited, but the president of the company reported no takers yet.

Wednesday sweep-ins were still taking place. Bob Stubbs was back from a four-and-a-half-month trip around the world to pick up incense and handicrafts for the Phoenix. Seventy-seven windowpanes were smashed at the Conservatory in Golden Gate Park. An Everyman's Free Store was operating in Mendocino. More riots were predicted for September, and this time storefronts were boarding up not only in the Haight but all around the Bay Area.

September 2.   The Muir Beach dances wound up with a Cosmic Car Show where Mouse, Kelly, Griffin and Wilson judged psychedelically decorated vehicles. The winners were a three-wheeled Morgan car, a customized Volkswagen sedan, a panel truck and a surrey-topped three-wheel motorcycle. The event raised $1,200 for the United Farm Workers' grape strike in Delano, California.

In Bakersfield, California, police stopped a Jefferson Airplane concert despite guitarist Paul Kantner's attempt to arouse the audience, "Come on, there's only five of them and five thousand of you!"

The Hearst Publishing Company announced a quasi-psychedelic youth magazine titled *Eye.*

September 3.   All Saints Church presented a concert by the Amplified Ohm, a rock band formed by In Gear proprietor Tsvi Strauch. Father Harris was applying for a dance permit for regular Saturday night dances at All Saints.

The *San Francisco Examiner* published a story ("Exclusive Chat with Acid King") for which a reporter armed with a photo of Owsley and a sketchy history of his activities had visited the chemist's whimsically medieval-looking house on Valley Street in Berkeley. The man who answered the door denied that he was Owsley, but the reporter deduced that he was from a peculiarity of the shape of his ear.

She was wrong. He was a house guest of Owsley's, a musician who had played lute for several of Timothy Leary's Psychedelic Celebration stage shows and looked nothing at all like Owsley. But since she was determined to have an interview, he sounded off until she figured she had her story: Drugs are better than booze, a man's home is his castle, the *Barb* was a better paper than the dailies because it wasn't "constantly violating one's right to privacy."

September 4. Senator George Romney told reporters that the Army had given him a calculatedly false impression of the war when he visited Vietnam; as he put it, "I was brainwashed." The public reaction was not to inquire how many other congressmen who had supported the war were still brainwashed, but to discount Romney as presidential material.

The same day that Romney spoke, Ralph Gleason reported the contents of an interview George Harrison had given to an English music magazine. To its own audience, it was as big news as the Romney speech: "I don't mind anybody dropping out of anything, but it's the imposition on somebody else I mind . . . It doesn't matter what you do, as long as you work."

September 5. The Beatles, now devotees of the Maharishi and practitioners of his Transcendental Meditation technique, announced that they were giving up drugs on his instruction.

September 7. Gunfire was reported at Morning Star. Police said it was due to a rivalry over a seventeen-year-old girl, but Lou Gottlieb blamed it on rabbit hunters. In Trinidad, Colorado, the pioneer rural commune known as Drop City was denied food stamps.

September 8. Bill Graham ended his summer program of keeping the Fillmore open six nights a week.

The Family Dog opened a branch in Denver, Colorado. The Denver Dog had a four-track recording studio as well as a dance floor, and the use of the same now-famous poster artists as the San Francisco dance hall. Helms announced plans for five or six Dogs worldwide, but admitted that the London Dog was in abeyance for the moment.

Why Denver? Helms gave a sort of Red Dog Saloon scheme as the reason, the attraction of a nearby rural retreat for musicians, and added that Denver was "one of the most sophisticated towns we visited." Opening night sophisticated Denver police walked right into the Dog and asked all of its patrons for IDs.

Another benefit for the Free Clinic at Longshoremen's Hall. The organizers had hoped to bring in at least $2,000, but proceeds were only around $500. After three months of operation and 12,000 patient visits, the clinic had only $150 in the bank. In the six weeks since donation cans were placed in the Clinic, less than $100 had been deposited.

September 10. Lynda Bird Johnson announced her engagement. The Hearst newspapers ran banner headlines for a story by columnist Bob Considine, "We're Clobbering Them in Vietnam." Chet Helms's house on Wilmot Street near the old Pine Street neighborhood burned down.

September 11. For the Straight Theater's second appeals hearing, the English actress Dame Judith Anderson spoke on behalf of the Straight and its plans to subsidize legitimate theater such as Shakespeare and modern dance with receipts from rock dances. With her was her nephew Luther Greene, one of the Straight's directors.

The Summer of Love was plainly drawing to an end. For a week there had been throngs of hitchhikers at the Oak Street freeway on ramp, a place that had become oddly traditional for hitchhiking although the fast lane at the bottom of a hill was a most unlikely place for a driver to want to stop.

The spare-change panhandlers disappeared from Haight Street along with the tourists, and it was no longer a struggle to get down the sidewalks. Fewer grimy, lost-looking teenagers huddled in doorways clutching lost-looking puppies or kittens. The I/Thou Coffee House, whose lines had reached out the door, was half empty. Haight Street had the tawdry, exhausted air of a beach town at the end of summer.

Peace and love, however, had not returned to the battered neighborhood. On the contrary, amphetamine and heroine were bigger problems than ever, and the Haight was a restless, fearful place. Page Street east of Masonic had always been rough, and as the nights grew longer an aura of strong-arm crime seemed to seep out of it into the rest of the neighborhood.

The press spotlight that had focused on the Haight-Ashbury all summer was looking for a new subject for the fall season. Aside from the riot of July 9, the police had maintained a low profile on Haight Street since April. The many hippies left in the Haight began to wonder how long the police would be cool once the news cameras disappeared.

The Haight might have been a burned-over territory, but the music business was doing better than ever. San Francisco was still the phenomenon of the music industry, despite the facts that it offered no major recording studios and that a number of bands, Steve Miller and Quicksilver among them, had not even signed record contracts. But *Surrealistic Pillow*, after twenty-five weeks in the Top Hundred list for albums, was still No. 5, right after the Beatles, the Stones, the Monkees and the Doors. The Moby Grape album was No. 29, the Fish were at No. 50, and the Dead at No. 122. The Airplane's new single, "The Ballad of You and Me and Pooneil," was No. 64 in its second week on the charts, and the No. 10 single was Eric Burdon's corny tribute to the Haight, "Warm San Francisco Nights."

The old Airplane and Quicksilver standard "Get Together" was No. 85 as recorded by the Youngbloods, a group of New Yorkers who had settled in Marin. It was the first single ever released because of demand created by an FM station's airplay of an album track. The station, of course, was KMPX. A market survey in August and September showed that KMPX was the most listened-to radio station in the area from seven to midnight among males eighteen to thirty-four.

KMPX was becoming a new home for the old Nevada Mafia—Jack Towle of the original Family Dog after his Western Front venture was denied a dance permit, Chan Laughlin of the Red Dog Saloon after Tom Donahue offered him a job so he could get early parole from prison, where he was serving time on his grass bust.

Governor Reagan urged sharp escalation in the Vietnam War. The director of the FDA claimed organized crime was pushing LSD. President Johnson called the leaders of the recent riots "wretched vulgar men" and "poisonous propagandists." In Washington there was an organization called Business Executives Move for Vietnam Peace. Eric Frank Dahlstrom pleaded not guilty to the killing of Shob Carter on grounds of insanity.

September 15.   Lou Gottlieb had pleaded no contest to the charge of running an organized camp, believing he would thus buy time to get Morning Star up to code. Now a Superior Court issued a restraining order that enjoined Gottlieb not to allow the public on his property and especially not to allow outdoor fires or nudity where visible from other properties. A new kind of policeman showed up to harass Morning Star, the Border Patrol. They claimed to be looking for Canadian runaways, and their justification was that the California border—that is, the Pacific Ocean—was only six miles away, and Morning Star was therefore within their jurisdiction.

September 16.   Golden Gate Park officials announced that the hippie invasion was over, presumably because the school year had begun. In fact, Hippie Hill was still firmly in hippie control. The Parks Department had bowed to necessity during the summer and allowed barbecuing in certain parts of the park because people were barbecuing there anyway. Now, they said, there was a problem of rats in the former barbeque pits. The *Examiner* made a great fuss about a once symmetrical elm tree that had been damaged during the summer and was symmetrical no more. Police estimated the summer invasion had actually numbered about 75,000 people.

September 17.   The California fall beauty show previewed hippie wigs. A group of Hindu religious musicians known as Bauls visited Provo Park. Ken Kesey, interviewed at San Mateo County Sheriff's Honor Camp, said he had installed a stereo system at the swimming pool and painted some psychedelic murals which the authorities had then painted over. They had also refused to let him donate blood because of his having used LSD.

September 18.   The Shire School opened for classes at its own building, a warehouse on 17th Street between Valencia and Mission, for the use of its ninety pupils, four accredited teachers and twenty volunteer adults. The school was immediately informed that it would have to render the building earthquake-proof at a cost of $5,000.

September 20.   The band called the Phoenix took the stage at the San Francisco Art Festival in Civic Center Plaza next to City Hall. Municipal court judges complained of noise and had the plug pulled.

September 21.   Lou Gottlieb's new gambit for Morning Star: the farm was on the market and his guests were "prospective buyers," just trying the place out. Possibly one or more of them could come up with his asking price, $7 million.

This date was the autumnal equinox, the official end of summer. Several observances were planned.

At Speedway Meadow there was a pow wow aimed at bringing about contact between hippies and American Indians. For all its interest in Indian lore, the Haight had had next to no communication with the 43,000 American Indians living in the Bay Area. Chief Rolling Thunder of the Traditional Tribal Council of the Western Shoshone Nation addressed a crowd of about 600.

That night, an event honored the birthday of Aleister Crowley, the English satanist. It was called Invocation of My Demon Brother after *Lucifer Rising,* a work in progress of the satanist filmmaker Kenneth Anger. The moon that night was in the sign of Scorpio; Anger himself was an Aquarius with Scorpio rising.

Anger and a shadowy Brotherhood of Lucifer rented the Straight Theater for a guarantee of $700 and built a satanic altar on the floor. They hired Ben Van Meter and Scott Bartlett to do the light show, which was built around slides of Crowley's own tarot cards and 400 feet of Anger's film. Behind the projection screen the Orkustra would play, calling itself the Wizard for this occasion. Orkustra leader Bobby Beausoleil was himself the star of the film footage being screened.

The event did not draw a large crowd, but the satanic mood was beyond dispute. At one moment in the brotherhood's invocations around the altar, the top of the Tibetan prayer wheel flew off and hit, of all people, the *Oracle*'s former art director, who was so badly hurt that an ambulance was called. Tough luck for the Straight Theater's insurance policy.

At the end of the show Van Meter returned the film to Anger, who handed it to someone else for safekeeping so he could leave for a post-invocation party. Anger had called it "my first religious film"; to non-satanists it had seemed to be merely shots of Bobby Beausoleil in weight lifter poses. During the night the film was stolen, and the culprit was widely assumed to be Beausoleil.

September 22.   The Straight cleaned up after the satanic service, the job made somewhat easier by the fact that after Anger left, his audience had looted the altar. The show had failed to make its guarantee in gate receipts, and Anger at first peevishly made out his check for $666.66 rather than $700.

The pow wow, continued meeting in the Panhandle, briefly visited by Senator Romney, who had met Emmett Grogan while touring Huckleberry House. In the evening the Straight hosted a meeting for the Indians attended by some 1,500 people. Rolling Thunder repeated a prophecy that had appeared in *Oracle* No. 8 of a "Day of Purification," a purging "gourd of ashes" which symbolized beneficent destruction. He connected it with an event scheduled for the Friday after next, the Death of Hippie ceremony.

The Free Clinic closed the doors of its medical section at 558 Clayton. Dr. Smith had expected funding from the Health Depart-

ment, but the department's attitude was that of Ellis D. Sox: There
was no emergency because there were already clinics in the city.
"And if I went to the supervisors for money," said Sox, "I would have
to ask for funds to set up a clinic at Hunter's Point too—that's just
as serious a situation."

September 25.   The Straight's dance-permit appeal was rejected
three to two. "Now I can understand how the hippies feel about our
society," said Bill Resner as if he were an innocent square. "For the
first time I feel totally alienated."

The board of supervisors voted unanimously to make Haight
Street one-way westbound from Masonic to Stanyan and Waller
Street one-way eastbound between the same blocks, in order to
facilitate automobile traffic. So much for the petition to make Haight
Street a mall.

September 26.   The Maharishi spoke to a capacity crowd at the
Berkeley Civic Auditorium. What a surprise. The Beatles' own guru,
who outranked even the mystical George Harrison of "Within You,
Without You," preached what he called "200 percent life: 100
percent material and 100 percent spirit." In other words, by practicing Transcendental Meditation you would achieve not only spiritual
refreshment and enlightenment but wealth.

The Straight Theater announced that the Straight School of Dance,
which had existed as a modern dance school in the Masonic Hall
adjoining the Straight, would move to the theater building and offer
public dance instruction. Said the poster: "The Board of Permit
Appeals presents . . . Dance Your Misery Away. Professional dance
lessons—5 hours for only $2.50. Instructors include Jerome Garcia,
Dr. P. Pen."

A dance school, it turned out, did not need a permit the way a
dance hall did. Among such "dance instructors" as the Grateful
Dead and Neal Cassady with his mile-a-minute mouth was an actual
dance instructor, the famous dancer and choreographer Ann Halprin. Two thousand "student body cards" were sold.

Dick Clark was in town to film *The Love Children,* and American-International, the leading exploitation studio, was doing a hippie film called *Wild in the Streets.* Joe McDonald quit Country Joe and the Fish. Timothy Leary lost his trial for smuggling marijuana and was given the maximum penalty, thirty years in prison plus a $30,000 fine. After a long hiatus the Psychedelic Rangers painted another fireplug several miles from the Haight.

September 29.   The Free City Collective published the first issue of *Free City Newsletter,* which included instructions on how to build a firebomb.

October 2.   Among three houses raided for marijuana this Monday was 710 Ashbury, the Dead House. The Grateful Dead were back from their touring, and their old ladies returned from their reconnaissance of New Mexico with the decision to stay around San Francisco. Since March the Dead had played only one paying gig each at the Fillmore and the Avalon, but innumerable free concerts in the park.

The chief of the State Narcotics Bureau led the raid himself, but it was a disappointing catch: an equipment handler, two business managers, six young women and only two members of the band, Bob Weir and Pig Pen. They were the two least drug-involved members of the band, a vegetarian and a hard-drinking blues-lifer.

On October 4, manager Rock Scully was busted again, this time for being the lessee of a house "for the purpose of unlawfully selling, giving away or using narcotics." The Dead held a press conference to charge that rich potheads on Russian Hill were being left alone while the cops were laying into scruffy hippies in the Haight. Lt. Norbert Currie responded that only 40 percent of the drug busts in the Haight these days were for marijuana, and that most were for speed and heroin.

The announcement of a Death of Hippie ceremony answered a spontaneous feeling in many quarters that the movement had gone wrong and needed to be cleansed of the ugly accretions of the summer. Free City, the Switchboard, the Flame, the Free Clinic, Happening House and a dozen other centers of organized activity participated. The date chosen for the ceremony was October 6, the first anniversary of the anti-LSD law. By now the Free Clinic's medical section was closed, the Switchboard was $1,000 in debt because of expenses and an embezzlement, and the Psychedelic Shop was still $6,000 in the hole. Even the Trip Without a Ticket had $750 of debts and was charged with various building-code violations, including one for a broken front door. The door had been kicked in a few weeks before when, incomprehensibly, the free store was burglarized.

The Death of Hippie press release showed a titanic effort to save the dream from its publicity: "The media cast nets, create bags for the identity-hungry to climb in. Your face on TV, your style immortalized without soul in the captions of the *Chronicle*. NBC says you exist, ergo I am. . . . and the reflections run in perpetual anal circuits and the FREE MAN vomits his images and laughs in the clouds because he, the great evader, the animal who haunts the jungles of image and sees no shadow, only the hunter's gun, and knows sahib is too slow and he flexes his strong loins of FREE and is gone again from the nets. They fall on empty air and waft helplessly on the grass."

Not everybody joined the Death of Hippie project. Some openly doubted that hippies were actually going to tear off their beads, as the Death of Hippie rhetoric suggested they would, and become something called the Free Man. The I/Thou ridiculed the project, and the *Haight-Ashbury Maverick* chided "our colleagues the Haight Avenue East Crowd" for declaring Hippie dead when new people were still arriving in the Haight. The *Berkeley Barb*'s reporter in the Haight observed that the attack on media was itself a calculated media event, "the same kind of media crap as the Be-In, the Summer of Love and all that, and the same people dishing it out."

In the early morning of October 6, policemen arrived at the Matrix with a noise complaint about Big Brother and the Holding Company's performance. The local precinct captain threatened to arrest the band, and the club manager retaliated by closing the doors of the Matrix "indefinitely." The Matrix had been suffering financially since the beginning of the year, when the management had decided it was wrong to run the Matrix as a club minors couldn't attend and the club took the unheard-of, and economically disastrous, step of voluntarily relinquishing its liquor license.

Following a Wake for Hippie at All Saints Church on Thursday, the funeral procession began atop Buena Vista Hill at sunrise on Friday. "Taps" was played, candles were held aloft. Hippie and media emblems were consigned to a fire: copies of daily newspapers and the *Barb*, beads, reputed marijuana. Some eighty people took part in a procession down Haight Street, which was adorned for the day with a banner that read, "Death of Hippie Freebie, i.e., Birth of the Free Man." They bore a cardboard coffin with a representative hippie inside. After a "kneel-in" at the corner of Haight and Ashbury, the procession moved on to its destination, the Psychedelic Shop, where a record player was turned up loud to drown out the unscheduled screams of a girl bumming out on acid. The Psych Shop window was filled with signs: "Be Free." "Don't Mourn for Me, Organize." "Nebraska Needs You More."

That afternoon the police began regular daily sweeps of Haight Street to pick up runaways. Any man without a draft card was presumed to be either a minor or a draft evader.

October 8.   Lou Gottlieb was obliged to do one of two things: pay a fine of $500 a day as long as his "guests" were at Morning Star, or have them arrested. Reluctantly, he told police to arrest fifteen people remaining on his property. Two girls from the East Bay testified that when they ran away to the Haight, a man imprisoned them and allowed his friends to rape them, and also tried to turn them out on the street as prostitutes.

Che Guevara died in Bolivia.

October 9.   As if a ripple had reached New York, two young people named Groovie and Linda were found murdered in an East Village crash pad run by the quasi-Digger named Galahad.

By the fall of 1967, probably 75,000 people had lived in the Haight-Ashbury psychedelic community, and many thousands of acidheads around the Bay who had never actually moved there had taken part in its development. Although there were holdouts who never took psychedelics, the Haight-Ashbury was basically the biggest LSD party in history. In order to grasp an event so vast and so subjective, it might help to look at the Haight in terms of the two factors that were acknowledged to affect an acid trip: the set and setting. That is, the mental preoccupations of the people involved and the situation they found themselves in.

In a broad sense, the setting was the historical context of America in the sixties. The fifties had combined great prosperity with a legacy of anxiety from World War II: the most frightening weapon ever invented, the atomic bomb, and the terrible knowledge that the human race was capable of mass evil on the scale of Nazism. To make things worse, the Soviet Union had shown itself to be an expansionist totalitarian state like Nazi Germany, relying on seductive symbols and ideas to spread its power. In fact Communism seemed to be a sort of political disease spread by ideas, and intellectuals, who had largely been sympathetic to the Soviet Union in the thirties and forties, had spent the fifties in isolation and disrepute.

Toward the end of the fifties, however, sick comics like Lenny Bruce and satirical comedy troupes like the Second City in Chicago and the Committee in San Francisco became popular by lampooning political figures and conventional beliefs. Dissenting voices pointed out that anti-Communist crusaders were in fact practicing totalitarianism by undermining freedom of speech, that in our prosperity and anxiety we had lost our way as a nation.

President Kennedy, elected in 1960 as commencement speakers all over the country were bravely denouncing the "rising tide of conformity," seemed to promise an end to the feeling of stasis. Radiating youth, energy, confidence and intellect, he made culture fashionable by inviting Pablo Casals and other artists to the White House and by appointing Harvard professors to government posts. The Kennedy glamour rubbed off on the arts, and painting, as if responding to the new mood, seemed to meet the public halfway with pop art.

Fun itself suddenly seemed permissible. Old *Batman* serials were revived in movie houses, and eventually a *Batman* television show was presented in the same ironically obtuse spirit. Advertisers catered to the teenagers of the baby boom generation as a Pepsi Generation that was free of their elders' hang-ups. One hang-up was certainly in retreat; sex was far less troublesome given the availability of birth control pills.

Kennedy presented himself as a partisan of civil rights, rather than as a neutral referee like Eisenhower; the White House doors were opened to Martin Luther King, who seemed to many young people the purest moral leader in the country. Idealism reasserted itself, and thousands of white kids participated in the campaign against racial segregation in the South.

Kennedy also acknowledged the danger of atomic war. To be sure, he presided over the Cuban missile crisis, but he at least talked about the *possibility* of peace. He referred to the adversary as the Soviet Union, not as the bogeyman "Russia," and to the highest Soviet official as *Chairman* Khrushchev—as an individual holding a certain office, not a faceless menace.

The left, isolated from the political mainstream for so many years, hoped to prosper in this more relaxed atmosphere, and indeed there was an outpouring of radical activism on college campuses. The traditional left parties, though, benefited little from the student movement. Much as young people were attracted to folk music as a hobby and a lifestyle rather than as an ideological "People's Music," college students saw leftist politics as an arena for self-discovery and self-assertion. They called themselves a new left, and sought to make radical changes in America that were untrammeled by traditional political doctrines or alliances.

Indeed, as many in the new left saw it, Marxism was in need of revision. The working class, for instance, was obviously not interested in serving as the force behind a revolutionary transformation of all values and social relations. But who could serve in its place? Perhaps the oppressed Afro-Americans, if they could be ideologically enlightened. Or maybe the student movement itself could take the starring role and change the world. Naturally, this meant depicting students as an oppressed class, and an account of the 1964 Free Speech Movement at Berkeley was casually entitled "Student as Nigger."

Another problem with Marxism was that the inevitable collapse of capitalism seemed rather too long in coming. The United States was in fact obscenely wealthy, a throwaway economy. Everything came in convenient throwaway packages; grocery stores were throwing away untold tons of edible produce simply because it didn't look appealing. Gas was so cheap and so many people were buying a new car every year or two that Detroit concentrated on style and ignored the idea of a fuel-efficient car that would last. There was even a name for this new way of engineering: planned obsolescence.

Thinkers looking at the long-term effects of this prosperity detected hitherto unforeseen dangers. Marxists had promised a paradise in which technology would free humanity from the mere struggle to survive. Now, with the possibility that modern technology would reduce the need for human effort indefinitely ("Robots will be doing all the work"), observers began to wonder what people would do with all their free time. In 1961 Robert Theobald wrote, "The schoolchild of today will live in an era when he will work only twenty hours a week. One of our most urgent tasks is to make this leisure time meaningful rather than boring."

Initially this line of thought was informed by the fear that bored masses might prove susceptible to anti-intellectual fascism, but other leisure theorists argued that leisure itself would power the total revolutionary transformation of all values. Machines would eliminate the need for human labor and therefore the existence of social distinctions based on wealth; without the "crutch" of a career to shape our lives, we'd have to face ourselves psychologically as never before. In January 1966, the director of the Western Behavioral Institute declared, "The superior man of the future will be the person who can cope with a world without work. . . . Rather, he will prize his ability to relax, to contemplate, to attend to the world around him, to be aware of his inner feelings, to enjoy others, to be what he is, to live in the present."

The exhilaration and sense of breakthrough suffered a blow when Kennedy was assassinated in 1963. How loath the nation was to accept the absurd murder of this glamourous young hero by a lone madman can be judged by the number of books attempting to uncover a conspiratorial design. People involved in the civil rights movement in particular looked with grave suspicion on the new president, a southerner. In fact, Johnson had a very liberal civil rights record; while the civil rights movement had many difficulties during his administration, they were largely internal—the growing popularity of black power and black separatism leaders who wanted whites out of leadership roles in their movement, or out altogether.

The real problem with Johnson was war. In the summer of 1964, as he was finishing out Kennedy's term, he openly sent thousands of military advisers to aid South Vietnam. In the 1964 election campaign he presented himself as a peace candidate against Barry Goldwater, but once the election was over Johnson further escalated the war and even adopted Goldwater's proposal to defoliate the Vietnamese jungle to make Vietcong supply routes more visible.

The general public was going along with the war, but to college students it gradually came to seem a conspiracy against American youth. In 1966 draft boards were allowed, for the first time ever, to induct college students who had low grades. In March 1967, the House Armed Services Committee threatened to end the 2-S college deferment altogether if antiwar demonstrations continued to take place on college campuses. In May 1967, three members of that committee demanded that the Justice Department simply disregard the First Amendment when it came to draft resisters.

It was in this setting—a thwarted sense of breakthrough, mobilization for war and a civil rights movement gradually turning hostile and separatist—that the Haight-Ashbury adventure took place. As for the mental set of the participants, the original hippie community did have a rough consensus insofar as everyone subscribed to bohemian values, mostly as gleaned from Beat Generation writings.

Bohemianism, often understood to be mere happy-go-luckyism, in its most important sense was a project of self-discovery and self-assertion on the part of young middle-class artists or would-be artists. Bohemians rebelled against the placid comfort that the middle class aimed for and the prudent endeavor by which middle-class comfort is achieved. Instead, they wanted a sense of grappling with real life, and preferred boldness to prudence, pleasure to restraint, and ecstasy, danger and the unknown to comfort. Ostensibly they sought "experiences" in order to grow as artists, and their poverty demonstrated their commitment to be artists at any cost.

Bohemians typically explore wild territories of the psyche—eroticism, the occult, physical danger, drugs—and are fascinated by the lives of the poor, the failed, the insane, the primitive. The hard lives of such outsider groups do have an authenticity often lacking in the middle class, though the bohemians who admire them are liable to misinterpret what they see by projecting their own situation as voluntary outsiders on these no-choice outsiders. Eventually this passionate exploration of the possibilities of life bears fruit or not; the bohemians become artists or they don't, they settle down or continue to seek experiences, and a new generation comes along to go through the same process in their own way.

The most recent generation of bohemians, the Beats, saw themselves as *victims*. Their attitude toward the squares was not the traditional bohemian contempt and disdain, but something less confident—something full of fear and resentment. The Beats also saw themselves as a movement or a social group more than previous bohemians had; in fact art, finally, was less important to them than Beatness. Anybody who read a poem, no matter how terrible, at a Beat coffeehouse was accepted as long as he expressed the necessary bile against the squares, the cold war, racism and other evils of the day. In a way, the Beats paralleled two other social groups that had arisen after World War II, the outlaw motorcycle gangs and the surfers. Each group had its thrill—fast cars, jazz and drugs for the Beats, bike riding for the bikers and surfing for the surfers—and each was more an in-group and a way of life than an art or sports community.

From the Beats the hippies inherited the idea of bohemia as a social group holding outsider political and philosophical values in common. They inherited the use of drugs as well, though they rejected much of the Beat style, above all the nihilistic mood. Another item from the Beat heritage they abandoned was the outsider group to emulate. Various generations of bohemians have favored one noble savage or another. For the Romantic bohemians of the nineteenth century it was the gypsy; the Beats' favorite among the "fellaheen of the world" was the American black, especially jazz musicians. But a growing sense of black nationhood had rendered blacks unwilling to serve as identity crutches for white kids. The holy primitives of the Haight were Hell's Angels and American Indians.

At first the art world had hotly disavowed the Beats, but by the middle sixties they were acknowledged to have been fighting the good avant-garde fight. Long after the Beat neighborhoods disintegrated, the avant-garde magazine *Evergreen Review* continued to write about the Beats and their preoccupation with drugs and the irrational spontaneity of jazz and Zen enlightenment. The early Haight hippies typically made an attempt to keep abreast of the avant-garde through *Evergreen* and similar sources.

The Zeitgeist of the sixties avant-garde was markedly different from that of the fifties. The leading art form, the art to which all the other arts aspired, had been abstract painting; now it was a sort of theater. A number of elements conspired in this direction. For one thing, there was the perennial avant-garde tendency to destroy a priori notions of what art is, and at the moment this tendency centered on breaking down distinctions between various forms of art. Since arts such as music and dance only exist in being performed, this inevitably led—as it had in Wagner's nineteenth-century Art of the Future—to the idea of uniting all the arts into a performance. The sixties also saw a revival of Artaud's and Brecht's theories about theater. Artaud's Theater of Cruelty confronted the audience with the inevitable squalor of life and established a kind of spiritual communion with it by means of primitive ritual. Brecht's Theater of Alienation might seem to be diametrically opposed—didactic, Marxist, intentionally untheatrical—but it was also meant to *change* the audience, and there were many attempts to fuse the two theories.

Lurking in the background was the disenchanted experience of the left intellectuals during the forties and fifties, namely the fear of anti-intellectualism and fascism. The accepted psychological explanation of fascism was that the authoritarian personality was taught to suppress its feelings and submit to its superiors, on the condition that it was allowed to take out all its hostilities on underlings and outsiders. In his introduction to *The Mass Psychology of Fascism*, Wilhelm Reich wrote: "Fascism is only the organized expression of the structure of the average man's character"—the average man, according to Reich, being thwarted and repressed. Obviously, it behooved intellectuals and artists to forestall a new outbreak of fascism by encouraging spontaneity and freedom from authority— even, perhaps, the authority of the artist over his audience.

All these tendencies converged in the heady experiments known as happenings or events or participatory theater. Here was the new unbounded art form of the future, the apotheosis of spontaneity, spiritual and social communion, perhaps a mass psychiatric exercise and, to boot, a hedge against fascism. In fact, audience participation was better ideology than practice, because many actors in happenings resented the audience leading the event in a direction they hadn't worked out. But as the current metaphor for art, this kind of theater incorporated not only painting and music but dramatic elements from other phenomena of the day, from the political satire of comics to the performance qualities of everyday life. The bohemian world was, after all, known as the "scene."

The notion of participatory theater was ever-present in the Haight-Ashbury. Ken Kesey hadn't known what to call his LSD party-adventures until it occurred to him that they were a kind of participatory theater, and he started charging admission and calling them Acid Tests. The early hippie rock dances with their multimedia aspects—music, dance, light shows, costume, body painting—were widely understood as pop art happenings. Daily life in the Haight had the usual theatrical quality of making the scene, and beyond that, people consciously organized moments of theater for their friends, even for unsuspecting strangers. This was called "blowing someone's mind," arranging some experience so completely unexpected—say, pulling from your pocket a tiny bell with a sweet, pure tone but decorated with a death's head, and ringing it an inch or two from the mind-blowee's eyes—that the person's mind would be "blown," destroyed. Mind-blowing had overtones of the psychodrama, koan and practical joke, and its ultimate practitioners were the Merry Pranksters.

The Diggers sprang from a theatrical troupe and inherited Artaud and Brecht along with a tradition of performing outside theaters. They became famous for free food and free crash pads, but most of their activities were strongly theatrical: the various street theater provocations they organized, the actional theater of the free stores, the symbolic Frame of Reference you had to walk through before you got your bowl of Digger stew. The Haight was the perfect theater, a large territory full of stoned people making the scene and vaguely waiting for something to happen. The Diggers had a political or supra-political purpose in all this, the creation of "life-actors" who would be uninhibited wild cards, freely acting out their feelings at every moment. Their vision was a Brechtian-Artaudian-Reichian synthesis, a declaration that acting was not merely the central art form but the key to spiritual, psychological and political salvation.

Even the supposedly staid Haight Street shop owners were involved in theater (many thought of their stores as environmental art, à la the constructions of Ed Kienholz). The Psychedelic Shop, of course, had theater seats in its window looking out on the passing drama of Haight Street. One day Richard Cherney of House of Richard told every person who came into his store in turn, "You're in charge!" and had him run the counter like a store owner—somewhat like the Diggers' tactic in their Free Stores, but proceeding from high spirits and not from the Digger ideology. Wild Colors had lost so much money to shoplifters that an employee was installed atop a ladder to watch the customers. As the days passed the ladder accumulated decorations that eventually made it look somewhat like a throne, and tourists asked store owner Peter Krug what famous hippie figure this enthroned watcher was. As a goof, Krug told them this was the Pope of the True Catholic Church. In time this pope started selling 1¢ indulgences, little cards that read "You are forgiven."

The theater motif was one thing that distinguished the hippie use of psychedelics from that of the Beats a few years earlier. The Beats had understood the world in terms of spontaneity, religion, psychiatry and so on, and had even envisioned a world freed from greed and war by psychedelics. But the theater motif proved a particularly effective handle for assimilating the psychedelic experience, otherwise so vast and formless, into everyday life.

The psychedelic experience is always exalted and supernormal, whether euphoric or frightening. LSD and mescaline suppress the mind's ability to discriminate according to levels of importance—the kind of thing that allows a mother at a noisy party to hear the sound of her baby crying upstairs—and to form persisting notions about reality based on them. This faculty causes us to focus on one thing and ignore many others. Eventually, whatever we are familiar with tends to become mere background as we go about our daily business, worrying about whatever we worry about and basically on the lookout only for changes in our environment. A chair becomes just a chair, something about which we have nothing more to learn. As adults we do not see a chair with the same intensity with which we examined one when we were children.

This faculty of discrimination is what William James called the reducing valve that screens out the near infinity of actual details in the world and relationships that exist or could be conjectured to exist among them. We sense the vastness of reality only at rare moments —a rocky cliff reveals more to an architect building on it or to a man whose life depends on climbing it than to the ordinary passerby. Solving a problem, appreciating a work of art or falling in love all have in common an aesthetic moment or sense of wonder that brings feelings of freshness, value and reevaluation of oneself. For that moment, as our ideas change, we are in touch with the vastness of reality in the happiest way, because we are moving toward a desirable result.

The stronger the psychedelic, the more strongly it suppresses the faculty of discrimination, right up to a featureless experience called the White Light, in which all details are equally important and all connections equally valid. In a sea of perpetually changing impressions, the meaning of anything can differ wildly from moment to moment. The exaltation of being stoned might be the dawn of birth, the moment of death or a mystical unity of the two. The world might be the play of eternal archetypes or nothing but the moment-to-moment flashing of spontaneous energy. A place might disclose its utter uniqueness, or it might reveal itself as being beyond time and space. This is what people mean when they speak of LSD hallucinations—not full-fledged visions of things that are not there, but extraordinary and uncontrollably shifting interpretations of things that are.

There are many possible ways to look at such an experience as LSD, but the Haight saw it as an avant-garde art tool—a gateway to experience itself, to spontaneity, to visions of unsuspected connections between things; an equivalent of the contemporary avant-garde art project that combined ritual, psychodrama, political amelioration and the expounding of all secret things. LSD was called a deconditioning agent, suitable for destroying the roots of war, racism, fascism and all other evils based on narrow-mindedness and repression.

But psychedelics are more than an intellectual challenge. The exaltation of the high has no real parallel in ordinary life, either in intensity or duration. Since the high is bound up with the perception of real things, unlike, for example, the effect of heroin, people coming down from LSD often feel that they have been unfairly cast out of a state of mind that is their birthright, and hence they go questing for a way to recover that experience, if possible without the drug. Inexpressibly poignant, this cast-out feeling has to be shared. Psychedelic users automatically congregate with other heads, even if they have to turn on their own friends (which they generally do anyway). LSD tends to form cabals of initiates.

There were collections of such cabals in many areas around the country in the middle sixties, but the Haight-Ashbury was the boldest of all. In part it was because San Francisco was a tolerant environment, in part because the community was blessed with a number of bold individuals who told acid heads that they were doing the right thing: Ken Kesey, Owsley Stanley, the outrageous individuals who started the acid dances and Haight Street shops and Digger stores. An important underlying factor was that San Francisco had a long-established psychedelic tradition not based on LSD. Most psychedelic communities around the country were LSD scenes, and LSD was distributed by the Timothy Leary network, which meant that psychedelics came freighted with the Leary cult and his books and quietist theories. The San Francisco tradition, though, dated back to the Beats, and until Owsley started making LSD the favorite drug was peyote, which could be ordered from cactus farms in Texas.

At the same time that LSD cabals were arising in bohemian communities, soft drugs such as marijuana and LSD were becoming popular among non-bohemians—college students and the liberal professional class. These people often saw the same bohemian values in LSD as the hippies did, but they were not themselves ready to live as bohemians, careless of the morrow. They were not, for instance, ready to smuggle marijuana across the Mexican border or score it in black neighborhoods or sell it to strangers, and they were certainly not ready to start illicit drug laboratories. Hippies, however, were already doing such things for their own enjoyment, so when college kids and professionals wanted drugs, they turned to the hippies, who were from their own middle-class background and relatively easy to deal with.

By this accident of history, hippies drifted into a lucrative gap in the drug trade. Overnight, much to their surprise, a lot of hand-to-mouth types found themselves with great wads of cash. Roger the Dealer found one day that he had $580 in cash, by far the most money he'd ever had in his life. He went down to Haight Street and collared a sidewalk buddy of his and said, "Hey, man, you ever flown in a jet plane? Well, neither have I. Let's see how far we can get on five hundred and eighty bucks!"

In effect there was now a class of *rich beatniks.* The flamboyant style of the early Haight owed a lot to the whimsical spending habits of these people to whom money was simply not serious. Dealing wasn't work, really—sitting around smoking grass all evening with a bunch of people and table-hopping at coffeehouses was what they'd have been doing anyway—but it paid just like work, or even better. By doing what came naturally, hippies found money raining down upon them, and they spent it on Mod or antique or handmade clothes, or on toys or Navajo jewelry or Persian rugs. They backed rock bands and stores on Haight Street—both convenient covers, it turned out, in case the IRS came around asking about your means of support. (Eventually the rock bands were able to reward their benefactors even more concretely. As rock sound technology evolved, the mountains of loudspeaker cabinets the musicians were obliged to cart around could also house mountains of marijuana.)

Early on, a number of political dropouts had found their way to the Haight. Fresh from the civil rights movement, they'd confidently turned to antiwar activism, but to their dismay the American people didn't rally to them. Many activists then dropped out of politics to explore LSD in hope of finding the root cause of war, be it the ego, private property, the nuclear family, technology or Western civilization itself. They added a desperate radicalism to the Haight, as well as an awareness of the possibility that the easy life there might be lulling hippies into playing "good Germans" to the atrocities of Vietnam.

True, the war was a serious problem, but here in the Haight how amazingly everything fit together. A community arose as if by magic. By late 1966, the dances, the light shows, the posters, the *Oracle,* the Diggers, the suggestive evidence that big-time rock stars were exploring psychedelics along with them—all these things had developed, often from unexpected quarters, all obviously part of one huge event. People were trying to face the most serious problems they saw, such as racism and nuclear war, and there was an ever-expanding hope of success.

In the very early days, the intellectual makeup of the community was not marked by noticeable factions. People shared the usual hodgepodge of bohemian tradition, dominated by the writings of the Beats but with plenty of room for yoga, Gurdjieff, Velikovsky and Marcuse. Aldous Huxley and Alan Watts were popular, naturally, since they wrote about psychedelics. A Beat inheritance was Zen, which described enlightenment not as something to be achieved over many painful rebirths but as a real possibility in the present life. Like Zen, the Chinese oracle book called *I Ching* recognized a reality made up of momentary situations rather than enduring entities—in this case, situations that could be understood by interpreting the chance configuration of falling coins. Psychedelic explorers in the Haight also discovered books of American Indian mysticism such as *Black Elk Speaks* and *Warriors of the Rainbow* that supplemented the more familiar mysticism of Hinduism, occultism and astrology.

The bohemian interest in psychology was served by a few books, notably *Gestalt Therapy* by Frederick Perls and Paul Goodman. Goodman had taught at the Experimental College at San Francisco State; Perls was teaching at the Esalen Institute in Big Sur, which had social links to the Haight (founder Michael Murphy once contributed an article to the *Oracle*), and Esalen-type sensitivity training was one of the novelties of the October 1966 Awareness Festival at San Francisco State. Freud was out of fashion and Reich was known largely through popularizers, above all the anarchist educator A. S. Neil, who described his method and theories in *Summerhill.* Jung's theory of archetypes was certainly well known in the Haight, adding a mystical dimension to the fantasy adventures of Tolkien's *Ring* novels and the Marvel Comics series.

Of course there was Timothy Leary, whose writings were available in the *Psychedelic Review,* his book *Psychedelic Prayers* (a loose rendering of the *Tao Te Ching*) and, above all, his manual of the stages of an acid trip, *The Psychedelic Experience*, which was based on the colorful descriptions of acid-like visions (and the reassuring warnings that they were mere mental projections) in *The Tibetan Book of the Dead.* But Leary's style was not the Haight's, although the *Oracle* was published by an admirer.

To the Haight a more important psychedelic intellectual was Ken Kesey, a special hero for his utter fearlessness and the sense he projected that an intrepid tripper was traveling to a real, if unknown, destination. The Prankster core group remained a tribe on the scene even after Kesey's flight to Mexico, but both Kesey and the Pranksters lost their self-confidence during his absence. He retained the celebrity of being the established author who had thrown himself into psychedelics when the rest of the respectable world had never heard of them, but many of the specific features of the Pranksters' trip—their Bus Movie, organized Pranking, their fascination with video and electronic equipment—remained unique to them. One Prankster contribution to the Haight was the Hell's Angels, though, and the Pranksters also influenced the fashion for surreal costumes and face painting.

Learyites and Pranksters were identifiable groups. So were the HIP merchants, though they did not start with an identifiable philosophy. They were reasonably typical of the early Haight crowd in terms of background: Richard Cherney (House of Richard) was an actor, Peter Krug (Wild Colors) a folkie, David Rothkop (I/Thou Coffee House) a teacher at San Francisco State, Bob Stubbs (Blue Unicorn, The Phoenix) a dropout. They tended to view the Haight as a community of artists and visionaries which had something to offer the world and which, in the face of the world's crassness and recurring spasms of violence, ought to make itself independent and self-sufficient until its message was accepted.

Their shops were an integral part of the Haight—indeed, they were what made the Haight a hippie neighborhood rather than just a neighborhood where hippies lived—but they were also businesses. They had to deal with the same regulatory agencies and economic situations as other businessmen. They formed a merchants' association, held meetings with politicians and policemen, founded and advertised in a newspaper generally congenial to their views, and issued public pronouncements as would a local chamber of commerce. And although it's unlikely that anybody who opened a shop on Haight Street before 1967 hoped to get rich off it, they did want to make money. Bobby Bowles, who had started his Peg 'n' Awl Leathers in a corner of Mnasidika, was a community-minded merchant who contributed freely to neighborhood projects. But he remembers reading the predictions that 100,000 hippies would visit the Haight in 1967 and thinking to himself, "Oh boy! If I can just get *one dollar* from each of them . . . "

Their rivals, the Diggers, were a striking contrast, and not only because they weren't businessmen. The Diggers had the most thoroughly worked out, conscious ideology of any group in the Haight. Basically it was the bohemian consensus plus new left politics reconsidered through psychedelic eyes, but from its early Mime Troupe roots it inherited a particularly aggressive manner and an exceptionally systematic vision of theater as revolution. It was a vision whose power derived from uniting everything: using the Free Store or street theater format to turn hippies into inherently revolutionary life-actors was political act and artistic statement in one, with suggestions of Zen, Reich, *acte gratuit.* The Diggers were the epitome of the avant-garde.

To the reader familiar with the usual psychedelic writings, which dwell on the LSD experience itself and its psychological or metaphysical ramifications, the Digger writings might seem to be written from a non-drug perspective by assertive young anarcho-existentialist rebels who liked to quote Mailer and Artaud. But they were in fact presenting a psychedelic vision. Like Leary, Kesey and other gurus, the Diggers claimed to know what LSD was about and how to achieve its promise—recovering childhood's lost "tense of presence," as an early Digger broadside put it, and escaping compromise with the "games" of everyday life.

The Digger program was for people to become life-actors, filling the world-stage with the kind of bold, satisfying gestures actors can make when their performance expresses their real feelings. To deal with the problems of living in human society, they promulgated their

Ideology of Failure, which was summed up in an early broadside: "When Love does its thing, it does it for itself, not for profit. . . . To Show Love is to fail." This was not the simple Kantian ethics it might seem—refusing to consider an act moral if there was any taint of self-interest—because to fail was not only to be moral, but to be free. If you have nothing, you have nothing to lose (and everyone, wrote the Diggers in the August 18, 1967 *Barb*, has something to lose: his "fixed mental institutionalized identity").

"A free person," they wrote in another part of the same *Barb*, "has no needs, no necessities, he is free to choose any alternative." But then how does a free person choose an alternative? The basis could be in Zen spontaneity or irrational *acte gratuit*. More to the point was the innocent, imprudent acid tripper in Peter Berg's 1966 play *Search and Seizure*, who confronted the police with his and their common humanity simply by being too stoned to regard the invisible line the police had drawn between themselves and their prisoners. The unpremeditated acts of an acidhead contributed to the model of what is moral, free and revolutionary.

And such acts were unarguable, undebatable. As in the happenings, where part of the action was left to chance and in effect God was made coauthor of the play, this doctrine amounted to an identification of Digger actions with the Absolute. Digger writings often suggested this: "The fuck-leader youth searcher and maker of voluntary life is a mutant." "Holy is a peacock mind."

With this original and high-powered ideology behind them, the Diggers really were free to do whatever they chose. Perhaps this is why some people found their motives a mystery. The HIP merchants, castigated by the Diggers as Uncle Toms and false witnesses, tended to regard the Diggers as their collective conscience and dutifully accepted their strictures like sermons, though sometimes they suspected the Diggers' "what's mine is yours and what's yours is mine" doctrine of being something of a shell game. When Bill Resner of the Straight Theater first met Emmett Grogan, Grogan was removing the refrigerator from the Straight. It was for the people, said Grogan. "*What* people?" demanded Resner.

In any case, one must distinguish between the core Diggers' ideology and what they were popularly thought to stand for. Many people in the Haight never heard of the Ideology of Failure and life-actors. What caught their attention was the brusque and provocative activism of the free food and Free Stores, with its suggestion of intransigent moralism. The press picked up on the same things and happily represented the Diggers as a sort of hip Salvation Army with an admirable doctrine of anonymity and nonexclusiveness—though there was nothing Salvation Army-like about a group that believed all institutions, from families and churches to outlaw gangs, were "horizontal and vertical pyramid hierarchies boxed and frozen for coordinating programmed corpses."

Most people on the street were not Pranksters, Learyites, merchants or Diggers, but there was an intellectual life outside these organized groups; for example, there was widespread interest in the nature and meaning of technology. This was a new subject without clear antecedents in former bohemias, and the most distinctive non-drug concern of the Haight.

To be sure, the leisure-challenge theory was in the air. The "robots will do all the work" vision of utopia was certainly widespread, the subject for instance of Richard Brautigan's famous poem "All Watched Over by Machines of Loving Grace" and one of the recurring ideas in the Leary-Snyder debate in *Oracle* No. 7. This vision was sometimes used to explain what was happening in the Haight, and was Lou Gottlieb's rationale for the Morning Star experiment: "We are running a pilot study in survival. The hippies are the first wave of the technologically unemployed." The reporter who wrote the "I Was a Hippie" series quoted a Digger as saying, "These kids are explorers. They're trying to find creative ways to live in a leisure age—ten years away, when machines and computers will do most of the work."

But there was also a more specific interest in the nature and direction of technology. Possibly it owed something to free-floating notions of good design left over from the Bauhaus school, but mostly it was a direct outgrowth of psychedelics. It was hard to ignore bad design, clumsy craftsmanship and shoddy materials when you were stoned. And from another aspect, two of the elemental questions that are liable to come up during an acid trip were, in the words of Alan Watts, "Where are we going to put it?" and "Who's going to clean up?" The problems of cleaning house and getting rid of garbage had parallels, an acidhead would see, in the question of where society was going to put its wastes and how the planet could be best managed.

As it happened, a philosopher of technology who had a following in the Haight had even taught a course at the Experimental College in 1966. He was Buckminster Fuller, the designer of the geodesic dome, which remains the lightest, least expensive and, for its weight, strongest way to enclose a space. Fuller believed that by efficient use of resources, including good design and recycling of materials, scarcity could be eliminated and everyone could "be a success." Reform of man's physical environment, rather than direct reform of man himself by laws and moral codes, could eliminate poverty, war and meaninglessness. In the process, ordinary human motivations such as greed, pride, patriotism and respect for tradition would have to be subordinated to the dictates of everyone's Phantom Captain, the fragment of the perfectly wise Universal Intelligence that constitutes the real self in everyone; Fuller never explained how this subordination would take place, except to suggest that there would be waves of enthusiasm for his ideas.

The interest in technology also created the popularity of Marshall McLuhan's *Understanding Media.* A slapdash work from the standpoint of scholarship, McLuhan's book offered exhilarating vistas of thought, such as a New Age wherein the whole world would become a Global Village in mystical union via its "externalized nervous system"—electronic communications. "Such a state of collective awareness," he wrote, "may have been the preverbal condition of man." McLuhan's theory that technology ("media," as he called it, suggesting the communications media in particular) was a series of extensions of various human physical capacities could have the same ring of elemental truth when you were stoned on acid as Leary's theory that LSD put you in contact with your molecules. McLuhan's book was the all-time most popular stimulus for pothead trips, and his idea that communications media were replacing the old world of jobs with one of "participatory roles" seemed to fit what was happening.

But all these visions of a harmonious rapprochement between man and technology were rejected by a large though disorganized body of neo-neolithics who considered technology a sin against nature, a quest for power which led to ever-mightier weapons and finally nuclear doom. Leary catered to this mood, for instance, with his theory that "metal belongs underground." Even people who tolerated technology collected *objets de nature* such as rocks, flowers, driftwood, fur and feathers for the beauty of their spontaneous forms. Such objects were considered "gentle" because they suggested the bounty of nature rather than the regimentation of society. They were reminders that life had gone on before human society and its commands and prohibitions, and would go on if human society collapsed.

The American Indians were of course here before the Europeans, and on some acid trips it seemed natural, even obligatory, to follow their Stone Age ways on their continent. The Indians also had the glamour of psychedelic experience, since peyote worship was common on the reservations. There were some white "peyote boys" in the Haight who were actually communicants of the Native American Church, and many times more who had never actually been to an Indian peyote meeting but wore headbands and turquoise jewelry as a badge of their sympathies.

More widespread in the Haight than the Indian cult was the simple feeling that the modern world was a meaningless, menacing place of atomic war and harsh competition, where it was too hard to find peace. There was a common fear that modern civilization would soon collapse under its dependence on so much elaborate technology; if atomic war didn't do it in, a natural phenomenon like an earthquake might. Then everyone would live in the same neolithic willy-nilly, and (poetic justice!) the voluntary primitive who was innocent of technological sin would be the one best equipped to survive in the post-catastrophic world.

There were many other currents of thought in the Haight—psychedelic Christians, mystical surrealists of the Fluxus Group sort,

Krishna devotees, simple druggies who looked on psychedelics as just another thrill. New left politics were not unknown, although organized left groups long considered the Haight as either an example of bourgeois self-indulgence or a plot to keep American youth from studying Marxism-Leninism. At the Human Be-In, the left was invited to join the revolution; the wary radicals tried, but the psychedelic community was bored by debate and uninterested in the usual political round of drafting position papers and orchestrating caucus fights. The Haight rarely followed the left routine of staging demonstrations and announcing demands. Instead, it felt it had an extra-political power, which it sensed in its ever-larger public gatherings, to change life totally.

The consensus, then, was that psychedelics might save the world from political and/or psychological repression and infuse it with a spirit of love, freedom, peace and creativity.

There were, however, a number of consequences to LSD besides deconditioning and bliss. Psychedelics are not a philosophy but an experience in which ideas are blown every which way. If taken for any length of time, LSD creates strange characteristic effects, all due to the mind's inevitable attempt to find some order in the storm.

The simplest were the visual riddles common to all psychedelic art, such as the ambiguous lettering of posters that, until you refocused and saw the letters, remained mere squiggles. Acidheads were also given to a peculiar noncomic punning that worked the same way. The phrase "ahead of his time," meditated on for an instant too long, would fall apart into mere syllables and different meanings (for example, "a head [an acid user] of his Time"). The song title "Dedicated to the One I Love" is transformed into the "One-Eye Love," obviously the unitary Godhead that sees through all our eyes. Once grasped, this principle made the perfect basis for a secret psychedelic code with which to pass on drug insights or simply to declare one's membership in the psychedelic brotherhood.

The ability to see things in a new light is intimately bound up with love and creativity, but an LSD-induced eight-hour dose of wild surmise often led in wayward directions. The ordinary yardsticks for evaluating other people were left far behind, so a nervous acidhead could observe some fractional part of a person's identity—a fleeting mood, or a clerk's need to insist on charging money—and blow it up into an ugly and unfounded vision. Conversely, with a thousand imaginable explanations for anyone's actions, other people could turn into utter mysteries, and the inscrutable interchanges between them could seem, depending on the acidhead's mood, either a blissful cosmic dance or a hideous collection of pointless games played by programmed, robotlike people. Worry and doubt could seem noble and Christlike or instead a vicious game of bringing other people down by dwelling on sinister possibilities, or even an attempt to bring about evil with "negative prayer."

The emotional flux of stoned people led to peculiarly unsteady relationships. Lovers who knew each other quite well might find themselves weirdly, inexplicably estranged. Or the reverse might happen—complete strangers could feel merged in perfect harmony. There were thousands of psychedelic romances in which two people, while high, saw in each other great wells of love and trust, only to see these feelings evaporate when they came down.

Life could become a fathomless and evanescent flow of events, which you were supposed to trust. "Trusting the flow" often made sense for the specific reason that someone completely ripped on LSD might be clumsy and ineffectual when he tried to influence the course of events. This trusting of the flow led to a kind of quietism, and an avoidance of things too complicated to understand; hence the popularity of simple food and things made of natural materials. A parallel development was the tendency of acidheads to speak in truisms. Trying to ask for a drink of water, a stoned person might labor for several minutes trying to put the request in the most universal terms possible as his mind focused randomly on various subjects: "I—or rather, this person, this one who speaks—wants; that is, expresses a need, its cells that metabolize those molecules that represent the vibratory form known as hydrogen combined with what humans, that is humans who speak English, call oxygen. . . ."

The dissolution of all solid boundaries, especially the distinction we feel between ourselves and the outside world, led to deep philosophical questions. Before psychedelics a college philosophy teacher might have given anything to get thousands of people to question so seriously the reliability of sense data, the nature of the self and the ultimate reality of the universe. The welling, oceanic feeling of an acid trip was felt as the presence of a single experience/entity pervading everything, the world and the individual alike, and acidheads described the essence of reality in terms suggesting this lack of individuation or discord: Peace, Love, Oneness, Harmony, Beauty, Bliss, Freedom. Or they might speak more abstractly of a transcendent Consciousness that was as one with Being. The spectrum of philosophical positions ranged from pantheism to solipsism.

One common development was what might be called gnosticism, because it resembled the strain in Western thought according to which the universe is not the work of a loving Creator but a trap, or at least a mistake, into which our souls have wandered from the perfect world that is their true home. The word "gnostic" derives from the Greek word for knowledge, and in the early centuries of Christianity it referred to people who followed one or another of the esoteric doctrines that the Gnostics devised in profusion. But one strain of Gnosticism associated the perfect world with the mind itself; Gnostic salvation was sometimes called "inheriting the First Mind." In the psychedelic community the experience of seeing everything disappear into a ceaseless froth of change and relativity often led spontaneously to the idea that reality had to be consciousness itself, rather than an *object* of consciousness. The corollary was that there must be some way of entering this reality of consciousness, by some special way of knowing. Allen Ginsberg quoted William Butler Yeats in *Oracle* No. 5: "This preposterous pig of a world, its farrows that so solid seem / Must vanish on an instant, did the mind but change its theme."

Ideas like gnosticism are so contrary to ordinary language and common sense that they could scarcely be put into words, only hinted at. Like the ancient gnostics, acid mystics would instead read their ideas into existing public texts—above all in rock and roll lyrics that cried out for such interpretation, such as those by Dylan and the Beatles that described life in terms of dream or illusion. All this secret philosophy with its codes and hints generated a great excitement. "There was a super-curiosity on the street in '66," recalls a Haight resident named Greg Reisner. "We thought there was going to be a *breakthrough*, and that it was imminent. I thought, There might be some room in this neighborhood where they've found a tunnel out. So I got into as many scenes as I could."

All psychedelic philosophy is an attempt to draw conclusions from an endlessly changing experience that in its very mutability seems paradoxically to reveal a unity. As the boundaries between things dissolve, everything tends to become One, and the same happens to ideas—they merge. Acidheads typically come up with grand syntheses of ideas they are sympathetic to, as Allen Ginsberg did in the article in *Oracle* No. 5 where he suggested that indulgence in sex and sensation may well "lead to contemplative awareness and cessation of desire"—that is, that two of his preoccupations would turn out to be the same. There were innumerable syntheses of the Hindu idea of the world as Illusion created by past karma, the gnostic feeling that it was a sort of mental error, the Marxist notion of "intellectual superstructure" determined by socioeconomic relations and the psychiatric concept of a delusional system which the psychotic projects on the world but which disappears when understood. All these ideas echoed the acidhead's experience of the simultaneity of the Absolute and the mundane, and they all held out the promise that this world is an illusion *as conceived*—the real world *is* here and now, but it is as different from what *appears* to be the real world as being stoned is from being straight, and it's just around some mysterious corner. Creating a grand synthesis often revolved around finding a verbal formula that would unite everything, if only verbally; the word "together," which could suggest being organized and effective in one's personal life as well as united with other people spiritually or politically, or even united with God, came in for heavy use.

As each acidhead came up with a grand synthesis that unified his own ideas, he was inclined to suppose that other heads' ideas and experiences were the same as his own—all One. It was a common experience for one head to turn to another stoned person and feel certain that both of them were thinking the same thoughts (it often happened, too). Even if they were thinking along different lines, by the time they started talking they would find common ground. In any case, insisting on your own opinion was taboo. Called "trying to lay your trip on people," it was inappropriate because we were all equal in the kingdom of the spirit, and anyway it smacked of bullying (a "power trip") to anyone as suggestible as a person stoned on LSD.

With all these attempts to find unsuspected unity in things, it was inevitable that the Haight should conclude that everyone there was "on the same trip." In the apocalyptic context of the time, that meant preparing for a total takeover of the straight culture of America. As Gary Snyder said in *Oracle* 7, "This is no time for caution." Many people put themselves on the line for this faith. In January 1967, against all conventional business wisdom, the Matrix nightclub voluntarily surrendered its liquor license—which had been so hard to get, and which had brought in more than half the club's revenue —so that minors need not be turned away from the sacrament of rock music.

Even the Diggers, so astute about the differences between themselves and the HIP merchants, labored under the delusion that the psychedelic community was unified on some level. At the Love Circus picket line they handed out leaflets reading, "The Diggers will not pay for this trip. As you buy a ticket, you kill the digger in yourself . . . yourself." The Diggers were also susceptible to the "What if all the hippies moved to Nevada?" line of thinking. What if hundreds of hippies invaded the FBI? What if people tore down the fences between their yards and copulated among the cabbages?

The middle-sixties idea of a unitary art embracing all others led, in the Haight, to the destruction of the idea of art—something the avant-garde, in its perennial wrestling match with any preconceived idea of what art is, had long flirted with. Again and again in 1967 one came across a statement said to be a Balinese proverb (sometimes a Balinese potter's answer to an anthropologist's question) to the effect that we Balinese "have no art, we just do everything as well as we can."

But the dissolution of the idea of art as a distinct human activity also dissolved the idea of bohemia as it had been known. Bohemia was no longer an estate of young artists; it had been swallowed up by a drug movement that did not expect its members to create art at all. The old distinction between bohemian and philistine, which in the fifties translated as hip versus square, was replaced by head (or doper) versus straight.

By the time the press started covering the Haight, its intellectual landscape was covered with all the ideas people had brought into the experience, wildly magnified by LSD. People in the Haight had no time to spell out the differences among themselves to reporters; it was unserious to do so, since the differences were illusory ("Words, you're just getting hung up in words") and the point was to save the world. Reporters asked people what was going on and got mystical answers and predictions that sheep would graze in city streets, gnostic hints and helpless assertions that the Haight was just a groovy place to be. (To *be*, that is, to really *be*—to sprout naturally from the ground of Being and assume the form you were meant to have.)

The reporters found people in the Haight often skeptical about the validity of newspaper stories yet absurdly credulous toward stories and rumors that originated in their own community. "There's this rich guy who took acid and he freaked out and he's down at the beach giving away everything he owns." "There was this dude at the Dead concert in the Panhandle who walked around for a couple of hours in the crowd before somebody noticed that his face was blue—sky-blue, man—and when they asked him whether he was Krishna he disappeared into thin air." "People who are stoned on acid are immune to radiation burns."

In particular there were rumors of conspiracies ("The CIA is poisoning the acid these days to make everybody go on bad trips"), but of course the Haight knew of real conspiracies in the semi-criminal world of drug dealing. The favorite figure in the conspiracy tales after the CIA was the Mafia. Some merchants charged that the Straight Theater was a Mafia front, the Straight crowd suspected the Diggers of being a Mafia theft ring with a shrewd "everything free" cover, and Diggers accused the Love Conspiracy of being part of "some mob."

In fact, the intellectual laissez-faire and the belief that the psychedelic community was unified cloaked tenacious differences. Political differences, for instance. Though the consensus was against the Vietnam War, the Haight was not solidly left-wing; many people were entirely apolitical and some quite conservative—Chan Laughlin of the Red Dog Saloon wrote editorials for a Republican newspaper in Nevada in which he opposed the Vietnam War on conservative principles—and many of the Haight's favorite writers, including Tolkien and Heinlein, were conservative-minded men. But differences faded from view in the excitement of the community's growth. Someone who was in the Haight searching for the key to world peace would come to feel that, after all, he and someone who had simply come looking for friends were "on the same trip"—peace and love, rightly understood, being the same. This was a refreshing and inspiring experience for those who felt it, a truly religious emotion.

In much the same spirit, the Haight-Ashbury had tried from the beginning to practice absolute tolerance and nonexclusiveness. This often worked, largely due to the technique of trusting the tribal spirit, of seeking the level where everybody was, in some way, on the same trip, in order to solve conflicts. The most thoroughgoing example of this was Morning Star, where utter tolerance of behavior and what they called voluntary primitivism—neolithic subsistence in exotic shacks—were explored as a sort of psychological and spiritual therapy. With anxiety neuroses this sort of thing worked brilliantly; with psychoses, less well; and with highly motivated hustlers, it could be a disastrous failure.

The Diggers had foreseen the dangers that were likely to result from publicity, and aimed to defend against them by playing nonexclusiveness to the hilt: anonymity, no leaders, no money, a continual shift of tactics to put the cops and the media off the trail. They were tactics, not principles: the Diggers did accept money, and Grogan, Berg and Cohon did speak to writers and allow themselves to be identified as Diggers. As for the opposition to leaders, it was easy for the core Diggers to say "don't follow leaders" when they themselves had natural leadership qualities and were bound to have a following. To that extent, the Digger crusade can be seen in terms of Weberian sociology as part of the endless conflict between charismatic and bureaucratic authority.

But shrewd as the Diggers were about the consequences of the publicity that various groups were seeking for the Haight, they contributed energetically to it with their magnetic myth of non-exclusivity. And the Diggers were the ones who began predicting how many people would flock to the Haight in 1967: 50,000, then 100,000, finally 200,000. The press treats concrete figures with awe, and it repeated these predictions so often that they became self-fulfilling prophecies.

If the press had come to the Haight-Ashbury with the intention of doing justice to this phenomenon, reporters would have spent months reconstructing the intense period of development and amazing coincidences that had made it a magical event. As it was, reporters had only a couple of days to make sense of this roiling, incomprehensible mob of weirdos and they fell back on the stock journalistic formula of Bohemia, Menace to the Nation's Youth: a panorama of indolence, promiscuous sex and madness. The dramatic and technological dimensions were basically invisible to them. Spokesmen for the neighborhood, in a clumsy attempt at ingratiation, allowed its thinking to be represented by the likes of Timothy Leary and the enigmatic slogan "flower power."

When the press repeated these shallow gleanings, the result was in effect an advertisement for the neighborhood, but not the kind that had been hoped for. The press advertised free love, free lunch in the Panhandle, tolerance for the crazy and the outcast, and a New Age governed by the power of love and innocence. So it brought in not only visionaries but insecure young people unable to find a place for themselves, dropouts content with the basics of life, outcasts and crazies, and—with the dissolution of the idea of bohemia—a sort of redneck bohemian indistinguishable from a wild kid attracted by the thrills of bohemia and its freedom from middle-class morality.

As the ideas of the community broke down, the institutions did the same. The free food had become irregular long before summer; the Digger crash pads, stymied by repeated troubles with police, were supplemented by truly dangerous places charging 25¢ or 50¢ a night.

The dealing economy, which had made the original community possible, suffered its regular seasonal drought during the summer of 1967 and in any case had become concentrated in fewer and fewer hands. The Job Co-op turned into an underground press distributorship and then collapsed. And so on. The only new institutions to emerge in the summer of 1967 were free rock concerts in the Panhandle and the free medical clinic.

So the Haight came crashing to the ground under the weight of population pressure. Many of the old-time hippies discounted the inexperience of the newcomers: they felt that if the new people took acid they must be on the same trip, though the old-timers' trip was the result of many experiences the newcomers hadn't had. And the newcomers could never feel the same ease about their membership in the community as the old-timers. They had joined an established entity, and they were faced with the choice of conforming exactly to some model of what it was to be a hippie, including dressing and speaking in an accepted way, or making a name for themselves by taking the trip to an extreme, usually by consuming more drugs than anybody ever had. Investigated by sociologists, interviewed by journalists, proselytized by gurus and preyed upon by criminals, the Haight was in the last analysis just too densely populated to work.

This was bitterly disappointing, but there were more surprises in store. As every age seems to discover anew, the most obvious problems of a time may not turn out to have been the most serious ones. The Vietnam War loomed in everyone's mind in 1967 as evidence of an inherent blood lust in the hearts of Americans. As a result the Haight spent much of its energy trying to dissociate itself from being American. This was one meaning of the Indian motif; as Gary Snyder wrote in his poem "A Curse on the Men in the Pentagon, Washington, D.C.": "I am killing the white man in me." The Haight was not alone in this analysis. As time went on, the war became a general invalidation of all authority and convention. In January 1967, the bridegroom at a Satanist wedding in San Francisco snapped to a reporter, "This wedding is as legitimate as the Vietnam War!" A day or two later, a Berkeley father defended his twelve-year-old son's use of drugs in the same terms. Eventually Vietnam would be invoked as license for everything from pornography to terrorist bombing.

In retrospect, though, the Vietnam War looks very little like an expression of the popular will. The government seems to have sensed that support for the war was perfunctory and liable to erode if the war ever made any harsh demands on the population as a whole. The government never introduced rationing, though during World War II it had even rationed things that were plentiful in order to give people on the home front the feeling they were doing their part. A Vietnam War surtax was added to the income tax in 1966, but it by no means covered the war's expense, which was basically borne by heavy long-term borrowing and slow devaluation of the national currency rather than by taxes. The most morally offensive aspect of the war, the extravagant use of firepower and modern war technology, was likewise a calculated move to avoid testing public support for the war. It was meant to hold American casualties to a minimum by fighting as much as possible from the air.

For anyone who chose to read them, there were clear signs that this was not a popular war: the paltry number of mothers of combat dead who wrote to Washington for Gold Star Mother status, the public opinion polls that reported the majority was against "pulling out" of Vietnam yet at the same time opposed to spending more money, sending more troops or committing the country for any specific number of years. In believing the news media's picture of an America solidly in favor of the war, the Haight wrestled with a problem larger than reality.

Nor did the dreaded leisure crisis develop as expected, and by the end of the sixties the challenge of a cybernetic Eden was in eclipse. The eclipse had actually begun in 1966. Throughout the fifties and early sixties, the United States had enjoyed agricultural surpluses it didn't know what to do with and had regularly shipped the excess abroad as foreign aid. But on December 23, 1966, the State Department announced that the United States could no longer "feed the world." In the seventies the talk was not of developing a New Man to live in the Post-Scarcity Age, but of disastrous world overpopulation and a future of perennial shortages.

Another kind of disappointment loomed in LSD itself. From the beginning this most ambiguous of experiences had been hard to evaluate. Was it a glimpse of heaven or of madness, a deconditioning agent, a sacrament, food for the spirit, instant yoga instruction, reality itself? And above all, how was it that this experience, so intimately woven with the experience of every perceivable object, went away when you came down from the drug? How did you deal with the fact that the million visions of the possibilities of life you saw were humiliatingly tied to the perversely unchanging self you brought into the experience?

Michael McClure and his Beat Generation friends had gone through the process of discovering psychedelics and reaching the limit with them just a few years before the Haight. He thinks of what was going on in his personal psychedelic cabal as a kind of "delusionary collusion": "If we colluded with each other in our use of psychedelics, we would come closer to the discovery of a Philosopher's Stone; we would find ourselves in control of time and space. It was very Faustian. Along with the greatest alchemical aspirations would go the Faustian desire to become at one with the universe-as-Messiah, and crash through time and space and be everything once and for all.

"I can't see in retrospect that anything was gained after the first couple of uses. Or whatever it takes to let that awareness and appreciation of reality in its manifold dimensions to come into being. To experience it over and over doesn't seem to lend anything. It's so beautiful and it promises so much, but there isn't any more that way."

What made the Haight unique was the fact that psychedelics were so new, and so many people were getting turned on at the same time, that the limits of the experience were not visible. The crowd energy of the baby boom generation and the teeming Haight-Ashbury dragged along even old-time acidheads who had lost much of their faith in LSD; it seemed that all this energy had to lead to something amazing.

So the Haight-Ashbury failed in several of its aims, and even found that certain of its concerns were phantoms. In this regard, as a human endeavor, it was par for the course. It is our lot to fail and be deluded much of the time, particularly in the fires of youth.

In retrospect, one thing is strikingly evident about the Haight-Ashbury. Even when deluded and doomed to failure, it was not (certainly not before it was swamped in the summer of 1967) the sink of know-nothingism and self-indulgence the press painted it to be. On the contrary, the Haight was almost inhumanly serious-minded and nobly intentioned. The problems it grappled with were acknowledged as some of the most serious of the day, and it was also bravely trying to deal with the great issues directly raised by the completely uncharted world of psychedelics. The Haight was not merely wrestling with the problems of war and technology and human nature on an intellectual level, but was also risking health and sanity and future and life itself in pursuit of answers. The Haight-Ashbury was not just a bunch of people getting stoned. It was heroic.

Eventually acid communities everywhere more or less adopted the Haight style. By the end of 1967 there were mini-Fillmores and Avalons all over the country, advertising with San Francisco-style posters their rock concerts featuring light shows. Fashions for buckskin, beads, Indian headbands, god's-eye yarn sculptures and rainbow diffraction gratings spread everywhere, fossilized into a sort of official hippie uniform. (Virtually the only fashion that came into the Haight from other hip communities was the floppy-brimmed Australian digger hat.) The prestige of the Haight reinforced such trends as the *I Ching* and the writings of Tolkien and Heinlein. Acidheads everywhere did their best to make alliances with their local equivalent of the Hell's Angels. The fashion that spread above all others was that of having larger and larger public gatherings to register the momentum of spreading psychedelic use.

But many things did not transplant well. The Acid Tests bogged down on the road because the Pranksters didn't find the necessary nonchalant readiness to participate in improvised psychedelidrama. The Los Angeles *Oracle* was short-lived, though less so than any other attempt to re-create the original. The Communication Company tried without luck to set up a counterpart free publishing operation on the Lower East Side of New York. None of the Digger-inspired free service organizations had the aggressiveness and invention of the original. *The Realist* reprinted some of the most important Digger writings in 1968, but it didn't lead to more open-access free food, housing and the like. Mostly the hints were used by individual communes or groups of communes for their private survival.

The superficial style of the Haight was adopted by advertisers as soon as they realized its youth appeal, an appeal that included the naive excitement of following the latest fad as well as the more intense resonance of psychedelic brotherhood. In March 1967, a major record label attempted its first psychedelic album cover, swirls à la early Wes Wilson that might have been derived from the Beatles' *Rubber Soul* cover, for the Platters' *Goin' Back to Detroit.* The next month brought new albums with paisley patterns, Persian rug arabesques, Italianate and art nouveau swirls, kaleidoscopic mandalas and wiggly psychedelic doodles. Then the Grateful Dead's first album sported an awesome Kelly collage with completely unintelligible calligraphy, and an industry of highly polished album cover art was born.

The advertisers' natural instinct was to pitch psychedelic advertising for rock music, blue jeans and other youth gear, but obviously they wondered how far they might run with it. At the end of November 1967, the Purex Corporation took a chance by advertising a detergent called News ("for people who want clean clothes without being taken to the cleaners") with a photo of a bearded man and his old lady in hip rags. There was even a conservatively psychedelic coupon.

But the psychedelic explosion of the sixties had far deeper effects on the American public than on advertising styles. The most obvious is a greater tolerance for deviant behavior and belief or—to use the current expression—for alternate lifestyles, a phrase that appeared in an HIP pronouncement written by Tsvi Strauch. To enjoy illegal marijuana was to put a small crack in one's unquestioning faith in the law, and to get stoned on it (not to mention experimenting with psychedelics) was enough to make a lot of people see that reality is not a simple, one-sided picture. The fashion for long hair on men signaled a loosening of the cold war parade-ground rigidity and also involved a progressive reevaluation, as hair grew longer, of the meaning of masculinity.

These things happened first in the younger generation, then in the general population as the times worsened and the government-organized "consensus" showed some slimy fingerprints. By the late seventies, with the Vietnam War rejected, a president discredited and driven from office, and marijuana decriminalized in a number of states, to Grateful Dead manager Rock Scully it was obvious: "America joined the hippies."

Naturally, the Haight had a more profound effect on people who lived there than on outsiders. The way of life itself had consequences. Not so much the dope trade, which became big business and eliminated most of the ordinary middle-range dealers, but the low-budget communal living situation.

Late in the sixties, California cracked down on groups of unrelated people living in the same apartment or house, especially when some of the members were on welfare. But there were ways around the law, and even today there are a number of communes in San Francisco drawing inspiration from the Haight, some even claiming to have been founded there. (For that matter, the law eventually forbade dwelling in an automobile, but the characteristic gypsy panel truck with paisley curtains in the windows can still be seen in the city's streets.) Far more communes were located outside the city, mostly in semi-rural communities to the north and south.

These communes, mostly groups of monogamous couples despite the hopes for group marriage, have maintained themselves as inexpensively as possible by buying their food collectively with other communes in food conspiracies largely inspired by the Diggers' work. Commune members might take part-time or short-term jobs, alternating with periods on welfare or food stamps, but most of them follow a craft interest in music or woodworking or the like. After 1967 a network of crafts fairs arose where they sold their wares or talents. The City of San Francisco, after long harassing the hippie musicians and street vendors who plied their trade around tourist spots, finally licensed them and characteristically turned the one-time menace to tourism into a tourist attraction itself.

The effects of LSD are almost too various to discuss. Psychedelics nearly always changed people, but in no particular direction. A resident at 1020 Page Street decided he was an orange, and bitterly resented it when people cast doubt on his orangeness—for instance, by asking him why an orange ate hamburgers. A long-time Haight resident named Mary Anne Kramer once spent four months in spiritual preparation for a single acid trip, avoiding meat and stimulants in the approved fashion. As usually happened after careful preparation, when she took the acid she had a cosmic experience that lasted for days. But what she experienced was total, instantaneous and profound understanding of . . . every course she'd taken in college. So while Timothy Leary was chanting his dropout mantra, she was dropping back in by enrolling at San Francisco State.

The one thing nearly everybody experienced from acid was the disappointment of realizing there was a point of diminishing returns, after which it was just a hall of mirrors. This discovery was probably hardest on people who had taken Timothy Leary seriously, because his official line was that LSD was not a glimpse of anything to be integrated into ordinary life, it was the one True Reality Itself. "The symbolic net which films and muffles your sense organs . . . must be dissolved chemically." "The only way out is biochemical." LSD was a "chemical door" through which you could leave the "fake-prop-television-set America" and find the Garden of Eden.

But you always came down afterward. Wasn't it inescapable that you were helpless in the grip of this hideous cosmic delusion? The satanism that flourished briefly in the late sixties sometimes resulted from this obsession: if you can't win, you might as well sell out big, to the very ruler of this evil universe. Even before that, however, there were people in the Haight who had lost their faith in LSD in a big way. Greg Reisner, who was caught up in the super-curiosity of 1966, had by the end of that year started taking another chemical door out, one that was to become more and more popular: heroin.

Though on an acid trip people are likely to attempt some sort of artistic expression like sketching, writing poetry or doodling on a flute or guitar, the Haight-Ashbury never became an art center. What it did turn out in quantities were woodworkers, metalworkers, jewelers, leatherworkers, exotic tailors and hash-pipe sculptors, not to mention the archetypal craftspeople of 1967, the bead stringers and candlemakers. It was natural for the Haight to work not in the fine arts but in the cousin of art closest to technology: domestic crafts to adorn and comfort everyday life.

Though the reporters who came to the Haight in 1967 were appalled by the dirt and discomfort, psychedelics usually incline people to seek comfort. When meaning and motivation are a mysterious whirl, and one can grasp only what is observable at the moment, it may become stunningly evident that the cupboard is badly designed, your shoes are heavy and stiff, you can't find a comfortable posture on your chair no matter which way you turn, and your stomach's upset.

Hence the organic life that arose in the seventies with its uniquely unemphatic hedonism. Light, simple, digestible food, inclining a little to blandness. Loose clothing, or nudity when the temperature is right. Sandals, or briefly in the early seventies, shoes with heels lower than the toes. Rooms filled with sunlight and the smells of plants or incense. Furniture designed to be pleasant or comfortable rather than practical, such as the water bed (invented by a State College student in 1967). Large wooden tubs for bathing. Northern California woodworkers have created extraordinary houses in this mode by using solid wood in smooth and rounded forms and lots of glass; the best of them combine quirkish shapes and trippy little corners with the comforts of a health spa.

Psychedelics interested many people in religion, but since their idea of a religious experience was derived from a drug, they were often looking for the equivalent of a drug experience. Throughout the ages mystics have warned that visionary states are only acts of divine grace or stages of spiritual growth, mere side shows, but since there was a market, gurus came along to promise these seekers states of wonder as automatic as any a pill can produce. The price they usually extract is total obedience, a bargain if the individual will is only a barrier to egoless bliss. Like some of the sensitivity therapy games that developed, these "ways" often involve re-creations of things experienced on LSD. For instance, the spellbinding notion that the guru knows the disciple's every thought reproduces the feeling that there is no distinction between inside and outside and no such thing as a secret.

More substantial than the attempt to re-create the psychedelic experience were the attempts to integrate what had been experienced. Integration meant not merely trying to relive the discovery that any individual is a part of various functioning patterns (not limited to the "I versus world" pattern) and ultimately of the incomprehensibly vast pattern of patterns that is the universe, but also understanding one's place and function. Gestalt therapy was eminently suited to this kind of exploration, and Esalen and various other sensitivity training groups drew much of their strength from the psychedelic movement.

The same insight of the world pattern of mutually interacting patterns extended to the study of man in nature as well as man in his personal relationships. The Haight-Ashbury provided a lot of the manpower for the ecology movement that bloomed in the late sixties. The interest in ecology was fed by both the anti-technological neo-neolithic mood and the Fullerite more-with-less philosophy, not to mention the revulsion many an acidhead felt upon discovering a picturesque rural stream that on second glance was polluted and dying. In Northern California, which is rich in renewable resources such as lumber and hydroelectric power, the ecology movement involved so little threat to the economy that it was soon accepted by straights as well as hippies.

Stewart Brand, the Trips Festival organizer, was interested in Buckminster Fuller from the start. In 1968 he founded the *Whole Earth Catalog*, a magazine that reviewed tools for their efficiency and also included book reviews and essays. It became the center for a nationwide class of Fullerite designers, ecologists, city people trying to live in the country, and many others who were simply fascinated by the descriptions of hundreds of tools and gadgets. With its telltale psychedelic slogans, "If we're gods, we might as well get good at it" and "We can't put it [the earth] together. It is together," *The Last Whole Earth Catalog* was published as a book in 1971, became a national best-seller and inspired numerous follow-ups.

The integration of psychedelic insights into the world of politics was slow to appear, perhaps because people were already aware of politics as a business of mutually interacting patterns and because most psychedelic thinking was anarchist or apolitical. But in 1974 California elected a governor who listened to rock music, admired Zen and seemed ready to see political problems afresh, without regard to conventional approaches. Jerry Brown certainly had a normal grip on the realities of political power and a great deal of political ambition, but he spoke to a desire for government by statesmanlike politicians who could put aside political expediency when their Phantom Captains had discerned the perfect solution to a problem.

These were only the broadest consequences of the adventure. In their ordinary lives, many people continued trying to integrate the psychedelic way of looking at things, that habit of examining a situation from as many different angles as possible in the hope of seeing it as it really is. And nearly everyone who was touched by the movement retains part of it in some way.

"Richard Alpert used to talk about the orange basketball," remarked Stewart Brand some years after the Haight had collapsed. "Psychologists raised some ducklings with a basketball and they imprinted on it as if it were their mother. Wherever the basketball rolled, they'd follow it.

"That's what the movement was to us. That was our orange basketball. Wherever it rolls, we'll follow."

The Death of Hippie ceremony had been theater. When it was over everybody went home and the Haight careened along the path it was already on, drawing in new residents as it grew steadily more uninhabitable. People still called themselves "hippies," or increasingly "freaks," instead of "Free Men," and the widely publicized image of the Haight as a holy place still cast a golden glow over what went on there. But what went on was farther than ever from peace and flowers.

The atmosphere of violent crime that spread over the Haight had multiple roots: the presence of naive potential victims, the population pressure of blacks being forced out of the Fillmore District by a redevelopment project, and heroin. The last, the drug most despised by psychedelic believers, had first come to notice in the summer of 1967 when a couple of Diggers, including Emmett Grogan, got into it. Though most smack was initially used as a rough-and-ready antidote for the depression that follows a couple of days of shooting amphetamines, it quickly showed its way of turning into a habit. The Haight, unfortunately, was rather defenseless against heroin because of the crude philosophy among newcomers that you had to be high to be cool, abetted by such things as Tim Leary's custom of speaking of all drugs as yogas.

After the Death of Hippie, Ron Thelin joined a group of Diggers on a cross-country trip to create life-actors and spread the gospel of "assuming freedom." Soon other shops were closing or contemplating closure, and a company called Haight-Ashbury Store/West House was eagerly picking up the vacated storefronts. The free food in the Panhandle was entirely gone, but bread at All Saints was available two or three times a week. The only public feeds were the barbecues that often accompanied rock concerts put on in the park by a group with Digger roots, Teddy Bear and the Thirteenth Tribe.

Digger activities diminished in the fall. At the All Saints office some of the community service people still called themselves Diggers, but the Trip Without a Ticket was closed. The Free Store goods were moved into the basement of All Saints and then distributed more clandestinely out of various apartments in the neighborhood. One of the All Saints Diggers, Rob Sutherland, talked himself into the managership of the Post Script Hotel, an old place being renovated down by the bayside wharves at the foot of Market Street, and filled it with moneyless hippies.

The Be-In had been planned as a preliminary to an exorcism of the Pentagon, and the Pentagon demonstration came off as planned on October 21, although the exorcism ceremony failed to make the building rise. In early November, Tom Donahue took over the programming of station KPPC-FM in Los Angeles. The son of San Francisco mayoral candidate Joseph Alioto opened a play he had written, *The High Mass*, which was advertised with a Fillmore-style poster by Bob Fried. In December, *Oracle* No. 11 had as its theme the City of God and featured speeches by Buckminster Fuller and Robert Theobald. On December 21, Owsley's LSD lab in Orinda, California, was busted. Uncompromising to the last, he told the arresting officers, "Even though you have a search warrant I consider you uninvited guests in my house."

The winter of 1967–68 ground along and the city government, which in the previous spring had refused to turn Haight Street into a mall, agreed to block off the street for occasional street parties with rock bands. On the whole, the Haight was heading toward much more violent police confrontations than the July 9, 1967 melee, in which only nine had been arrested. In February 1968 there were riots between street people and the police Tactical Squad that destroyed whatever optimism about love may have remained. Dr. Smith of the Free Clinic saw a young man being beaten by a tac squad cop although the boy was already unconscious, and Smith ran out into the street to give first aid. He introduced himself as a doctor, and to his shock, the tac squad officer made after *him* with his riot stick. Smith did not stay around to point out that even in time of war medical men are allowed to treat the wounded.

When a white man assassinated Martin Luther King in April, any hope for peaceful race relations in the Haight was shattered along with every store window on the street. More merchants moved out. The cover of *Oracle* No. 12 showed a body lying corpse-like on Mount Tamalpais and the first story in the issue was Lew Welch's pessimistic essay "Final City/Tap City." This was the last issue of the *Oracle*, though the name and format were later appropriated by a group of Sufis in Marin County.

On March 18 the entire staff of KMPX walked off the job to protest new management restrictions on which records they could play and, incidentally, the fact that although the station's revenues increased eightfold, no general salary increases had been made since the rock DJs had first broadcast on the station. Unionized as the Amalgamated Associated American FM Workers of the World, Ltd., they were back at work two months later at a new station, KSAN-FM. While they were out of work, their strike fund put on several benefit shows, including the first U.S. screening of the Beatles' "home movie" *Magical Mystery Tour*—the Straight Theater's finest hour, though the film did not arrive until three or four o'clock in the morning.

Some *Berkeley Barb* contributors split off to found their own underground paper, the *Express-Times*, early in 1968. For several months their attempt to put out something more tough-minded than the *Oracle* and less on the Berkeley revolutionary high horse than the *Barb* caught the radicalized mood of the street perfectly. The

Express-Times also introduced the novelty of readable text and clean, harmonious layout to the underground press, which had tended to the crowded, smudgy look of the *Barb,* if not to the optical conundrums of the *Oracle.*

The original Mime Troupe core of the Diggers, now calling themselves Free City, moved back into the public spotlight for a few months in 1968. With the slogan "How do you want to live?" they organized free goods distribution points, instituted a 1 percent tithe of hip stores to finance free activities and started daily poetry readings on the steps of City Hall, accompanied by free food and sometimes belly dancing. Bureaucrats and puzzled passersby were exhorted to abandon property, jobs and anything that delays gratification. The Free City people predicted that on the summer solstice the city of San Francisco would "enter into eternity," and they evidently believed that "outbreaks" of personal anarchy were imminent. (In a late 1967 interview, Peter Berg had said, "We will become the political dynamic of the new society because we are *living* a new civilization.") On the solstice, with music and events going on in five separate parks, they drove a truck full of belly dancers through the Financial District and the city of San Francisco ostensibly entered eternity.

Free City helped close another short-lived institution. On May 1 the Carousel Ballroom, which had been run as a dance hall in competition with the Fillmore and the Avalon for two and a half months by a group including members of the Dead and the Airplane, hosted a Free City Convention. A public announcement of the convention read, "Bring food, women, etc." and it was a rowdy anarchist event. In the morning, Headstone Productions discovered that someone had changed the "Free City Convention" sign on the marquee to read "Free Cunt." The ensuing police pressure, plus Headstone Productions' expensive lease and the drop in dance attendance after the Martin Luther King assassination, forced the Carousel to shut down. Bill Graham leased the place for himself and renamed it the Fillmore West, to parallel his recently opened Fillmore East in New York.

In the summer of 1968, the Haight-Ashbury was still attracting hundreds of runaways every week, but it was a changed neighborhood. Even the music scene had changed. The old Fillmore was closed in favor of the Fillmore West. The Family Dog, having lost a fortune on its Denver ballroom, could no longer afford the striking posters that made it nationally famous (and incidentally provided a major part of its income). Beginning in July the posters were printed in black and white rather than in color. In September the Board of Permit Appeals closed down the Avalon on a noise complaint.

The Haight seemed to hit rock bottom in 1969. Thirty-six storefronts were vacant, and the remaining eighteen or so had metal gratings or boards over their windows. It is said that house cats did not dare to walk on the street that year; they hid behind bushes because needle freaks—speeders and junkies—were hunting them for food. Haight Street was unpleasant and dangerous even by noontime. The Straight Theater finally folded after a year and a half of struggles with Free City and other neighborhood groups. It had lost money from the start, and with the Haight as it was, it could only continue to lose.

In the summer of 1969 the Family Dog, reorganized as Associated Rubber Dog, opened for business again at an old dance hall in the dying Playland amusement park on the westernmost edge of the city, just across the highway from the Pacific Ocean. Shortly after it opened, the workers in the city's various light show companies, now numbering 500 individuals, went on strike for higher wages. Helms was in deep financial trouble as it was, but he attempted to negotiate with them and the result was the Common, a sort of parliament and group therapy for everyone interested in the future of the Family Dog at the Beach. Bill Graham was considerably more tough-minded. He simply canceled light shows at the Fillmore West, and was able to point out that his attendance did not drop at all. This effectively finished off the light shows, because the Family Dog at the Beach would close in only a few months and the other rock and roll venues in town couldn't afford light shows at all—even the latter-day shows that had grown heavily capital-intensive and used a minimum number of employees.

The momentum of ever-larger public gatherings that began in San

Francisco had seemed to falter in a nationwide grab bag of un-imaginative rock concerts. In March 1969, a number of San Fran-cisco rock figures, including Tom Donahue of KSAN, managers of the principal rock bands and Jann Wenner and Ralph Gleason of the year-and-a-half-old magazine *Rolling Stone,* planned to show the country how to put on a proper festival. Their ambitious plans for the Wild West Show included a free citywide multimedia arts festi-val with light events from the hilltops and music of all kinds through-out Golden Gate Park, to be financed by paying concerts. The paying concerts were the sticking point; in the deepening paranoia of the time, Wild West fell victim to the same sort of conflict over commu-nity representation and control that had cursed the Straight Theater and the Family Dog.

On August 15, 1969, one week before the aborted Wild West Show was to have happened, the crowning achievement of mass psychedelic gatherings took place, but not in San Francisco. The Woodstock Festival in Bethel, New York, was attended by 450,000 people. San Francisco was spurred to make one last attempt to top the series. The Rolling Stones tour that fall had stirred unquenchable rumors that the Stones were going to give a free concert, and the Stones finally held it near San Francisco at the Altamont Raceway on December 6. In its way, it was the topper of all the giant rock festivals, because it was the end of the series. The nasty atmosphere of panic and hostility near the stage made it the symbolic dead end of a generation's adventure. At the concert a black man, Meredith Hunter, was killed and countless others severely beaten.

The real dead end was the dream that this was a blessed genera-tion, immune to the darkness of the heart that has always caused violence and oppression. The same week as the Altamont Festival, a grand jury in Los Angeles was investigating a one-time Haight resident named Charlie Manson in connection with a series of ritual murders. A Manson associate, Bobby Beausoleil (who had been bouzouki player with the Orkustra, the Digger band), was already in jail for murder. In the fall of 1970 the rock stars Jimi Hendrix and Janis Joplin died within three weeks of each other—of barbiturates and heroin, respectively. Shortly thereafter, *Rolling Stone* published an interview in which John Lennon of the Beatles said, in so many words, The dream is over.

Innocence was not all there was to the dream, and it was not the Haight-Ashbury's dream alone, but it was preeminently the Haight's. Making sense of what happened has been the task ever since.

The institutions evolved in the Haight's brief two years did not, on the whole, last very long. Institutions themselves were suspect, and certainly were hard to maintain when the personnel were taking psychedelics. Ten years after the Summer of Love, Bob Stubbs, the last of the HIP merchants on Haight Street, closed the Phoenix. That left only two institutions from 1967, the Haight-Ashbury Switchboard, some of whose operators had never heard the names of its founders, and the Free Clinic, which for some time had been chiefly concerned with alcoholism and psychiatric care. The Free Clinic had been the greatest success, inspiring nationwide about 500 similar clinics, which differed from traditional charity clinics in not having religious connections, judgmental attitudes or long forms to fill out.

The hippie newspapers folded quickly. In 1968 and 1969 the only paper reporting on the Haight, apart from occasional stories in the *Express-Times,* was the straight *Haight-Ashbury Record.* Chester Anderson gave up trying to form his own Communication Company and edited the rock magazine *Crawdaddy!* for some months. The Digger faction of com/co put its mimeo machines at the service of Free City publications, where they were used in such innovative ways that the Gestetner Company itself was impressed. Com/co had always done a lot of printing for the Black Panther Party, and one story is that the Gestetners ended up with the Panthers.

The Haight-Ashbury Legal Organization (HALO) was a one-summer operation and did not continue, though it helped form the network of lawyers specializing in defending drug cases that later pushed for marijuana law reform. Happening House was doomed; Leonard Wolfe survived an attempted takeover by a group of Learyites, but his enterprise was out of steam and the Free Clinic took over the downstairs of 409 Clayton. The Shire School and the Settlement House vanished from sight.

Rock and roll continued to flourish, however. Even after closing both Fillmores in 1971 and his several announced "retirements," Bill Graham remained the most important rock and roll concert promoter in the country. The Rolling Stones and Bob Dylan automatically went to him to manage their tours. The San Francisco rock bands remained unusually active for aging rockers—partly because they had won bold contracts from their record companies which gave them unprecedented control over what they recorded and how it was presented. Jefferson Airplane, now called Jefferson Starship, continued to be one of the most popular bands in the country. The Grateful Dead, in pseudo-retirement, gave concerts at irregular intervals which were regular mini-be-ins for their fans—known as Dead Heads and still a heavily psychedelic crowd. Quicksilver and Country Joe and the Fish continued to have periodic reunions. The various Charlatans started groups of their own: Mike Wilhelm's folk-rock Loose Gravel, Richie Olsen's dixieland Powell Street Jazz Band, Dan Hicks' sophisticated and ironic country-jazz-Hawaiian group The Hot Licks. Only Big Brother and the Holding Company seem permanently retired.

The dance-poster scene died when Graham closed the Fillmore, but the original poster artists had already moved on to new projects. They helped to create a new school of album-cover design, itself partly made possible by the San Francisco bands' tough contracts. Kelly did the first Grateful Dead album, Moscoso designed the first Steve Miller Band album, Rick Griffin did Quicksilver, Mouse designed the cover for the English "supergroup" Blind Faith. Mouse and Kelly had been making T-shirts since 1966, and like highly polished album cover art, printed T-shirts became a staple of the rock and roll world. Mouse and Kelly's Monster Company was for years a substantial business employing dozens of people.

Altogether the poster artists upset the predictions that they would move away from posters in the direction of gallery art. They did some gallery art, but they kept busy in popular art as well. In 1968 Moscoso and Griffin began working with the cartoonists Robert Crumb and S. Clay Wilson on a new kind of comic book called *Zap Comix*. Surreal, flamboyantly vulgar and often very funny, *Zap* (and its erotic counterpart, *Snatch*) set the form for a new kind of late-adolescent entertainment its fans called "comix." It was a San Francisco business at the start; the principal comix publisher, Rip Off Press, began in the Fillmore District loft of the light-show artist Ben Van Meter. By 1968, underground comix already supported a bookstore, Gary Arlington's San Francisco Comic Book Company.

Apart from Stewart Brand's *Whole Earth Catalog* (and its successor, *Co-Evolution Quarterly*), only one major national publication came out of the Haight-Ashbury movement: *Rolling Stone.* The first tabloid-format issue of the biweekly rock newspaper appeared on October 18, 1967, financed by a total investment of $7,500, and against great odds the magazine became a success. In keeping with its name, *Rolling Stone* followed the center of interest freely. By the late seventies it was the twenty-seventh largest publication in the United States in terms of newsstand sales, and described itself as "a general interest magazine covering American culture, politics and arts, with a special interest in music."

As a physical center of people, the Haight worked like a cyclone— tugging them in from all over, whirling them up in the air and scattering them in every direction. Very few people stayed continuously in the Haight through the mid-seventies. The move was in the direction of the country, but the distance varied; a lot of spare-changers never got past Telegraph Avenue in Berkeley.

Certain cabals naturally stuck together. A number of the original Family Dog and Red Dog Saloon people found their way back to the Comstock Lode country of Nevada, where the air is clean and life is frontier-rugged. The barren-looking area is home to a surprisingly large number of low-visibility hipsters, though not many live in Virginia City itself, where the old Red Dog Saloon became Kitty's Long Branch. It was 1972 before the jackrabbit population around Virginia City recovered from the gun-happy Red Dog summer of 1965.

When Ken Kesey got out of jail, he returned to Oregon to operate a dairy farm near Eugene, and a number of Pranksters—many of whom were Oregonians—settled in nearby Willamette Valley towns. Other Pranksters wound up at the Hog Farm, a mountaintop commune in Los Angeles whose public face was the comedian Hugh Romney, now known as Wavy Gravy. The Hog Farm is a sort of community-service commune that has provided medical help at rock festivals and sponsored ecological charities. The Pranksters' Bus Movie, numerous tapes of Acid Tests and Neal Cassady monologues are still stored in the Prankster Archives shack at Kesey's farm. The Bus with its thirty layers of paint is parked nearby.

Many public figures of the Haight-Ashbury migrated north to the woods of Marin and Sonoma counties: musicians, poster artists, merchants. Marin in particular, with its tricky maze of tiny mountain roads, was full of perfect hideaways for rock musicians and a life of psychedelic hedonism. In Sonoma, the area west of Santa Rosa and particularly around the Russian River resort towns became thick with Haight Street alumni, where such diverse sorts as Ramon Sender, Blind Jerry, Ben Van Meter, the Jacopettis, Peter Krug and Chester Anderson have lived within a few miles of each other.

The biggest move to Sonoma County had taken place in 1967 when the Diggers were shunting people up to Morning Star Ranch. After Morning Star was closed down, a number of communards moved to the neighboring Wheeler Ranch, which had adopted Lou Gottlieb's open-land philosophy. Both places served as launching pads for smaller rural communes. *Simpático* groups would form at Morning Star or Wheeler and move out to some old farmhouse in the vicinity, or further north to Mendocino or Humboldt counties. Morning Star had always had contact with communes in New Mexico through Ramon Sender and Stewart Brand. The Diggers themselves, through Emmett Grogan, had picked up the gospel of achieving self-sufficiency and getting back to nature down in such places as El Rito and Placitas, New Mexico, and a number of Diggers and Morning Star people migrated there. They also moved to the traditional rural bohemia of Big Sur, especially around Gorda and Limekiln Creek, but a number of Diggers settled in San Francisco.

The Haight experience had a way of changing people's careers. The great exception seems to be the light-show artists. After the light-show scene closed down in 1969, most of the original artists returned to what they'd been doing before. Bob Carr's Retina Circus show became a multimedia design company. Bill Ham took his show to Europe for a few years before returning to his old place on Pine Street.

Otherwise a spin in the Haight-Ashbury was likely to give somebody a new life. Before the Haight the Hell's Angels had largely been lumpen-proletarian bikers who fooled around with drugs but bought them in small quantities like anybody else. The Haight taught them, as it taught a lot of others, that there was a lot of money in the dope trade; and unlike a lot of others, the Angels were a brotherhood and a lot tougher than ordinary hippie dealers. In 1972 the attorney general of California charged that the Hell's Angels were in effect a massive dope ring, and the U.S. Customs Service estimated that Angels had shipped $31 million worth of drugs to the East Coast in the preceding three years.

For the less organized elements in the Haight, the picture is vague. In March 1967, when the move to the country was beginning, it was estimated that about 7,000 hippies lived in the neighborhood. By late summer so many sociologists were doing field studies in the Haight that they considered forming their own professional organization, but there was no way that social scientists could have kept track of what happened to the 75,000 who had passed through. Possibly the most extensive and thorough study was the Haight-Ashbury Research Project, organized in 1968.

To the project's director, Dr. Stephen Pittel, the population drawn by the 1967 publicity splash seemed to fall into three categories. The smallest, making up about 15 percent of the 250 people in his sample, he classed as psychotic fringe and religious obsessives—people who could not carry on an ordinary, secular conversation. About 40 percent were believers in the mystique of the Haight and had come because they saw it as a model for the rest of the world. The remaining 45 percent or so were attracted by the no-hassle lifestyle of the dropout, with a minimum of work and a maximum of getting stoned.

Pittel saw these three groups as being on different trajectories from the start. The psychotic fringe came from cold, authoritarian families and many of them ended up on heroin or other hard drugs. Most were still living rootlessly in derelict neighborhoods when the study ended—those who hadn't committed suicide or died drug-related deaths. The believers in the Haight, by contrast, came from supportive families. They never felt they had completely broken contact with their parents, and when they left the Haight it was relatively easy for them to organize themselves and return to school or choose a career. The in-between group, the dropouts, came from families that demanded high achievement from their children but actually discouraged their independence. The members of this class in Pittel's study migrated to communes or quasi-communes in the country— not deep in the country, where life was too hard, but just outside the suburbs. They continued to be marginally employed and organized their lives around crafts and the pleasures of family and friends. In short, they were the ones at the end of Pittel's study who still looked like hippies.

Pittel's study shows clearly the basic differences that had seemed infinitesimally small to the community itself, as well as the sort of people that the news media and word of mouth attracted to the Haight. But from these general findings, it is impossible to generalize about the destinies of individuals, particularly among the original Haight crowd. Here are some examples.

Bob Stubbs. The original owner of the Blue Unicorn coffeehouse and the Phoenix head shop had already opened a branch of the Phoenix in Mill Valley, another in North Beach and a bookstore on Haight Street by 1970. Despite the neighborhood's decline and a disastrous 1973 fire, he kept the Phoenix open until June 1976. After that he returned to his home state of Hawaii to run the Maui Phoenix and the Sundance Incense and Trading Company, his import firm, and to farm.

Norman Stubbs. Bob Stubbs' brother tried to market a sitar-like musical instrument of his invention in 1967, then switched to making leather goods. His business mushroomed so fast that for years his wholesale leather company was still known as East-West Musical Instruments.

Ramon Sender. After Morning Star, Wheeler's Ranch and the

Banana Patch commune on Maui, the Trips Festival organizer returned to Sonoma County and bought land near Morning Star and Wheeler's with the proceeds of a book he wrote with the ecology writer Alicia Bay Laurel. He has initiated people into a religious Order of the Morning Star.

Wes Wilson. The Fillmore poster artist planned to become a commercial artist after leaving Bill Graham's employ, but he lacked the professional training to cash in on his by-then-world-famous style. He retired to develop an original technique for making stained glass: annealing colors onto a solid sheet of glass, rather than piecing together designs out of bits of colored glass held together by leading. His Windows for the New Jerusalem are in many Marin and Sonoma homes.

Ben and Rain Jacopetti. In late 1966 the Open Theater and Trips Festival couple left Morning Star Ranch and moved back to Berkeley. When KMPX went acid rock, Ben arranged for the ski shop where he worked to be one of its first advertisers, using the Congress of Wonders actors for the first of their long series of KMPX ad spots. In 1969, working on the script of a projected Congress of Wonders movie, he began hanging out at KSAN and ended up as a director and sometime disc jockey. In 1974 his wife published *Native Funk and Flash*, a book documenting the colorful ornamentation lavished on everyday objects (especially blue jeans) by Northern California hippies. As adherents of the religion Subud, Ben and Rain have changed their names and are now Roland and Alexandra Jacopetti.

Chet Helms. After the failure of the Family Dog at the Beach, Helms sold antiques, a natural outgrowth of the Edwardian hip trip. He developed an interest in massage and in 1975 became a licensed masseur.

Jerry Sealund. "Blind Jerry" ran his health food store on Page Street until 1969, when he was robbed twelve times in eleven months, then moved out. He had helped with the All Saints bread-baking operation and consulted with the Black Panthers on their free breakfast program. His new store was Organic Groceries in Santa Rosa.

Peter Krug. Wild Colors grossed $40,000 in 1967, of which Krug netted $6,000. After the neighborhood got too rough for him in 1968, he opened a shop in North Beach, but he had already concluded that the merchant has overhead and worry while the craftsman has the fun. He moved to an unincorporated town in Sonoma County and began making jewelry and paraphernalia.

Straight Theater. Some of the Straight staff went as far as New Mexico when the theater finally closed in 1969, but the founders stayed in San Francisco. Bill Resner ran the first head shop in the Pacific Heights district, the Paisley Penguin Fine Trippery, and later sold classic cars in Marin County. He died in 1982. Bill and Hillel Resner had been partners in the Tulip Recording Company, an eight-track studio in San Francisco. Luther Greene had a video/film studio in the city, Studio C.

Emmett Grogan. The pioneer Digger remained active in the Free City Collective for a couple of years and then returned to New York. In 1971 he published a novelistic autobiography, *Ringolevio: A Life Played for Keeps*, and in 1976 a thriller titled *Final Score*. On April 1, 1978, he was found in a New York subway dead of a heroin overdose.

Peter Cohon. The Digger luminary has become a well-known actor under his new name Peter Coyote. He played Keys, the sympathetic scientist in the movie *E.T.* In 1976 Governor Brown appointed him, along with the poet Gary Snyder, to the California Arts Commission.

Chester Anderson. The Communication Company founder took over the editorship of *Crawdaddy!* in 1968, and upon its demise (another magazine later used the name *Crawdaddy* with permission) he retired to the woods of Mendocino and Sonoma counties, where he occasionally supported himself as a typographer. His Greenwich Village novel *The Butterfly Kid* has been reprinted, and he has written a novel about the Haight, *Everything Free*.

Patrick Gleeson. The San Francisco State professor who had dabbled in Vietnam Day Committee and Digger activities was denied tenure in 1968. Down and out, his academic career over, he turned to music in 1969. He has played keyboards and Moog synthesizer with the Herbie Hancock band and as a studio musician, and owns a 24-track recording studio in San Francisco, Different Fur.

Larry Miller. The primal FM rock disc jockey has stayed in radio. In a controversial move he returned to KMPX during the 1968 strike and consequently was not welcome at KSAN with the other ex-KMPX jocks. He went to work at radio stations in Detroit, Los Angeles, San Diego, and Babylon, New York.

Si Lowinsky. The Vietnam Day Committee activist who managed the Print Mint on Haight Street in 1967 and 1968 got interested in art at his job. He ended up working at the Phoenix Gallery in San Francisco, which held the first California show of the Dutch visionary artist M.C. Escher.

Ashley Brilliant. The ex-college professor who became a Hippie Hill fixture with his bullhorn and sheaf of "Pot Shots" poem-epigrams quit performing in October 1967, and started publishing Pot Shots on 3-by-5-inch cards with cartoon illustrations. Eventually they were franchised worldwide (from the beginning Brilliant had avoided puns and other untranslatable effects) and were even available on T-shirts. They have been syndicated by the Chicago Tribune-New York News syndicate.

Don McCoy. The wealthy owner of the Marin Heliport building where many rock bands rehearsed and original owner of 715 Ashbury began a commune at 690-acre Rancho Olompali, near Novato in Marin County, at the end of 1967. The next year, after a difficult period when there had been two arrests, a fire and two drownings at Olompali, his relatives put his property into conservatorship because of his announced intention to give away all his earthly goods. But by then he had met a guru in India named Chiranjiva, who preached that a new era, the age of Shiva's Omnipotent Imagination, had begun in 1966. Among the others besides McCoy who became followers of "Father," as Chiranjiva is known, are Lou Gottlieb of Morning Star, who returned to show business in the late seventies, and Ron Thelin of the Psychedelic Shop, who lives in rural Marin.

This list could be multiplied with many less famous names, from the All Saints Digger who wound up managing a chain of bookstores to the policeman who walked a beat in the Haight and later opened an occult bookstore. One generalizes about the people who passed through the Haight-Ashbury at one's peril.

The buildings that had housed so much psychedelic intensity went through ceaseless urban recycling in the years after 1967.

The Fillmore Auditorium (1806 Geary) became Muhammad's Mosque No. 26 for some years, then the Elite Club.

The Avalon Ballroom (Sutter and Van Ness) was remodeled as the Regency II Theater, with theater seats built on the old ballroom floor and an escalator installed on the staircase. Inside the theater one can still see the pilasters on the walls that added such peculiar effects when the light show was projected on them.

The Psychedelic Shop (1535 Haight) became Bohemienne Bazaar East, then part of House of Richard, then the office of a community organization that served breakfasts to minors. Recently it has been empty.

House of Richard (1541 Haight) became United Health Alliance, a food stamp outlet, and the office of a candidate for the Board of supervisors, among other things. It has also been empty. The original address at 405 Shrader is empty.

Mnasidika (1510 Haight) became the Silmi Market, a grocery, and has also been empty.

The Blushing Peony (1452 Haight) became successively Middle Earth Clothing, the Righteous Rag, Oola Bula Clothes, the Cola Boutique.

The Phoenix (1377 Haight) became Family Affair Hairstyling, then Recycled Records.

The Print Mint (1542 Haight) became Stan's Furniture.

Love Burgers (1568 Haight) left, but the Pall Mall bar in which it was located survived the whole period.

The Free Frame of Reference (520 Frederick) became the God's Eye Ice Cream Parlor and God's Eye Theater in 1967. It has been a weaving studio and a residence in recent years.

The Trip Without a Ticket (901 Cole) became Consolidated Upholstery, then Ironwood Café.

Tracy's Donuts (1569 Haight) became the Haight-Ashbury Kitchen, the Family Cooking Company, and the Gold Cane.

The I/Thou Coffee Shop (1736 Haight) became the Brother Juniper Inn, run by the Holy Order of Mans, then the Lee Way Inn, the Pentecostal Church of Daemon, a real estate brokerage and Daljeet's, a clothing store.

The Drogstore Café (1398 Haight) became Magnolia Thunderpussy catering service. For a long time it was the Psalms Café, most recently Yellow Rose, a Tex-Mex restaurant.

Wild Colors (1418 Haight) is Raffi's Café.

In Gear (1580 Haight) is the Soft Touch Boutique.

The Straight Theater (1748 Haight) was painted with revolutionary murals when it closed in 1969: a marijuana leaf against a red star and a clenched fist. The murals declared it to be the People's Ballroom, but it lay unused from 1969 until it was demolished in 1981.

All in all, the surprising thing about the Haight-Ashbury at the beginning of the eighties is how few storefronts are vacant. In 1965 any observer would have recognized the Haight as a declining neighborhood, with its eighteen vacant storefronts, and after the brief spurt of 1966–68 it soon became as bad as a neighborhood can get —a heroin-infested slum where somebody could get knifed for a bag of groceries.

But the Haight did a remarkable job of pulling itself out. Neighborhood institutions such as the Free Clinic, Huckleberry's (since closed), the churches and communes united to stave off an urban redevelopment plan, and in so doing, showed that there were a lot of people living there who considered it home and were going to stick it out. By the mid-seventies property values were up to five times what they had been at the lowest ebb in 1969, many buildings were freshly painted and businessmen were taking the chance of renting storefronts. Haight Street was still a bit seedy and edgy, and not altogether safe at night, but the neighborhood looked livable again. Like the rest of San Francisco, it drew a sizable gay population, and there were more restaurants, and on the whole better goods in the shops, than in 1967. Of course, it was no longer the crest of a historical wave, although the mystique of the old Haight had everything to do with why some people were living there.

But it now has a new mystique. The Haight was again an example for the world, an example of what could be done if people decided to stick it out when things got tough in their neighborhood. Dr.

Smith of the Free Clinic often entertained visitors from other cities who were curious about this parent of the free clinic movement, and is fond of taking them around the neighborhood to point out its renaissance.

"I tell my visitors, 'Look around,' " he says. " 'Have you ever heard of a neighborhood that has gone through a major heroin epidemic —and that's what we had, a major heroin epidemic in 1969—and neither turned into a slum nor gotten redeveloped?' "

That, in some quarters anyway, was the new mystique of the Haight: that it has survived the bitterest disappointments and most violent disruption, and then pulled itself out. By comparison with 1967, a chastened vision, but like the old one, still a vision of hope.

Abshear, Susan, 148
Acid Tests, 34–35, 37, 38–39, 41–50, 57–58, 100–103, 252, 275
Adams, Carolyn, 43
Adler, Lou, 190, 207, 209
Albin, Peter, 36, 74
Alpert, Richard, 34, 90, 124, 137, 186, 201, 281
America Needs Indians, 18–19, 46–47
American Indians, 7, 18–19, 59, 64, 186, 239, 250, 257, 263
amphetamines, 80, 81, 197, 237, 283
Anderson, Chester, 117, 128–29, 138–39, 141, 143–44, 176, 181, 196, 215, 230, 289, 292, 296
Anderson, Dame Judith, 236
Anderson, Ray, 23, 69, 139
Anger, Kenneth, 239–40
Angry Arts Week, 177–78
Anonymous Artists of America, 103, 223
Arthur, 70
Arthur, Gavin, 141
Artists' Liberation Front (ALF), 82, 94, 145–47
Associated Press, 21
atomic bomb, 51, 66, 245
Avalon Ballroom, 60–62, 81, 128, 149, 199, 214, 287, 298
Awareness Festival, 94–95

Babbs, Ken, 13, 34, 43
Baez, Joan, 106
Baillie, Bruce, 47, 85–86
Balin, Marty, 16–17, 72, 158
Barger, Sonny, 27–28, 33
Batman, Billy and Digger, 216
Batman Festival, 60
Beatles, 4, 8, 37–38, 52–54, 110, 153, 198–99, 208, 212, 220, 233, 235, 237, 241, 266, 285
Beats, 5, 21, 66–67, 78, 249–51, 257, 274
Beausoleil, Bobby, 240, 288
Be-In, 121–28, 130–31, 150, 204, 264
Berg, Peter ("the Hun"), 89–90, 260, 270
Berkeley Barb, 16, 25, 63, 98, 105, 120–23, 132–33, 151–52, 154–55, 176–77, 188, 197, 202, 215, 224, 243, 260, 285–86
Best & Company, 170
Bhaktivedanta, Swami, 123, 129–30
Big Brother and the Holding Company, 37, 47, 59, 71–72, 74–75, 83, 97, 126, 136, 145–47, 206–8, 210, 233, 243
Black Panthers, 187, 196, 289
Blues Project, 74, 75, 208
Blue Unicorn, 19–21, 92, 258, 294
Blushing Peony, 77, 154, 298

bohemianism, 249–51, 268–69
Boise, Ron, 14, 15, 42, 94
Bowen, Michael, 120, 122, 123, 135
Bowles, Bobby, 259
Brand, Lois, 85
Brand, Stewart, 19, 39, 41, 43–45, 47,
    67, 85, 94, 280–81, 291, 292
Brautigan, Richard, 145, 199, 261
Brilliant, Ashley, 297
Brown, Edmund G., Jr. "Jerry," 281,
    296
Brown, Edmund G. "Pat," 101–2
Bruce, Lenny, 21, 246
Buchla, Donald, 47, 94
Butterfield Blues Band, 60, 74, 75, 93,
    132, 133, 206–7
Byrds, 8, 206, 208
BZ, 193, 213

Cahill, Thomas, 131–32, 164, 184
Calliope Company, 101–2, 221
Calm Center, 137, 189
Carter, John Kent ("Shob"), 224–27,
    231
Cassady, Neal, 13–14, 34, 39, 43, 48,
    103, 241
Cassen, Jackie, 133, 170
Castell, Luria, 28, 33, 57
Chamber Orkustra, 116, 146, 240
Charlatans, 8–9, 17, 18, 28–31, 73, 213,
    223, 290
Cheetah, 70, 223
Cipollina, John, 40–41
civil rights movement, 16, 57–58, 81–82,
    246–48, 256
clean-ins, 131, 224
Cohen, Allan, 127
Cohen, Allen, 88, 94–96, 107, 113, 120,
    122, 156, 163, 165, 209, 231
Cohen, Sidney, 186
Cohon, Peter, 90, 193, 220–21, 270, 296
com/co (Communication Company),
    128–31, 134, 135, 141, 146,
    149–54, 157, 164–65, 167–68, 176,
    180–81, 187–88, 196–97, 215, 221,
    222, 230, 275–76, 289
Committee Theater, 18–19, 21, 31, 41
Country Joe and the Fish, 26–27, 63,
    73–74, 126, 151–52, 177, 180,
    185–86, 188, 190, 206–7, 219, 237,
    242, 290

Dahlstrom, Eric Frank, 225, 227, 238
Davis, R. G., 22, 31, 68, 82, 179
Death of a Hippie ceremony, 242–44
Demetrios, 56
Denver Dog, 235–36
Diggers, 82, 106, 108–10, 113–21, 124,
    129–32, 135–38, 142, 144–50, 157,
    166, 169, 186, 188, 194, 196–97,
    209, 216, 220–21, 252, 259–61,
    268, 270–71, 283–84, 298
    artistic-political actions of, 103–5, 109,
        114, 116, 145–47, 155–56, 171,
        177, 180, 191, 252–53
    dissent among, 183–84, 216, 230,
        270–71
    free food and clothes distributed by,
        97–99, 108, 113, 116, 125, 130,
        137–38, 167, 200, 201–2, 210, 212,
        226, 271, 284
    publications of, 90–92, 93, 119, 129,
        131, 168, 189, 196, 206
DMT, 52, 189
Donahue, Tom ("Big Daddy"), 11–12,
    23, 29, 71–72, 158, 174–75, 182,
    200, 284–85, 288
Donovan, 53, 78, 190
Doors, 128, 237
Drogstore Café, 112–13, 176, 299
Drop City commune, 85, 235
Durkee, Steve, 85
Dylan, Bob, 5–6, 8, 35–36, 37, 53, 54,
    74, 87–88, 121, 148, 153–54, 184,
    266, 290

ecology movement, 280–81
Epstein, Brian, 212, 233
Erkskine, Stuart, 110–11
Express-Times, 285–86, 289

Family Dog, 28–31, 33, 44, 58–63, 134
    Helms's leadership of, 59, 60–70, 74,
        75, 134–35, 144, 149–50, 167, 171,
        235–36, 287, 295
Fariña, Mimi, 102, 106
Ferguson, Michael, 9
Ferlinghetti, Lawrence, 21, 26, 62
Fillmore Auditorium, 38, 42, 57–70, 75,
    78, 81, 126, 149, 153, 178, 287,
    298
Fillmore District, 6–7, 35–36, 93, 138,
    218, 219, 221–22
Final Solution, 36, 72, 75
First Annual Love Circus, 150
Flame, 226, 228, 230
folk music, 5–6, 26–27, 60, 247
folk-rock, 8, 35–36, 37
Fonteyn, Margot, 217, 220
freaking out, 13
Free City Collective, 216, 226, 242, 286,
    289
Free Clinic, 201, 223, 240–41, 243, 272,
    289, 299–300
Free Speech Movement, 16, 106, 110,
    214, 247

Freiberg, David, 40–41
Fugs, 32, 39
Fuller, Richard Buckminster, 77, 262, 280, 284

Garcia, Jerry, 37, 48, 73
Gerrans, Art, 118, 148, 157
Gestalt Therapy (Perls and Goodman), 257
Ginsberg, Allen, 16, 25, 30, 32, 33, 39, 119, 122–24, 126–27, 130, 131, 142, 159–63, 266, 267
Gleason, Ralph J., 17, 29, 31, 35–36, 53, 62, 82, 101–2, 116, 143–44, 158, 179, 206, 235, 288
Gleeson, Patrick, 296
gnosticism, 266–67
Gottlieb, Lou, 44–45, 84–86, 148–49, 204–5, 215, 217–18, 235, 238, 239, 244, 297
Graham, Bill, 31–33, 35–36, 38, 41, 44–50, 60–66, 72, 81, 82, 94, 101–2, 108, 111, 128, 153–54, 157–58, 178, 191, 203, 235, 286, 287, 290
Grateful Dead, 39, 42–43, 47–48, 50, 56, 57, 61, 70, 72–74, 83, 87, 94, 95, 101–2, 106, 126, 128, 133, 151, 163, 174, 177–78, 195, 207–10, 218, 230, 233, 237, 241, 242, 276, 290
Gray Line Bus Company, 171, 175, 178, 179, 193–94
Great Society, 29, 36, 72
Greene, Luther ("Spike"), 82–84, 296
Griffin, Rick, 123, 141, 219, 234, 290
Grogan, Emmett, 90–91, 97–99, 109, 118, 129, 137, 144, 146, 149, 176, 183–84, 186, 209–10, 221, 228, 240, 260, 270, 283, 292, 296
Grossman, Albert, 74
Gurley, Jim, 36, 71, 74, 139

Haight-Ashbury Maverick, 215, 243
Haight-Ashbury Legalization Organization (HALO), 195, 289
Haight-Ashbury Research Project, 293–94
Haight-Ashbury Settlement House, 77
Haight Independent Proprietors (HIP), 108, 131, 132, 136–38, 181–82, 258–60, 268, 269
Halprin, Ann, 47, 241
Ham, Bill, 9, 23, 29, 49, 68, 94, 132, 213, 293
Happening House, 156, 158–59, 212, 229–32, 289

happenings, theatrical, 21, 251–52
Harmon, Ellen, 9, 28
Harris, Leon, 136, 159, 169, 211–12, 234
Harrison, George, 112, 212, 227, 235
Harrison, Lou, 49
Hayward, Claude, 117, 128–29
Hell's Angels, 15–16, 27–28, 78, 95, 106, 115–16, 126–27, 130–31, 135–36, 206, 250, 258, 293
Helms, Chet, 36, 59–65, 74, 134–35, 139, 144, 163, 206, 236, 287, 295
Hendricks, Chocolate George, 115–16, 129, 232, 233
Hendrix, Jimmy, 209, 288
heroin, 228, 237, 242, 255, 278, 287, 300
Hilton Inn Tiger Room, 170
Hilyard, Roger, 68, 132
Hinckle, Warren, III, 143–44, 153
hippies, 5–6, 250, 255–56
Hodgeman, Eric, 213–14
Hoffman, Abbie, 232–33
Holding Company, 75
Hollingworth, Ambrose, 141–42
Holy See, 63, 139
Hopi Indians, 186
House of Richard, 20, 154, 253, 258, 298
Huckleberry House, 204, 240, 299
Hughes, Lynn, 18
Hunter, Bob, 8–9, 23
Hunter's Point riot, 93–94
Hunter, George, 57

I Ching, 24, 103, 135, 146, 155, 257, 275
In Gear, 77, 234
Inner Space, 203
I/Thou coffee shop, 77, 89, 91, 176, 223, 237, 243, 258, 298–99

Jacopetti, Ben and Rain, 22–24, 44, 85–86, 292, 295
James, William, 254
jazz, 53, 60, 67, 69, 250
Jefferson Airplane, 16–17, 23, 28–32, 36, 72–74, 126, 188, 194, 199, 205, 207, 234, 237, 290
Job Co-Op, 100, 136–37, 187, 194–95, 272
John Dillinger Computer, 145–47
Johnson, Lynda Bird, 236
Johnson, Lyndon B., 34, 51, 214, 223, 229, 230, 238, 248–49
Jomo Light Disaster, 70
Joplin, Janis, 74–75, 207, 208, 288
Juvinall, Andrew, 116

Kandel, Lenore, 107, 119, 122, 126, 146, 195
Kantner, Paul, 16–17, 40
Katz, Matthew, 72, 199
Katzman, Sam, 176, 221
Kelly, Al, 9, 23, 28, 57, 65, 219, 234, 290
Kennedy, John F., 22, 246–48
Kerouac, Jack, 13, 163
Kesey, Ken, 12–16, 19, 26–28, 45–50, 58–59, 94–95, 100–103, 110, 143, 188, 212, 239, 252, 255, 258, 291–92
    see also Acid Tests
King, Martin Luther, 246, 285
King, Mrs. Martin Luther, 180
Kiva, 171–72, 181, 203–4
KMPX-FM, 139–40, 158, 174, 182, 200, 217, 237–38, 285, 297
Kot, "Hairy Henry," 115–16, 129, 135–36
Krassner, Paul, 109, 142
Krug, Peter, 26, 92–93, 100, 137, 138–39, 215, 253, 258, 292, 295–96

Lark Shipping Company, 153
Laughlin, Chan, 8, 11, 18, 238, 270
Leary, Timothy, 7, 13, 19, 34, 54, 67, 81, 82, 83, 89, 111–12, 121–22, 132–34, 143, 159–63, 176, 181, 201, 242, 255, 257–58, 261, 263, 278
leftist politics, 179–80, 245–48, 263–66
Lennon, John, 23, 53–54, 194, 212, 289
Lesh, Phil, 37, 73, 208–9
Levine, Steve, 114, 124, 156, 158
Levi Strauss & Company, 188
Levy, Howard B., 194
Life, 52, 70
light shows, 9, 23, 29, 38, 39, 55, 57, 66–70, 106, 133, 170, 287, 292–93
Lisch, Arthur, 136, 154, 166
Locks, Seymour, 67
Look, 194
Los Angeles Times, 95
Love Book, The (Kandel), 107–8, 112, 156, 195
Love Burgers, 154, 165, 298
Love Conspiracy Commune, 150–51, 189
Love-In, 165
Love-Ins, The, 176, 221
Love-Pageant Rally, 96–97
Lovin' Spoonful, 12, 30–31, 75
Lowinsky, Si, 297
LSD, 4–5, 7, 11, 13, 19, 47, 55–56, 80–81, 90–91, 125, 127, 156, 160–63, 175, 185, 190, 193, 197, 227–28, 253–57, 259–60, 264–68, 274, 278–80
LSD Rescue, 224
Luce, John, 194

McCartney, Paul, 139, 190, 208
McCoy, Don, 297
McClure, Michael, 83, 107–8, 112, 115, 146, 274
McDonald, Joe, 26–27, 73–74, 242
McGlothlin, William, 185
McGuinn, Jim, 206
MacInnes, Colin, 53
McKenzie, Scott, 201, 209
MacLean, Bonnie, 203
McLuhan, Marshall, 19, 262–63
Mamas and the Papas, the, 201, 209
Manson, Charlie, 288
Marbles, 29, 47
marijuana, 78–80, 197, 224, 255–56
    movement for legalization of, 20, 220, 222, 277
Matrix, 16, 28, 72, 149, 243, 268
Max, Peter, 170
Melton, Barry, 73–74
Melvin, Milan, 200
Meredith, James, 52
Merry Pranksters, 12–16, 18, 26, 28, 58, 59, 95, 258, 291–92
    see also Acid Tests
Metevsky, George, 90–91
Methedrine, 188–89, 228
Miller, Larry, 139–40, 158, 174, 297
Miller, Stanley ("Mouse"), 65, 123, 143, 178, 219, 234, 290
Steve Miller Band, 206–7, 237
Minault, Kent, 89, 90
Mnasidika, 20, 77, 200, 298
Moby Grape, 128, 199, 207, 237
Moffett, Melinda, 110–11
Monkees, 132, 208–9, 237
Monterey International Pop Festival, 190, 197, 201, 205–9
Morning Star Ranch, 196, 204–5, 215–16, 217–18, 229, 235, 238, 239, 244, 270, 292
Moscoso, Victor, 149, 219, 290
Mother's, 11–12, 23, 36, 61
Mount Tamalpais festivals, 202, 215
multimedia events, 18–19, 23, 32, 170, 252
Murcott, Billy, 90–91, 97–99
Murphy, Michael, 142
Mystery Trend, 36, 50, 75

New York, N.Y., 56–57, 70, 170, 176
Nixon, Richard M., 51
Noonan, Allen, 187–88

Northern California Psychedelic
  Cattlemen's Association, 150, 213
Nureyev, Rudolf, 217, 220

obscenity laws, 22, 107–8, 112, 149,
  154–56, 182, 185, 195
Om Festival, 230–31
Open Theater, 22–24, 46–47, 68, 78, 85
Oracle (The City of San Francisco
  Oracle), 88–91, 95–96, 99, 106,
  112–14, 119–24, 133, 140–42,
  154–55, 159–62, 167, 171, 181,
  186, 202–4, 231–32, 261, 268, 275,
  284, 285
Orkustra, 116, 146, 240
Owsley (Augustus Owsley Stanley III),
  3–4, 35, 40, 42, 57, 73, 95, 125,
  175–76, 223, 234, 255, 284

Panic, Milan, 175
PCP, 214
peyote, 19, 255
Phillips, John, 190, 201, 205
Phoenix, 92, 239, 258, 289, 294, 298
Pig Pen, 145–47, 242
Pittel, Stephen, 293–94
Poon Tang Trilogy, 68, 118
poster art, 63–66, 149, 154–55, 182,
  218–19, 290
Pounds, William, 117–18
Print Mint, 112, 126, 132, 168, 187,
  297, 298
Psychedelic Review, 7, 13, 34
Psychedelic Shop, 76, 87, 91, 99–100,
  106–7, 132, 137, 174, 189, 195,
  243, 253, 298
psychedelic trade, 80–81

Quicksilver Messenger Service, 40–41,
  56, 74, 83, 102, 126, 163, 177,
  206–7, 210, 237, 290

Ramparts, 128–9, 143–44, 153
Reagan, Ronald, 102, 106–7, 135, 155,
  238
Red Dog Saloon, 8–11, 17–18, 28, 75,
  291
Reisner, Greg, 267, 278
Resner, Hillel and Bill, 83–84, 241, 260,
  296
Rifkin, Danny, 44, 57, 73
riots, 16, 93–94, 138–39, 191, 218–23,
  234
Rivers, Travis, 70, 74, 112
rock and roll, 5–6, 10, 17, 26–27, 29,
  36–37, 52, 54, 55, 63, 70–75, 290
rock dance concerts, 55–56, 60, 63–70,
  252
  see also specific bands and events

Roger the Dealer, ix, 79, 256
Rohan, Brian, 195
Roller, Alfred, 66
Rolling Stone, 288–89, 291
Rolling Stones, 37, 53, 154, 206, 214,
  223, 233, 237, 288, 290
Romero, Elias, 67–69
Roundhouse, 139
Rubin, Jerry, 121, 122, 126, 232–33

Sachs, Jeffrey Allen, 229
Sandoz Pharmaceuticals, 52
San Francisco Chronicle, 17, 18, 27, 44,
  61, 109, 119, 152, 185, 193, 199,
  243
San Francisco Examiner, 19–20, 179–80,
  234–35, 238
San Francisco Mime Troupe, 21–22, 64,
  68, 81–82, 89–90, 98, 104–5,
  114–15, 144, 167, 178–79, 185–86
  benefit shows for, 31–33, 35–36, 57
San Francisco State College, 6, 19, 67,
  76–77, 107–8, 154
San Francisco Steamboat Company, 158
Savio, Mario, 106, 110, 214
Scherr, Max, 63
Scott, Chloe, 49
Scully, Rock, 44, 57, 206, 277
Scully, Tim, 189
Sealund, Blind Jerry, 108, 295
Search and Seizure (Berg), 89, 109, 260
Sender, Ramon, 44, 85–86, 149, 294–95
Shankar, Ravi, 208, 227
Shulgin, Alexander, 175
Sierra Club, 51–52
Simpson, David, 219–20
sleep-ins, 165, 168
Slick, Grace, 36, 72, 74
Smith, David, 201, 223, 232, 240–41,
  285, 300
Snofox, Bobby, 116
Snyder, Gary, 119, 121–22, 124, 127,
  159–63, 261, 268, 272, 296
solstice celebration, 209–11
Sox, Ellis D., 164, 179, 224, 241
Spector, Phil, 157
speed, 188–89, 228, 242, 287
Spring Mobilization Against the War,
  177–80
Stepanian, Michael, 128, 195
Stern, Rudi, 133, 170
Steve Miller Band, 206–7, 237
STP, 189, 199, 203, 207
Straight Lightning, 83
Straight Theater, 82–84, 171, 215, 222,
  223–24, 233, 236, 240, 241, 260,
  269, 296, 299
Strauch, Tsvi, 77, 108, 131, 234, 276
Stubbs, Bob, 20, 92, 234, 258, 289, 294

Students for a Democratic Society
  (SDS), 31, 73, 90, 93, 213
Summer of Love, 171–72, 192, 196, 204,
  213–14, 226, 230–31, 236–37
Superspade, 110, 185, 225–26, 231
sweep-ins, 196, 234
Switchboard, 119, 230, 243, 289
Syracuse, Russ ("the Moose"), 29

technology, 261–63
theater, 21–24, 251–53
Thelin, Ron and Jay, 76, 88, 91, 99–100,
  108, 131, 137, 141, 186, 189, 196,
  223, 284, 297
Theobald, Robert, 248, 284
Thompson, Frank, Jr., 183
Thompson, Hunter, 15, 82, 143
Thompson, John, 190
Time, 25, 216
Tobacco, 136, 184
Toly, Signe, 23
Towle, Jack, 28, 238
Toynbee, Arnold, 194
Traps Festival, 82
Tree, Christopher, 68
"Tribal Stomp," 59
"Tribute to Dr. Strange, A," 28–30
"Tribute to Ming the Merciless, A,"
  33
"Tribute to Sparkle Plenty, A," 30–31
Trips Festival, 41, 44–50, 57, 58, 61, 63,
  76, 78, 143
Turk, Gut, 65

Unobsky, Mark, 8
USCo, 19, 85

Van Meter, Ben, 68–69, 118, 132, 240,
  292

Velvet Underground, 56–57
Vietnam Day Committee, 25–28, 52, 63,
  82, 296, 297
Vietnam War, 34, 51, 87, 166, 194, 214,
  223, 229, 230, 235, 236, 248–49,
  256, 270, 272–73
Village Voice, 228
Voulkos, Peter, 36
Voznesensky, Andrei, 62

walk-ins, 168–69
Warhol, Andy, 56–57, 70
Warlocks, 31, 37, 39
  see also Grateful Dead
Watts, Alan, 57–58, 75, 122, 142,
  159–63, 257, 262
Watts riot, 16
Weed Patch, 154
Weir, Bob, 208, 242
Welch, Lew, 60, 119, 166–67, 285
Weller, Tom, 190
Western Front, 213, 219, 238
Wild Colors, 92–93, 100, 137, 187, 253,
  295–96, 299
Wild Flower, 72, 75, 83, 97
Wild West Show, 288
Willner, Phyllis, 115, 129
Wilson, Wesley, 46, 64–66, 143, 188,
  190–91, 219, 234, 295
Winterland Auditorium, 93, 150, 195
Wolf, Leonard, 156, 158, 289
Woodstock Festival, 288
Works, Don, 7, 10
World's First Idea-In, 196

Youth Concepts, 170

Zappa, Frank, 33
Zig-Zag T-shirts, 65

ABOUT THE AUTHOR

CHARLES PERRY, associate editor of *Rolling Stone*, has written widely on music and popular culture. His interest in the Haight-Ashbury movement began with his participation in these events as a Berkeley hippie. Perry was born in Los Angeles in 1941, and studied at Princeton and the University of California. He lives in Sylmar, California.